Praise for

ATTENTION DEFICIT DISORDER:
A Different Perception

"A clear and positive viewing of our remarkable children with practical tips for the parent."
—*Stephen C. Davidson, M.Ed.*, of "Safe Kids" of Georgia, Founding member

"I highly recommend it to parents and educators.
—*Jack Neerincx, Ph.D.*, Supervising Psychologist, Gaston County Schools, North Carolina

"This book helped me understand ADD better and helped me with practical strategies on how to deal with these children in the classroom."
—*Anne Bennett*, Special Education Teacher, K-8th grades

"Thom Hartmann's conceptualization of Attention Deficit Hyperactivity Disorder is innovative and fresh. Rather than portraying the syndrome as a crippling disease, Mr. Hartmann demonstrates that ADHD can be associated with creativity, high achievement, and a most successful adaptive style."
—*Edward Hallowell, M.D.* and *John Ratey, M.D.*, authors of *Driven to Distraction*

"ADDers aren't abnormal, they are uniquely gifted individuals in their own right. Thom Hartmann describes these ideas, in a book that belongs in the hands of every educator, counselor, doctor, and parent."
—Review, the *Learning Disabilities Newsletter*

"Author Thom Hartmann has laid out a controversial but appealing theory."

—*Time* Magazine

"Why are Attention Deficit Disorder and related conditions so common? Could they in some way be advantageous? These questions and some possible answers are woven through this book, providing basic factual information about ADD with a twist that helps readers recognize the value—sometimes quite special—of people who have it."

—*Dale E. Hammerschmidt, M.D., F.A.C.P.,* Assoc. Prof. of Medicine, University of Minnesota

"It is refreshing to find a book that places ADD in a framework that does not imply dysfunction.... The metaphor of a "hunter in a farmer's world" fits so many of the ADD youngsters and adults with whom I have worked."

—*Margaret M. Dawson, Ed.D.*, The Center for Learning and Attention Disorders

"If you want an inside view of how ADD persons think and function in society, you should buy this book."

—*Dirk E. Huttenbach*, M.D., Psychiatrist specializing in child and adult ADD

"This book did for our family what years of being in and out of therapy failed to accomplish. It helped us to understand and appreciate each other's unique way of doing and seeing."

—*Janie Bowman*, mother of an ADD adolescent

ATTENTION DEFICIT DISORDER

A Different Perception

Also by Thom Hartmann

ADD SUCCESS STORIES
A Guide to Fulfillment
for Families with Attention Deficit Disorder

THINK FAST!
The ADD Experience
(with Janie Bowman & Susan Burgess)

BEYOND ADD
Hunting For Reasons In the Past & Present

FOCUS YOUR ENERGY
Hunting for Success in Business
with Attention Deficit Disorder

THE PROPHET'S WAY
Touching the Power of Life

ATTENTION DEFICIT DISORDER

A Different Perception

THOM HARTMANN

Grass Valley, CA
1997

ATTENTION DEFICIT DISORDER: *A Different Perception*
ISBN 1-887424-14-8 (trade paper)

 For information address the publisher: Underwood Books, PO Box 1609, Grass Valley, California 95945. The author can be reached via email at: mythical.net.

Distributed by Publisher's Group West
Manufactured in the United States of America

10 9 8 7 6 5 4 3 2
Second Edition

The ideas in this book are based on the author's personal experience with ADD, and as such are not to be considered medical advice. This book is not intended as a substitute for psychotherapy or the medical treatment of Attention-deficit Hyperactivity Disorder and the various medications described herein can only be prescribed by a physician. The reader should consult a qualified health care professional in matters relating to health and particularly with respect to any symptoms which may require diagnosis or medical attention.

Library of Congress Cataloging-in-Publication Data:
Hartmann, Thom, 1951-
Attention deficit disorder: a different perception /
Thom Hartmann --Rev. ed.
p. cm.
Previously published in 1993.
Includes bibliographical references and index.
ISBN 1-887424-14-8
1. Attention-deficit disorder in adults. 2. Attention-deficit hyperactivity disorder. I. Title.
RC394.A85H38 1997
616.85'89—dc21 97-23214
CIP

Dedicated to

Carl and Jean Hartmann

Gottfried Müller, founder of Salem

Joy Kutz, whose work lives on in our hearts

Foreword

Michael Popkin, Ph.D.

Every once in a while someone comes along who takes a body of knowledge and tilts it in such a way that a new view of the information raises up in a flash of hope and encouragement. Thom Hartmann is one of those people, and through this book he has finally put the concept of ADD into a context that we can appreciate.

With as many as 10% of the western world's children suspected of having ADD, I've often wondered how nature could have made such a mistake. Or was it a mistake? Perhaps we were just overdiagnosing—labeling more children as ADD than was warranted. Thom Hartmann's insight into this phenomenon offers a third alternative—one that both reaffirms the wisdom of nature and the value of all human beings.

As the author and director of Active Parenting, I have spent the past dozen years developing programs to help parents. Each of these programs is based on the idea that the purpose of parenting is "to protect and to prepare children to survive and to thrive in the kind of society in which they will live." All of the skills that we teach to parents in Active Parenting, from discipline to communication to encouragement, are designed to instill in children those qualities that will enable them to thrive in a contemporary democratic society. To approach the critical job of parenting without looking at the world in which our children will live—and the qualities and skills necessary to thrive in that world—makes as little sense as, well, let's say trying to hunt wild bear in the middle of a cornfield.

Yet Thom Hartmann has illuminated the fact that this is exactly the situation that ADD children and adults find themselves in, namely, hunters in a farming society. Although tremendously frustrating for the ADD person, there is nothing innately defective about the condition—at least as it is reframed in this book. It is simply a matter of having some of the right skills for the wrong time.

There is also something very encouraging in how ADD is presented as a continuum rather than an either/or phenomenon. The signs of ADD, which were clearly presented and consistent with current thinking as espoused by the American Psychological Association, becomes a mirror in which I suspect many readers will see aspects of themselves. That these signs are presented as strengths, as well as areas that may need to be compensated for in a society of Farmers, will not only offer encouragement and practical solutions to those who see themselves on the Hunter side of this continuum, but offer a fascinating insight into the evolution of humankind and society.

Dr. Michael Popkin, founder and president of Active Parenting Publishers based in Marietta, Georgia, developed the first video-based parent education programs in 1983. Since then Dr. Popkin has authored and produced several programs, as well as books, on parenting, loss education, and self-esteem education. Prior to founding Active Parenting Publishers, Dr. Popkin was a family therapist practicing in the Atlanta area. Dr. Popkin can be reached at Active Parenting Publishers, 810 Franklin Court, Suite B, Marietta, GA 30067.

Author's Preface

From Minimal Brain Damage to Hyperactivity to ADD

Every noble work is at first impossible.

—Thomas Carlyle

In the spring of 1980, I sat in the living room of the apartment of Dr. Ben Feingold, overlooking the Golden Gate Bridge in San Francisco, listening to him describe his search for a solution to the problem of hyperactivity. At the time, I was Executive Director of a residential treatment facility for abused and abandoned children, and most of the children referred to us had been diagnosed with "hyperactivity" or "minimal brain damage" (or MBD, a term later softened to "minimal brain dysfunction"). I was acutely interested in what Dr. Feingold had to say.

As a pediatric allergist, Dr. Feingold had noticed over the years that a number of his patients with skin disorders (particularly psoriasis) had identifiable allergies. When certain foods or food additives were removed from a child's diet, particularly those containing salicylates (the aspirin-like compounds contained in some foods and many food-additives), sores and crusty skin patches vanished.

But there was an odd side effect to these skin-disease cures: the children's behavior also changed. Many of Dr. Feingold's young patients, in addition to being victims of skin diseases, had been diagnosed with hyperactivity or minimal brain dysfunction. But when the skin-disease-causing foods or food additives were removed from their diets, the hyperactivity quite often disappeared, or was reduced so dramatically that parents and teachers noticed the change.

On the basis of these findings, Dr. Feingold built his theory that minimal brain dysfunction or hyperactivity results from a food or food-additive allergy. His first book, *Why Your Child Is Hyperactive* (Random House, 1975), eventually sparked a nationwide movement. "Feingold parents" set up "Feingold groups," to discuss ways to keep children away from salicylate-containing foods and food-additives. Papers were published, both condemning and supporting Feingold, and across the nation thousands of parents reported dramatic changes with his dietary program.

We tried the Feingold diet at the institution I headed, with excellent results on several children. This early institutional trial became the basis for a report on National Public Radio's *All Things Considered* program and dozens of newspaper and magazine articles. I published an article about our results in *The Journal of Orthomolecular Psychiatry*.

But there were some children with hyperactivity or minimal brain dysfunction—perhaps a majority—

whom the Feingold diet did not help. This troubling inconsistency led many professionals to discard Feingold's hypotheses in whole, and the movement that bears his name is now, several years after his death, just a shell of what it once was.

Yet Dr. Ben Feingold was a pioneer. In the opinion of many people, he discovered a key to one facet of what was later recognized to be not just one disease (the minimal brain dysfunction or hyperactive syndrome), but part of an entire spectrum of behavior disorders, including attention deficit disorder, hyperkinesis, and learning disorders such as dyslexia.

Since Feingold's time, psychiatry has largely separated hyperactivity from ADD. They are now seen as two separate (although sometimes overlapping) things.

Hyperactivity involves restless or excessive (hyper) activity. Hyperactive children are often described as being "on fire," as if they have "ants in their pants." Feingold noted these descriptions, and observed that they were probably having the normal reaction to an allergy—an itch—in the brain.

Attention deficit disorder, on the other hand, may occur without any presence of a hyperactive state. ADD is more clearly described as a person's difficulty focusing on a single thing for any significant period of time. Such people are described as excessively distractible, impatient, impulsive, and often seeking immediate gratification. They often disregard the long-term consequences of their actions, so focused are they on the moment and its rewards. They're usually disorganized and messy, because they bounce from project to project, too impatient to clean up the debris from their last activity (be it making their beds or organizing their desks). But, while ADD children usually have problems with schoolwork, they're not bouncing off the walls like their hyperactive peers.

A third category, "attention deficit hyperactive disorder" (ADHD) represents those who have both ADD and hyperactivity. This includes the majority of hyperactive children, although not all, and was the first category to be recognized in medicine more than seventy-five years ago.

While Ben Feingold believed he had found a "cure" for hyperactivity, he was baffled by his diet's failure to cure children of short attention spans. The hyperactive kids he treated no longer needed restraint or drugs, and a few became quite "normal" on his diet, but many still showed signs of the ADD syndrome which did not respond to diet.

Initially, he'd concluded that children who didn't respond had food allergies not yet discovered (such as an allergy to milk or wheat which are nearly impossible to avoid), or that his subjects were "cheating" on the diet. But a few months before he died, Dr. Feingold shared with me his concerns about this apparent inconsistency in the theory. He wondered out loud if there might be several different disorders lumped into what he had seen as a single category.

Feingold, again a prophet, was right. ADD is now increasingly being recognized as a separate syndrome from hyperactivity, something that is not generally "cured" by dietary change, other than the modest improvements which may result from using sugar in moderation.

It is interesting to note, however, that ADD children and adults often report an inordinate craving for sugar and, occasionally, exhibit some symptoms of hypoglycemia. They may also be more sensitive to the highs and crashes that come from sugar, alcohol, caffeine, and illicit drug consumption (and may benefit from avoiding those substances). But as we will see in a later chapter, these sensitivities may have little or nothing to do with symptoms of a "disease." It is quite probable that they are, instead, indicative of a biochemistry ideally suited to certain fundamental tasks.

Acknowledgments

For the preparation of this manuscript thanks go to those many ADD adults who shared their life stories so others could learn from their successes and failures.

Dianne Breen, who helped give birth to this book, and Dirk E. Huttenbach, MD, an expert in the field of child and adult ADD, were invaluable in providing anecdotes, information, and some of the core concepts which shaped the ideas presented here. G.W. Hall and Carla Nelson did a marvelous job of editing the early manuscript, and Fran and all the folks on CompuServe were a big help.

I owe a special acknowledgement to Dave deBronkart, who liberally shared his knowledge and experience with ADD, and proofread this book so thoroughly that it would not be inaccurate to say that he wrote parts of it. On the subject of ADD, Dave is the most knowledgeable layman I've met, as well as an articulate public speaker and outspoken defender of this world's ADD/Hunters.

Special thanks go to Susan Barrows, one of the world's great proofreaders, who caught at least a hundred typos in the early draft of this book while simultaneously offering valuable editorial assistance, and new and important insights into ADD.

Thanks also to Kyle Roderick and Alexis Fischer

for useful suggestions which added to the content of this book.

An excellent resource for parents of ADD children is the non-profit organization CH.A.D.D., which has chapters nationwide. For the address of a local chapter near you, write to CH.A.D.D., 499 N.W. 70th Ave., Suite 308, Plantation, FL 33317. For educational resources on ADD to individuals and support organizations, write to Attention Deficit Disorder Association (ADDA), PO Box 972, Mentor, OH 44061.

And special thanks are due to my wife, Louise, whose patience and support have helped bring this work (and so many other projects) to fruition.

Some of the money you paid for this book will go to benefit the work of the international Salem projects. For more information about Salem, write to: The Salem International Foundation, Star Route Box 60C, Frostburg, MD 21532; The New England Salem Children's Village, Stinson Lake Rd., Rumney, NH 03266; or: Kinder-und Jugendhilfswerk Salem, 95346 Stadtsteinach, Germany.

Contents

Introduction

Edward M. Hallowell, M.D.

Thom Hartmann is a businessman who is also a philosopher, world traveler, spiritualist, hiker, trainer of soldiers, author, lecturer, husband, father, son, and all-around lively human being. He is a twentieth-century pioneer, an adventurer, or as he would say, a hunter.

His idea of the hunter in the farmer's world, which he develops in this newly re-issued book, is just one of his many innovative ideas. This idea came to him when he was reading in bed one day. Never a quiet moment in the Hartmann brain. It is a fascinating idea, one that people from many different walks of life have found extremely helpful in learning how to fit best into today's world.

I won't sound-byte the idea here, but rather report what I have heard from many people around the country, that they have found this idea, as well as Thom's other books and lectures, practical and right on the mark. People mention Thom's name, and their energy level starts to rise.

What Thom offers is help, hope, and heart, as well as considerable thought and life experience. I commend both him and his books to all readers.

Edward Hallowell, M.D., is in private practice in adult and child psychiatry. He is the co-author with John J. Ratey, M.D., of Driven to Distraction and Answers to Distraction.

Author's Introduction

Hunters and Farmers Five Years Later

There must be no barriers to freedom of inquiry. There is no place for dogma in science. The scientist is free, and must be free to ask any question, to doubt any assertion, to seek for any evidence, to correct any errors.

—J. Robert Oppenheimer, (*Life*, October 10, 1949)

In the five years since the first publication of this book and my presentation of the Hunter/Farmer concept as a possible explanation for why we have ADD in our gene pool, there have been many changes in the thinking of people who study the subject. There have also been many changes in the overall view of psychiatric and physiological disorders in general, particularly those with a genetic basis.

The publication of *Why We Get Sick: The New Science of Darwinian Medicine* by Randolph Nesse M.D. and George Williams Ph.D. (Times Books) signaled a turning point in the minds of many. The book, thoroughly researched and brilliantly well-written, makes the strong and scientifically-defendable case that we are creatures living out of our element, humans with bodies and brains designed to live in a primitive natural environment and still carrying around the physical and psychological tools necessary to that environment. These include things from morning sickness to cystic fibrosis to depression. Our modern lifestyle, evolved just over the past few thousand years, represents not a norm for human life, but an incredibly brief flicker of momentary history in the 200,000 year life-span of *Homo sapiens* (people like us) on the planet.

Robert Wright's book *The Moral Animal* carries the model a step further, dealing with the subject of "Darwinian psychology," and pointing out in dramatic detail how behaviors ranging from depression to aggression to infidelity were adaptive and useful in the very-recent history of the human race.

The March 27, 1995 issue of *Time* featured a cover story on the functions of the brain and the latest research into why our brains behave the way the way they do. Evolutionary notions of behavior played an important part in that article, including the recent discovery by researchers that those people most likely to have the gene that causes the brain to crave fatty foods and thus produce obesity are also those people whose ancestors over the past 10,000 years came from parts of the world where famines were common. What was an adaptive behavior for primitive peoples has become maladaptive in a world where most "hunting" is done at the supermarket.

The 1996 publication by psychiatrists and physicians Anthony Stevens and John Price of the book

Evolutionary Psychiatry: a New Beginning (Routledge) summarized much of this research, and has provided a deep mine of material for future researchers. For example, they tell the story of the Ik, a group of hunter-gatherer peoples in Uganda whose rates of life-threatening psychological and physical illnesses exploded when they were forcibly moved from their natural hunting grounds and forced to engage in agriculture. Other examples abound in this well-researched work.

WHERE HAVE ALL THE HUNTERS GONE?

Additionally, new advances in anthropology and paleontology have answered one of the most vexing questions about the Hunter/Farmer theory: "*Why is the leftover Hunter/ADD gene only present in a minority of our population, and where have all the hunters gone?*"

In popular literature, Riane Eisler (*The Chalice and the Blade* and *Sacred Pleasures*) has explored early cultures and shows the fundamental differences between what she calls "cooperator" and "dominator" cultures. (We in western civilization are members of the latter.) Similarly, Daniel Quinn (*Ishmael* and *The Story of B*) writes about "Leavers" and "Takers" to describe a similar cultural division. About five thousand years ago, these cultural schisms set the stage for a mass extermination of hunter/gatherer peoples which continues to this day in remote parts of Africa, Asia, and the Americas.

A brilliant study published in the February, 1994 issue of *Discover* magazine detailed the exact answer to the question of when and how this happened, and has since been corroborated by other researchers. Using an analysis of language patterns and DNA, researchers found that 3,000 years ago Africa was almost entirely populated by thousands of different (genetically and in language) tribes of hunter/gatherer peoples. Population density was low and, apparently, strife was minimal.

Then a group of Bantu-speaking agriculturists in the northwestern part of Africa were apparently infected with what University of California professor of Native American Studies Jack Forbes calls the "cultural mental illness" of *Wétiko* (a native American term for the amoral and predatory behavior of the European invaders). *Wétiko* is the term that Forbes applied decades ago to describe what Eisler and Quinn today call "dominator" and "taker" cultural mass psychology.

In his penetrating and thought-provoking book *Columbus and Other Cannibals*, Professor Forbes points out how *Wétiko*, which he calls a "highly-contagious form of mental illness," originated in Mesopotamia around 5,000 years ago. From there, it spread across the fertile crescent and into Syria, eventually infecting northern Africa, Europe (via the Roman conquerors who carried Wétiko), Asia, and, with the arrival of Columbus, the Americas.

The Bantu-speaking farmers of northwest Africa, culturally contaminated by *Wétiko* beliefs in the "correctness" of genocide, systematically spread across the entire African continent over a 2,000-year period, destroying every group in their path. The result is that now fewer than one percent of the entire African continent's population are hunter/gatherers, and the languages and cultures of thousands of tribes—developed over 200,000 years of human history—have been lost forever. Entire ethnic groups were wiped out and have now vanished from the Earth.

The reasons the *Wétiko* farmers were so successful in their conquest of Africa (and later, Europe, Asia, Australia, and the Americas) is fourfold:

1. Farming is more efficient than hunting at producing food. Because it's about ten times more efficient at extracting calories from the soil, the population density of farming communities tend to be about ten times higher than those of hunting communities. And so their armies were ten times larger.

2. Farmers become immune to the diseases of their own animals. Measles, chicken pox, mumps, influenza and numerous other diseases originated in—and are still often carried by—domesticated animals. When the farmers of Europe first came to the shores of the Americas, they killed off millions of native Americans through accidental infection with these diseases, to which the local hunters had not developed immunities. (This later escalated with the deliberate infection of entire tribes with smallpox-infected blankets by the *Wétiko*-infected invaders.)

3. Farming is stable. Farmers tend to stay in one place, and that gives rise to specialization of function. The butcher, baker, candlestick maker, and weapons maker came into being, and armies were formed. Factories were a logical extension of farming technologies, and so farming peoples became even more efficient at producing weapons and technologies of destruction.

4. The *Wétiko* culture taught that slaughter could be justified on religious grounds. From its beginnings in Mesopotamia, *Wétiko* taught that the slaughter of other humans was not only acceptable, but could even be "a good thing" because it was ordered or sanctioned by their gods. The most bizarre instance of this can be seen during the Crusades, when Europeans slaughtered "heathens" in order to "save their souls." A close second is "the winning of the American West," in which Americans (whose Declaration of Independence says the Creator gave people the right to life, liberty and the pursuit of happiness) decreed that the same Creator gave white Europeans a "Manifest Destiny" to overtake the whole continent, and used this religious argument to justify killing the "heathen" residents.

While indigenous hunting peoples often had conflict with neighbors over borders and territories, these conflicts served to strengthen the cultural and independent identities of both tribes involved. *Wétiko* warfare, where every last person in the "competing" tribe is put to death, is something that no anthropologist has ever found in the history or behavior of any past or modern non-*Wétiko* hunting/gathering peoples. The *Wétiko* agriculturists, however, viewing non-Wétiko humans to be as exploitable as the land, have a history littered with genocide, slavery, and exploitation.

And so, over the past 5000 years, on every continent and among every people, hunter/gatherers have been wiped out, displaced, slaughtered, exterminated, and oppressed by *Wétiko* farmers/industrialists. Today, fewer than 2% of the world's human population are genetically pure hunter/gatherer peoples, and only a remnant of them is found in our gene pool, and that only as the result of enslavement and assimilation.

THOSE WHO WOULD DISEMPOWER FOR THEIR OWN GAIN

The *Wétiko* domination continues in our modern world.

We live in a society so psychologically sick that Mafia kingpins who sell dope and prostitution and order the murder of others live in expensive houses in "nice" neighborhoods. We honor those who have "attained success," even if they do it by selling death-dealing substances like tobacco. "Dog eat dog" is a cliché and norm in our culture, and the idea of cooperating instead of dominating is considered quaint and "nice" but idealistic and ineffective. It's assumed that to be successful in business one must lie and cheat, and our political leaders are trusted by such a pitiful minority of citizens (fewer than 20% in recent polls) that it's doubtful our governments could continue to operate if they didn't control the police, the prisons, and the tax apparatus (which is enforced by the police and prisons).

In the middle of this cultural milieu, we find those of the "helping professions." The majority enter these fields because of an honest and sincere desire to be of service to others. Much good is done and many lives are improved and even saved, and we rightfully have afforded these people a place of honor in our society. Yet within and on the fringes of these professions are also exploiters who proffer dubious advice or outright quack technologies. These controversial treatments range from injecting children with radioactive substances prior to "scanning" their brains, to hugely-marked-up herbal supplements accompanied by inflated claims, to expensive and prolonged (often for years) brand-name "therapies."

Essential to the success of the exploiters is the concept of sickness.

It is well known in the business world that if you can convince people something is wrong with them, you can then make a lot of money selling them a remedy. It's been done with facial hair, body odor, leg hair, wrinkles, varicose veins, "bad" breath, and dozens of what used to be ordinary parts of the human condition. Convince people there's something wrong with or embarrassing about their normal functions and you can get rich selling them mouthwash, douches, depilatory creams, wrinkle removers, suntan aids, diet pills, and a host of other products.

Similarly, exploiters on the fringes of the medical arena depend on the notion of sickness or abnormality to peddle their wares: to sell, they depend on convincing you that there's something about you that's intolerable, something that is wrong, something you need to change. In this context we hear some speakers and authors talk about the "importance of taking seriously" ADD.

Their message is not, "If you feel you have a problem, I have some solutions that may work," but, rather, "You are sick and I am not, and you must unquestioningly let me help you with my cure."

If we agree there is a need but we question the treatment, *our* intentions are challenged: "Why are you questioning me when I'm only trying to help you and your child?"

I will be among the first to say that being a Hunter in this Farmer's world is fraught with difficulty: nobody can deny that. The failures, evident in our prisons and schools and street people, offer loud testimony to the seriousness of ADD in today's society.

But to say, "Everything is okay with our culture and society, so it must be *you* that's seriously screwed up and needs treatment," is totally disempowering. It robs people of their humanity and dignity. It subjugates them. It is *Wétiko*.

I much prefer a rational middle ground, well articulated by Harvard Medical School associate professor of psychiatry Dr. John Ratey in his foreword to my 1995 book *ADD Success Stories*:

> After Thom Hartmann's first two books on ADD, the metaphor of the hunter began to provide many ADDers with an acceptable label for their quirkiness and a way of looking at themselves that was full of hope and permission.
>
> Just as the diagnosis of ADD itself often helps in replacing guilt with hope, so does an appealing metaphor like that of a hunter (which smacks of Robin Hood and Madame Curie) help in giving many people a sense of purpose and direction.
>
> This sort of personal mythology can provide a platform that looks to the future with promise and approval—never masking the problems of the brain but instead offering role models to gui ADDer into a more optimistic and forward-lo journey.
>
> While this new reframed version of who are should never excuse foibles or open the do self-indulgence, being granted permission t who they are often drives individuals to reach viously unattempted heights. When the shac of shame are lifted, the future can be approac with a cleaner, crisper, more energetic viewpoi

WHERE DO WE GO FROM HERE?

And so, five years after the first publication book, we are left with the ongoing questions: *W ADD, where did it come from, why do we have i where do we go from here*?

While scientists do not yet know for sure wh... the mechanism or cause of ADD is, we *do* know from numerous studies that when we describe and define people, they will most often live up to that expectation.

Tell a child he's "bad" often enough, and he'll most likely become bad. Tell her she's "brilliant," and she'll strive to achieve brilliance.

Not only do we live up to the things others tell us out loud about ourselves, we also live up to the unspoken assumptions.

The most famous example of this is the study in which a group of elementary school students were divided into two groups, balanced as much as possible by the researchers to be identical in the average of their abilities and intelligence. Then the teachers were told that group A was the highly intelligent group, and that group B was the lower intelligence group.

By the end of a single semester, group A had significantly outperformed group B academically. This wasn't just the grade the teacher gave them; it was *their actual performance* on a standardized test. Their real-life performance was substantially affected by what the teacher expected of them—even when the teacher didn't realize it.

Children *can* find and achieve their best when the adults around them help them do so.

Particularly as children, we respond to other's expectations of us. We live up to their assumptions, and we perform up to their and our belief of our ability to perform.

While there has never, ever been a study positively correlating grades in school with psychological success or adjustment in later life, there have been many which show that childhood self-esteem is a significant and generally accurate predictor of adult competence. (The book *Emotional Intelligence* by Daniel Goleman contains a wealth of this research.)

So when my son, at age 13, was diagnosed with ADD and was told that he had a "disease" that is "similar to diabetes, but instead of your pancreas being damaged and not producing enough insulin, your brain has been damaged and isn't producing enough neurotransmitters," I knew in my gut it was a lousy, disempowering story.

Not only was the message, "You're broken and we're the only ones who can fix you," but there was also an implicit, "You're broken and can never be *really* normal." In my opinion, that message profanes the sacred reality of human life and human diversity by putting people in neat little categories (which, it turns out, aren't so neat) and by then telling them that their future can only be good if they follow the dictates of the person who has redefined them.

This is well illustrated by a short semi-autobiographical story by Joe Parsons, a writer I met on the Internet. I reprint it here with his permission:

> "Dad! Dad! Look at my report card!" I let the screen door slam behind me and stood in front of my father, clutching my now-wrinkled report card.
>
> "What do you have there, Dave Jr.? Report card? Let me see it." He glanced at my grades—two C's, a D, and an A-minus. He looked down at me, frowning.
>
> "Didja see the comments, Dad? Didja? I brought that F in math up to a D! I'm gonna pass it! And look at what my teachers said, Dad!" I had read my report card over and over as I ran home. Three of my teachers said I was making "good progress" and my English teacher said, "Dave Jr. has a refreshing and creative point of view." My father kept looking at my report card, then at me. He didn't say anything for a long time.
>
> Finally, he said, "Son, these grades just aren't very good, but I know you're doing the best you

can." He sat me down on the sofa and looked at me. He seemed to be real sad. "Let me explain it to you again, son; you know those pills I have to make you take?"

"Yeah, Dad, the Ritalin... so I can pay attention better in class; they're really helping."

He looked even sadder. "Yes, son. It's a very strong medicine we have to give you because you have this very serious disease called Attention-Deficit-Disorder.'" He said it slowly, to make sure I would understand. "You see, you're not like the other kids. There's something wrong with your brain that makes you different from the other... normal... kids. When the teacher says that you have a..." he looked at the report card again. "...'refreshing and creative point of view,' what she's really saying is that you can't fit in and say things the way the other kids do."

"Is that a bad thing, Dad?"

He put his hand on my head. "I'm afraid it is, Son, but we're just going to have to live with your being ... different."

"But my teacher said I was doing a lot better, Dad; she said I was creative! Isn't that a good thing, Dad?"

He smiled at me again, but he still looked sad. "Your teacher is just trying to make you feel better, son. She doesn't realize that your disease is going to make you mess up everything you do in your life. The sooner you realize that, the easier it will be for you. I just don't want you to be disappointed, son."

I started to feel sad, too. I looked down at my father's shoes. "What am I going to do, Dad?"

"Just do the best you can, son. The main thing is not to get your hopes up." He put his arm around my shoulders. "As long as you always real-

> ize that you're different from the normal people that aren't sick like you are, you'll be a lot happier."
>
> "Okay, Dad. I'll try to remember." I took the report card from him and went to my room. I sat on my bed and read the words over and over: "good progress...refreshing and creative point of view."
>
> Soon tears blurred the words and I tossed the card on the floor. I knew Dad was right: I would always mess up.
>
> I was glad he reminded me.

I know this father meant well; he was doing the best he knew how, to respond to what he'd been told about his son's situation.

Unlike the father in this story, I spent the first year after my son's diagnosis (and the sermon by his psychologist that he isn't "normal") trying to find a deeper understanding of what this thing called ADD was. I read everything I could find, and talked with friends and former associates in the child-care industry. I learned that the three cardinal indicators of ADD are *distractibility*, *impulsiveness*, and *a love of high stimulation or risk.* (If you toss in the inability to sit still—hyperactivity—you have ADD-H or ADHD.) While I'd never seen it written anywhere, I also intuitively knew that people with ADD had a different sense of time from those without ADD.

And the more I looked at it, the more it seemed that this "illness" could also be an asset under some circumstances.

After six months of hyperfocused research, I was reading myself to sleep one night with *Scientific American.* The article was about how the end of the ice age, 12,000 years ago, brought about a mutation of grasses leading to the first appearance on earth of what we today call wheat and rice. These early cereal grains led to the development of agriculture among humans, and that point in history is referred to as the Agricultural Revolution.

As the article went into greater detail about how the agricultural revolution transformed human society, I got a "Eureka!" that was such a jolt I sat straight up in bed. "People with ADD are the descendants of hunters!" I said to my wife Louise, who gave me a baffled look. "They'd have to be constantly scanning their environment, looking for food and for threats to them: that's distractibility. They'd have to make instant decisions and act on them without a second's thought when they're chasing or being chased through the forest or jungle, which is impulsivity. And they'd have to love the high-stimulation and risk-filled environment of the hunting field."

"What are you talking about?" she said.

"ADD!" I said, waving my hands. "It's only a flaw if you're in a society of farmers!"

From that concept came what was originally a metaphor, an empowering story that I could tell my son (for whom I originally wrote this book) and others to explain their "difference" in a positive light. Since that time, we've discovered that this "story" may in fact be factually accurate: science is rapidly corroborating many of those original observations and theories.

So where we go from here is forward, into a future where people with ADD are not embarrassed or ashamed to say they are different, where children are helped in schools with appropriate interventions and tailored educational environments, and where teenagers and adults recognize in advance that some jobs or careers or mates are well-suited to their temperament and others are not. From that self-knowledge all ADDers can gain a greater measure of success in life.

We go forward as Hunters.

Northfield, VT
June, 1997

Chapter One

ADD as a State of Mind

Know the true value of time. Snatch, seize, and enjoy every moment of it. No idleness, no laziness, no procrastination. Never put off 'til tomorrow what you can do today.

—Lord Chesterfield

Somewhere between six and twenty million men, women, and children in the United States have attention deficit disorder or ADD. Millions more individuals possess many ADD-type characteristics even though they may have learned to cope so well that they don't think of themselves as people with attention-related problems.

If you are an adult who has experienced chronic issues with restlessness, impatience, poor listening skills, or a difficulty doing "boring" jobs like balancing a checkbook, you already know what it feels like to experience some of the challenges associated with ADD. And if you're the parent of an ADD child, the chances are high you have at least some ADD traits yourself.

This book is the first I know of to present the idea

that ADD is not always a disorder—but instead may be a trait of personality and metabolism; that ADD comes from a specific evolutionary need in the history of humankind; that ADD can actually be an advantage (depending on circumstances); and that, through an understanding of the mechanism which led to ADD's presence in our gene pool, we can recreate our schools and workplaces to not only accommodate ADD individuals, but to allow them to again become the powers behind cultural, political, and scientific change which they have so often historically represented.

You will see that this state of mind evolved naturally. It's not at all a malfunction—to the contrary, it's a coherent, functioning response to a different kind of world and society than that in which many of us live.

If, as you read this book, you see yourself described, it may hit you as a revelation. I've shared this information with many ADD adults, and invariably they are startled, concerned, and ultimately pleased to finally understand one of the principal forces which have shaped their lives.

This knowledge frees them to reframe the way they view their jobs, their relationships, their frustrations—which are usually legion—and their goals. It helps them set new courses and directions which may lead to greater success in life than they ever dreamed possible, or directs them to therapy or medication that will help them adjust to life in a non-ADD world and workplace.

If you're the father or mother of an ADD child, odds are high that you're an ADD adult yourself, to some extent. While long viewed as a condition that mostly affects young boys (the diagnosed prevalence in children is around 7:1, male-to-female), some authorities find that the rate of ADD among adults is 1:1, male-to-female. This gender differential may be skewed by many factors, including the fact that adult women are more likely to seek psychiatric care and therefore have a higher rate of diagnosis later in life. On the other hand, boys in our culture are, according to some studies, trained to be more aggressive and outspoken than girls. Combine this with ADD, and we may have a situation where ADD boys stand out more visibly than ADD girls, and therefore, at least in childhood, are more likely to be diagnosed.

This book does not advocate the abandonment of traditional diagnostic or treatment tools, including drugs such as Ritalin and behavioral modification therapy, for ADD. Indeed, you will see a strong case made for the proposition that such tools are often the salvation of people with ADD.

It is my hope that this book will help us remove the stigma of "illness" or "deficit" associated with a diagnosis of ADD and related conditions. A second, and equally important, goal is to provide specific tools to "work around" the dilemma of being an ADD "Hunter" in a contemporary society which is largely structured for and by non-ADD "Farmers," a concept we will explore in detail.

The individuals with whom I've shared this theory have found it both positive and transformational. This is the spirit in which this book is offered, with the sincere hope that it may help more teachers, psychologists, psychiatrists, and parents to empower and enable rather than label as sick or disabled ADD children and adults.

Chapter Two

How to Recognize Attention Deficit Disorder

Genius all over the world stands hand in hand, and one shock of recognition runs the whole circle round.

–Herman Melville (Hawthorne and His Mosses, 1850)

ADD is not an all-or-nothing diagnosis. There appears to be a curve of behaviors and personality types, ranging from extremely-non-ADD to extremely-ADD. Although there has not yet been enough research in the field to know the shape of this curve, it probably resembles a bell curve, with the majority of "normal" individuals falling somewhere in the center, showing a few ADD-like characteristics, and a minority (perhaps somewhere around 20-30 percent of the population) being split up on the two extreme ends of the spectrum.

Since a large body of research indicates that ADD is a hereditary condition, the distribution of this curve may well reflect the intermixing over the years of the genetic material of ADD and non-ADD individuals, blurring the edges of both types of behaviors. Placed along the spectrum of ADD individuals you will find people who typically exhibit some or all of the following characteristics:

❖ **Easily distracted.** ADD people are constantly monitoring the scene; they notice everything that's going on, and particularly notice changes or quickly changing things in their environment. (This is the reason why, for example, it's difficult to have a conversation with ADD people when a television is on in the room; their attention will constantly wander back to the television and its rapidly-changing inputs.)

❖ **Short, but extraordinarily intense, attention span.** Oddly enough, this isn't definable in terms of minutes or hours: some tasks will bore an ADD person in thirty seconds, other projects may hold their rapt attention for hours, days, or even months. ADD adults often have difficulty holding a job for an extended period of time, not because they're incompetent but because they become "bored." Similarly, ADD adults often report multiple marriages, or "extremely intense, but short" relationships. When tested for attention span on a boring, uninteresting task, ADD people tend to score significantly lower than others.

❖ **Disorganization, accompanied by snap decisions.** ADD children and adults are often chronically disorganized. Their rooms are a shambles, their desks are messy, their files are incoherent; their living or working areas look like a bomb went off. This is also a common characteristic of non-ADD people, possibly related to upbringing or culture, but something usually separates messy ADD folks from their non-ADD counterparts: non-ADD people can usually find what they need in their messes, while ADD people typically can't find anything. An ADD person may be working on a project when something else distracts him, and he makes the snap decision to change priorities and jump into the new project- leaving behind the debris from the previous project. One ADD adult commented that "the great thing about being disorganized is that I'm constantly making exciting discoveries. Sometimes I'll find things I didn't even know I'd lost!"

❖ **Distortions of time-sense.** Most non-ADD people describe time as a fairly consistent and linear flow. ADD individuals, on the other hand, have an exaggerated sense of urgency when they're on a task, and an exaggerated sense of boredom when they feel they have nothing to do. This sense of boredom often leads to the abuse of substances such as alcohol and drugs, which alter the perception of time, whereas the sense of fast-time when on a project leads to chronic impatience. This elastic sense of time also causes many ADD adults to describe emotional highs and lows as having a profound impact on them. The lows, particularly, may seem as if they'll last forever, whereas the highs are often perceived as flashing by.

❖ **Difficulty following directions.** This has traditionally been considered a subset of the ADD person's characteristic of not being able to focus on something they consider boring, meaningless, or unimportant. While receiving directions, conventional wisdom has it that ADD people are often monitoring their environment as well, noticing other things, thinking of other things, and, in general, not paying attention. In other words, ADD people frequently have difficulty following directions, because the directions weren't fully received and understood in the first place.

Another theory to explain this is that ADD people are very independent, and tend to dislike being told what to do. They prefer to think for themselves, and may therefore place less importance on other's directions.

But the most likely explanation for this, according to some authorities in the field, is that people with ADD have difficulty processing auditory or verbal information.

When you say to a "normal" person "Go to the store and pick up a bottle of milk, a loaf of bread, and some orange juice, then stop at the gas station and fill up the car on the way home," the "normal" person will create a mental picture of each of those things as they hear them described. They picture the store, the milk, the bread, the juice, and the gas station. This congruence of verbal and visual images makes for high-quality memory.

But an ADD person may only hear the words- without creating the mental pictures so vital to memory. They drive off to the store, repeating to themselves, "Milk, bread, juice, gas; milk, bread, juice, gas ..." until something distracts them and they lose the entire memory.

This problem with auditory processing is fairly well documented among children with ADD. However, the percentage of its prevalence among the general, non-ADD population is unknown. It may be that ADD people are only slightly more likely to have this problem, or it may be a cardinal symptom/problem.

One ADD adult described it this way: "I find my comprehension of long chains of words is improved, vastly, by a picture. That way my brain can directly absorb the pattern. If you un-pattern it and translate it into a linear string of words, then I'm forced to absorb the string and reconstruct the pattern."

This may also account for the so-very-common reports from parents of ADD children that their kids are television addicts and hate to read. Reading requires the processing of auditory information (words sounded out within the brain into internal pictures), whereas television is purely external visualization. At the residential treatment facility I ran in New Hampshire, we found it useful to remove the televisions altogether from the residences of ADD children. After a few months, the kids began reading, and the habit persisted after the reintroduction of television.

There's also a debate about the cause of the ADD/auditory processing problem.

One camp says that it's the result of a hard-wiring problem in the brain—the same mis-wiring problem that causes other ADD symptoms.

The other camp theorizes that converting auditory information to visual information is a learned behavior, acquired by most people about the time they become proficient with language, between ages two and five. Because ADD people "weren't paying attention," they may be more likely to have simply missed out on learning this vital skill.

Since the skill of converting words to pictures can be taught to ADD people with relative ease, the latter theory appears probable. Just say to an ADD child, "Will you please visualize that?" and watch for the characteristic movement of their eyes toward the ceiling, which usually means they're creating an internal mental image. If this is done each time instructions are given to an ADD child, eventually (often in a matter of weeks) the child will learn this basic skill of auditory processing and it becomes second nature. (For ADD adults, Harry Lorayne's Memory Book is wonderful, with its heavy emphasis on several methods to teach this skill, along with what Lorayne calls original awareness, which is merely a painless method of teaching yourself to pay attention.)

❖ **Exhibit occasional symptoms of depression**, or daydream more than others. ADD individuals who are relatively self-aware about the issues of sugar and food metabolism often report that depression or tiredness follows a meal or the consumption of sugary foods. This reaction may be related to differences in glucose (sugar) metabolism between ADD and non-ADD people, which we'll discuss in more detail later.

Another possibility is that ADD people are simply bored more often by the lack of challenges presented by our schools, jobs, and culture, and this boredom translates for some people into depression.

❖ **Take risks.** ADD individuals seem to have strong swings of emotion and conviction, and make faster decisions than non-ADD types. While this trait often leads to disaster (I've spoken with several psychiatrists who suggest that, in their experience, American prison populations may be up to 90 percent ADD), it also means that ADD individuals are frequently the spark plugs of our society, the shakers and movers, the people who bring about revolution and change. ADD expert Dr. Edna Copeland, in a 1992 Atlanta speech, referenced a recent study which indicates that about half of all entrepreneurs test out as being ADD.

Evidence is strong that many of our Founding Fathers were also ADD (see the chapter titled *Hunters Who Have Changed the World*). If they hadn't been, the United States of America might never have come into being. ADD risk-takers may have predominated in the early Americas because those were the people best suited to undertake the voyage to this continent and face the unknown.

❖ **Easily frustrated and impatient.** To "not suffer fools gladly" is a classic ADD characteristic. While others may beat around the bush, searching for diplomacy, an ADD individual is most often direct, to the point, and can't understand how or why such bluntness might give offense. And when things aren't working out, "Do Something!" becomes the ADD person's rallying cry- even if the something is sloppy or mistaken.

WHAT THE EXPERTS SAY

The American Psychiatric Association's DSM III-R defined a person as having attention deficit hyperactive disorder (ADHD) if they meet eight or more of the criteria paraphrased here. As of this writing, this is the only "official" method for diagnosing ADHD, in children or adults:

1. When required to remain seated, a person has difficulty doing so.
2. Stimuli extraneous to the task at hand are easily distracting.
3. Holding attention to a single task or play activity is difficult.
4. Frequently will hop from one activity to another, without completing the first.
5. Fidgets or squirms (or feels restless mentally).
6. Doesn't want to, or can't, wait for his or her turn when involved in group activities.
7. Before a question is completely asked, will often interrupt the questioner with an answer.
8. Has problems with job or chore follow-through, and this difficulty doesn't stem from some other learning disability or defiant behavior.
9. Can't play quietly without difficulty.
10. Impulsively jumps into physically dangerous ac-

tivities without weighing the consequences. (This is different from garden-variety thrill-seeking, and more accurately characterized by a child running into the street without looking first.)

11. Easily loses things such as pencils, tools, papers, etc., which may be necessary to complete school or other work.
12. Interrupts others inappropriately, butting in when not invited.
13. Talks impulsively or excessively.
14. Others report that the person doesn't seem to be listening when spoken to.

The three caveats on these diagnostic criteria are that the behaviors must have started before age seven, not represent some other form of classifiable mental illness, and occur more frequently than the average person of the same age. The term ADHD-RS, the RS representing Residual State, is used to describe this condition in adults.

CONDITIONS THAT MAY MIMIC ADD, AND VICE-VERSA

Several conditions may mimic certain characteristics of ADD, causing an inaccurate diagnosis. These include:

❖ **Anxiety disorders.** ADD may cause anxiety when people find themselves in school, life, or work situations with which they cannot cope. ADD differs from garden-variety anxiety disorder in that an anxiety disorder is usually episodic, whereas ADD is continual and lifelong. If anxiety comes and goes, it's probably not ADD.

❖ **Depression**. ADD may also cause depression, and sometimes depression causes a high level of distractibility that's diagnosed as ADD. Depression, however, is also usually episodic. When depressed patients are given Ritalin or other stimulant drugs, which seem to help with ADD patients, depressed patients will often experience a short-term "high" followed by an even more severe rebound-depression.

❖ **Manic-Depressive Illness.** Manic-depression is not often diagnosed as ADD because the classic symptoms of manic-depressive illness are so severe. One day a person is renting a ballroom in a hotel to entertain all his friends; the next day he's suicidal. Yet ADD is often misdiagnosed as manic-depressive illness. A visit to any adult-ADD support group usually produces several first-person stories of ADD adults who were given lithium or some other inappropriate drug because their ADD was misdiagnosed as manic-depressive illness.

❖ **Seasonal Affective Disorder.** This recently discovered condition appears to be related to a deficiency of sunlight exposure during the winter months and is most prevalent in northern latitudes. Seasonal affective disorder (SAD) symptoms include depression, lethargy, and a lack of concentration during the winter months. It's historically cyclical, predictable, and is currently treated by shining a certain spectrum and brightness of light on a person for a few minutes or hours at a particular time each day, tricking the body into thinking that the longer days of spring and summer have arrived. Seasonal affective disorder is sometimes misdiagnosed as ADD, and vice versa, but seasonality is its hallmark trait.

MAKING A DIAGNOSIS

Most likely, looking at the American Psychiatric Association's criteria, you saw bits of yourself and others. While numerous books and therapists offer elaborate (and sometimes expensive) tests for ADHD/ADD, it's important to remember that, according to the American Psychiatric Association, the only true diagnostic standard is to "hit" on their specified criteria, viewed through the lens of their three caveats. While elaborate and time-consuming tests may be interesting, and may provide useful insights into other facets of personality, none are officially recognized by the American Psychiatric Association, which is the final arbiter of these matters in the United States.

This is important for the consumer to realize, since some practitioners or clinic managers state that a diagnosis of ADD requires that you pay them for a test. Such is not the case.

❖ **The Hallowell-Ratey criteria.** In 1992, psychiatrists Edward M. Hallowell and John J. Ratey developed, through years of clinical practice, study, and observation, their own set of criteria for spotting probable ADD, particularly in adults. While this isn't an "official" set of diagnostic criteria, since its first appearance in their book *Driven to Distraction* it has become one of the more common standards against which both lay people and clinicians measure the probability of a person having ADD.

In publishing this, they added this caveat: *The following criteria are suggested only. They are based upon our clinical experience and constitute what we consider to be the most commonly encountered symptoms in adults with Attention Deficit Disorder. These criteria have not been validated by field trials, and should be regarded only as a clinical guide. Consider a criterion as being met only if the behavior is considerably more frequent than that of most people of the same mental age.*

According to Hallowell and Ratey, ADD may be present when we see a chronic disturbance in which at least twelve of the following criteria are present (quoted from *Driven to Distraction: Recognizing and Coping with Attention Deficit Disorder from Childhood through Adulthood [Simon & Schuster, 1995] with the kind permission of the authors):*

1. **A sense of underachievement, of not meeting one's goals (regardless of how much one has actually accomplished).** We put this symptom first because it is the most common reason an adult seeks help. "I just can't get my act together" is the frequent refrain. The person may be highly accomplished by objective standards, or may be floundering, stuck with a sense of being lost in a maze, unable to capitalize on innate potential.
2. **Difficulty getting organized.** Organization is a major problem for most adults with ADD. Without the structure of school, without parents around to get things organized for him or her, the adult may stagger under the organizational demand of everyday life. The supposed "little things" may mount up to create huge obstacles. For want of the proverbial nail—a missed appointment, a lost check, a forgotten deadline—their kingdom may be lost.
3. **Chronic procrastination or trouble beginning a task.** Often, due to their fears that they won't do it right, they put it off, and off, which, of course, only adds to the anxiety around the task.
4. **Many projects going simultaneously; trouble with follow-through**. A corollary of #3. As one task is put off, another is taken up. By the end of the day, week, or year, countless projects have been undertaken, while few have found completion.
5. **Tendency to say what comes to mind without necessarily considering the timing or appropriate-**

ness of the remark. Like the child with ADD in the classroom, the adult with ADD gets carried away in enthusiasm. An idea comes and it must be spoken; tact or guile yields to child-like exuberance.

6. **A restive search for high stimulation**. The adult with ADD is always on the lookout for something novel, something engaging, something in the outside world that can catch up with the whirlwind that's rushing inside.

7. **A tendency to be easily bored**. A corollary of #6. Boredom surrounds the adult with ADD like a sinkhole, ever ready to drain off energy and leave the individual hungry for more stimulation. This can easily be misinterpreted as a lack of interest; actually it is a relative inability to sustain interest over time. As much as the person cares, his battery pack runs low quickly.

8. **Easy distractibility, trouble focusing attention, tendency to tune out or drift away in the middle of a page or a conversation, often coupled with an ability to hyperfocus at times.** The hallmark symptom of ADD. The "tuning out" is quite involuntary. It happens when the person isn't looking, so to speak, and the next thing you know, he or she isn't there. An often extraordinary ability to hyperfocus is also usually present, emphasizing the fact that this is a syndrome not of attention deficit but of attention inconsistency.

9. **Often creative, intuitive, highly intelligent**. Not a symptom, but a trait deserving of mention. Adults with ADD often have unusually creative minds. In the midst of their disorganization and distractibility, they show flashes of brilliance. Capturing this "special something" is one of the goals of treatment.

10. **Trouble in going through established channels, following proper procedure**. Contrary to how it

often appears, this is not due to some unresolved problem with authority figures. Rather, it is a manifestation of boredom and frustration: boredom with routine ways of doing things and excitement around novel approaches, and frustration with being unable to do things the way they're supposed to be done.

11. **Impatient; low tolerance for frustration**. Frustration of any sort reminds the adult with ADD of all the failures in the past. "Oh, no," he thinks, "here we go again." So he gets angry or withdraws. The impatience has to do with the need for stimulation and can lead others to think of the individual as immature or insatiable.

12. **Impulsive, either verbally or in action, as in** impulsive spending of money, changing plans, enacting new schemes or career plans, and the like. This is one of the more dangerous of the adult symptoms, or, depending on the impulse, one of the more advantageous.

13. **Tendency to worry needlessly, endlessly; tendency to scan the horizon looking for something to worry about alternating with inattention to or disregard for actual dangers.** Worry is what attention turns into when it isn't focused on some task.

14. **Sense of impending doom, insecurity, alternating with high-risk-taking.** This symptom is related to both the tendency to worry needlessly and the tendency to be impulsive.

15. **Mood swings, depression, especially when disengaged from a person or a project.** Adults with ADD, more than children, are given to unstable moods. Much of this is due to their experience of frustration and/or failure, while some of it is due to the biology of the disorder.

16. **Restlessness**. One usually does not see in an adult the full-blown hyperactivity one may see in a

child. Instead one sees what looks like "nervous energy:" pacing, drumming of fingers, shifting position while sitting, leaving a table or room frequently, feeling edgy while at rest.

17. **Tendency toward addictive behavior.** The addiction may be to a substance such as alcohol or cocaine, or to an activity, such as gambling, or shopping, or eating, or overwork.

18. **Chronic problems with self-esteem.** These are the direct and unhappy result of years of conditioning: years of being told one is a klutz, a space-shot, an underachiever, lazy, weird, different, out of it, and the like. Years of frustration, failure, or of just not getting it right do lead to problems with self-esteem. What is impressive is how resilient most adults are, despite all setbacks.

19. **Inaccurate self-observation**. People with ADD are poor self-observers. They do not accurately gauge the impact they have on other people. This can often lead to big misunderstandings and deeply hurt feelings.

20. **Family history of ADD or manic-depressive illness or depression or substance abuse or other disorders of impulse control or mood.** Since ADD is genetically transmitted and related to the other conditions mentioned, it is not uncommon (but not necessary) to find such a family history.

In addition to requiring 12 out of 20 hits on this test, Drs. Hallowell and Ratey add that, as with the DSM criteria, these characteristics must include a childhood history of similar behaviors and not be explainable by other medical or psychiatric conditions.

The DSM says a psychiatric diagnosis isn't warranted unless something's wrong—unless there's some significant impairment of a major life function. My friend and editor, Dave deBronkart, found that he meets the criteria for ADD on the above tests. When he told an ADD expert that he was quite successful in his life nonetheless, the response was, "You probably have something wrong with you and don't even know it."

This is symptomatic of how pathology-obsessed our culture has become, often to the disadvantage of people (particularly children) who are forced to wear the label of "something wrong."

In contrast, this book offers new insights, perspectives, and tools that many find useful and compatible additions to the traditional view of ADD.

"As a physician I've worked among indigenous hunting societies in other parts of the world, from Asia to the Americas. Over and over again I see among their adults and children the constellation of behaviors that we call ADD.

"Among the members of the tribes of northern Canada, such as the caribou hunters of the McKenzie Basin, these adaptive characteristics—constantly scanning the environment, quick decision-making (impulsiveness) and a willingness to take risks—contribute every year to the tribe's survival.

"These same behaviors, however, often make it difficult for tribal children to succeed in western schools when we try to impose our western curriculum on them."

–Will Krynen, MD

Chapter Three

Hunters in Our Schools and Offices: The Origin of ADD

There is a passion for hunting, something deeply implanted in the human breast.

—Charles Dickens (*Oliver Twist*, 1837)

The earliest theories about attention deficit disorder characterized it as a diseased state which had to do with brain damage or dysfunction. At various times it has been lumped in with fetal alcohol syndrome, mental retardation, various genetic mental illnesses, psychiatric disorders resulting from early trauma or childhood abuse, and the theory that parental smoking led to fetal oxygen deprivation.

Prior to the early 1970s, when ADD was first characterized as a specific disorder, ADD children and adults were largely treated simply as "bad people" (even though attentional deficits have been recognized in the psychological literature since 1905). They were the kids who always got into trouble, the James Deans of the world, the rootless and unsettled adults like Abraham Lincoln's father, The Lone Ranger, or John Dillinger.

More recent research, however, has demonstrated a high incidence of ADD among the parents of ADD children. This discovery caused some psychologists to initially postulate that ADD was the result of growing up in a dysfunctional family; they suggested that ADD may follow the same pattern as child or spousal abuse, moving through generations as learned behavior. The dietary-cause advocates contended that children pattern their parent's eating habits, and this accounts for the generational patterns of ADD. Other studies suggest that, like Down's Syndrome or muscular dystrophy, ADD is a genetic disease, and a specific gene* has been identified by scientists as the leading candidate.

But if ADD is a genetic disease or an abnormality, it's a popular one, possibly afflicting as many as 25 million individuals in the United States. (Some estimates put ADD as occurring in 20 percent of males and 5 percent of females. Other estimates are much lower, hitting a bottom of 3 percent of males and .5 percent of females.) With such a wide distribution among our population, is it reasonable to assume that ADD is simply a quirk? That it's some sort of an aberration caused by defective genes or child abuse?

When the condition is so widely distributed, inevitable questions arise: *Why? Where did ADD come from?*

The answer is: people with ADD are the leftover

* The A1 variant of the D2 dopamine receptor gene

hunters, those whose ancestors evolved and matured thousands of years in the past in hunting societies.

There is ample precedent for genetic "diseases" which, in fact, represent evolutionary survival strategies. Sickle-cell anemia, for example, is now known to make its victims less susceptible to malaria. When living in the jungles of Africa where malaria is endemic, it was a powerful evolutionary tool against death by disease; in the malaria-free environment of North America, it became a liability.

The same is true of Tay-Sachs disease, a genetic condition which hits mainly Eastern European Jews, and confers on them a relative immunity to tuberculosis. And even cystic fibrosis, the deadly genetic disease common among Caucasians (one in twenty-five white Americans carries the gene), may represent a genetic adaptation—recent research indicates the cystic fibrosis gene helps protect its victims, at younger ages, from death by such diarrheal diseases as cholera, which periodically swept Europe thousands of years ago.

It's not so unusual, apparently, for humans to have, built into our genetic material, protection against local diseases and other environmental conditions. Certainly, Darwin's theory of natural selection argues in favor of such bodily defenses. Those individuals with the immunities would survive to procreate and pass along their genetic material.

As the human race moved from its earliest ancestors, two basic types of cultures evolved. In the areas which were lush with plant and animal life and had a low human population density, hunters and gatherers predominated. In other parts of the world (particularly Asia), farming or agricultural societies evolved.

SUCCESSFUL HUNTERS

Be it pursuing buffalo in North America, hunting deer in Europe, chasing wildebeest in Africa, or picking fish from a stream in Asia, these hunters needed a certain set of physical and mental characteristics to be successful:

❖ **They constantly monitor their environment.** That rustle in the bushes could be a lion or a coiled snake. Failure to be fully aware of the environment and notice the faint sound might mean a swift and painful death. Or, that sound or flash of movement might be the animal the hunter was stalking, and noticing it could mean the difference between a full belly and hunger.

I've walked through forests and jungles with modern Hunter-types, in the United States, Europe, and East Africa, and one characteristic always struck me: they notice everything. A flipped-over stone, a tiny footprint, a distant sound, an odd smell in the air, the direction in which flowers point or moss grows. All these things have meaning to Hunters and, even when walking quickly, they notice *everything*..

❖ **They can totally throw themselves into the hunt; time is elastic.** Another characteristic of a good Hunter is the ability to totally focus on the moment, utterly abandoning all consideration of any other time or place. When the Hunter sees the prey he gives chase through gully or ravine, over fields or through trees, giving no thought to the events of the day before, not considering the future, simply living totally in that one pure moment and immersing himself in it. When involved in the hunt, time seems to speed; when not in the hunt, time becomes slow. While a Hunter's ability to concentrate in general may be low, his ability to utterly throw himself into the hunt *at the moment* is astonishing.

❖ **They're flexible, capable of changing strategy on a moment's notice.** If the wild boar vanishes into the brush, and a rabbit appears, the Hunter is off in a new direction. Orderliness is not particularly important to a Hunter, but the abilities to make a quick decision and then act on it are vital.

❖ **They can throw an incredible burst of energy into the hunt,** so much so that they often injure themselves or exceed "normal" capabilities, without realizing it until later. Not unlike that quintessential of all Hunters, the lion, they have incredible bursts of energy—but not necessarily a lot of staying power. Given the choice of describing themselves as the tortoise or the hare in Aesop's famous fable, a Hunter would always say that he or she is the hare.

❖ **They think visually.** Hunters often describe their actions in terms of pictures, rather than words or feelings. They create outlines in their heads of where they've been and where they're going. (Aristotle taught a memory method like this, with which a person would visualize rooms in a house, then objects in the rooms. When he gave a speech, he'd simply move from room to room in his memory, noticing the objects therein, which were reminders of the next thing he had to talk about.) Hunters often aren't much interested in abstractions, or else want to convert them to a visual form as quickly as possible. They tend to be lousy chess players, disdaining strategy because they prefer to go straight for the jugular.

❖ **They love the hunt, but are easily bored by mundane tasks** such as having to clean the fish, dress the meat, or fill out the paperwork. Donald Haughey, a former senior executive with Holiday Inns, tells the story of how Kemmons Wilson, the legendary founder of Holiday Inns, had a group of executives he called Bear Skinners. Wilson would go out into the world and shoot the bear (negotiate a new hotel site, bring in new financing, open a new division, etc.), and his Bear Skinners would take care of the details of "skinning and cleaning" the deal.

❖ **They'll face danger that "normal" individuals would avoid.** A wounded boar, or elephant, or bear, can kill you—and many a Hunter has been killed by his would-be prey. If you extend this analogy to warfare, where the Hunters are often the front line infantry or the most aggressive officers, the same is true. Hunters take risks. Extending this metaphor, Patton was a Hunter, Marshall a Farmer.

❖ **They're hard on themselves and those around them.** When your life depends on split-second decisions, your frustration and impatience threshold necessarily tend to be low. A fellow Hunter who doesn't get out of the way of a shot, or a soldier who defies orders and smokes on a dark night showing the enemy your position, cannot be tolerated.

PEOPLE WITH ADD ARE DESCENDANTS OF HUNTERS

So, the question: where did ADD come from? If you compare the list of classic ADD symptoms, and the list of the characteristics of a good hunter, you'll see that they match almost perfectly. In other words, an individual with the ADD collection of characteristics would make an extraordinarily good hunter. A failure to have any one of those characteristics might mean death in the forest or jungle.

Chapter Four

"Normal" People: The Origins of Agriculture

When tillage begins, other arts follow. The farmers therefore are the founders of human civilization.
–Daniel Webster (*On Agriculture*, January 13, 1840)

Since ADD is a collection of skills and predilections necessary for the success and survival of a good Hunter, we're left with the question, "What about non-ADD people?" Where did their skills evolve from, and why do they represent the majority of the people in our culture?

The answer lies with the second basic type of human culture which primitive man produced: the agricultural society. In this sort of community, farmers were the ones who provided sustenance and survival. And the skills of a good Farmer are quite different from those of a good Hunter.

To go through a list parallel to those of a Hunter, we find that a good Farmer:

❖ **Isn't easily distracted by his or her environment.** It may take three or four weeks to plant all the seed or rice shoots necessary for a complete crop, and the window of good weather may be very limited. If the Farmer were to be distracted while planting, and wander off to investigate a noise in the forest, or spend days trying to figure out why one plant was slightly larger than another, the crop wouldn't get planted—and he or she would starve.

❖ **Farmers sustain a slow-and-steady effort** for hours every day, days every week, weeks every month. While it could be argued that there are bursts of energy needed during harvest time, most Hunters would say that such bursts are nothing compared to chasing a deer fifteen miles through a forest. And the Farmer's bursts need to last all day, often for days or weeks at a time. Even in high gear, a Farmer's efforts would be characterized as fast-and-steady.

❖ **Farmers see the long-range picture,** and stick to it. While subtle or limited experiments are useful for Farmers, to bet the entire crop on a new seed might lead to disaster. A Farmer isn't looking five minutes ahead, or an hour ahead (like a Hunter), but must, instead, look years ahead. How will this crop affect the soil? What impact will it have on erosion? Will it be enough to sustain the family or village through the winter? I've visited terraced hillsides supporting rice paddies or olive trees built by long-sighted farmers in Israel, Greece, and China that are still farmed more than 3,000 years after they were constructed: Farmers have the long view.

❖ **Farmers are not easily bored.** They pace themselves when living, the same way they pace themselves when farming. During the summer when things are growing, or during the winter when not much can be done, farmers find constructive tasks to occupy their time such as building furniture, chopping firewood, or weeding the garden. They don't mind repetitive tasks or things that take a long time to accomplish because that's the nature of farming. Given Aesop's model, a farmer would describe him or herself as the tortoise who ultimately wins the race through slow and steady effort.

❖ **Farmers are team players,** and often very sensitive to others' needs and feelings. Because Farmers often must live and work together, particularly in primitive farming communities, they must cooperate. Japanese society is perhaps the most exaggerated example of this, evolving from an almost purely agricultural base. They think in terms of abstract notions and feelings, considering the future and the good of the community, and are patient chess players. Teamwork is a powerful asset of a Farmer.

❖ **Farmers attend to the details.** A Farmer must make sure all the wheat is threshed, all the cows are milked completely, all the fields are planted, or he or she courts disaster for the entire community. If a cow isn't milked completely it can become infected; a crop put into ground that's too wet or too dry might rot or wither. Einstein's "God is in the details" might be a favorite saying of a farmer.

❖ **Farmers are cautious.** Farming doesn't often demand that a person face short-term danger. Farmers learn, instead, to face the more long-term dangers. They're often better planners than they are fighters.

❖ **Farmers are patient with others.** The patience that it takes to watch a plant grow for five months is easily translated into patience with a co-worker who wants to explain a problem or situation.

FARMERS AS NON-ADD INDIVIDUALS

A quick review of the Farmer's characteristics (obviously simplified for purposes of explanation), and a comparison of them with the Hunter's skills, shows that one could easily recharacterize ADD and non-ADD persons as Hunters and Farmers. Although most people don't fit into such neat categories, it's still possible to see the archetypes demonstrated in people we all know.

Individuals who are almost pure Hunters are classified as classic ADD. Individuals who are almost pure Farmers are classified as slow, careful, methodical, and, sometimes, boring. Since Farmer characteristics are less likely to be risky and dangerous (for reasons explained), these extremely non-ADD people are not often classified by psychologists. They don't get into trouble, and tend not to stand out in our society.

Accepting the idea that there's probably a bell curve to these behaviors, though, we can posit a norm which incorporates both Hunter and Farmer behaviors, with swings in both directions on either side of the center line.

An interesting footnote to this hypothesis is the observation that Europeans often view Americans and Australians as "brash and risk-taking." Americans and Australians often view Europeans as "stodgy and conservative." Accepting the notion that ADD is an inherited trait, consider the types of people who would risk life and limb for a journey across the Atlantic in the seventeenth century—they'd have to be either desperate Farmers or normal Hunters. Similarly, Australia's early white population was often descended from prisoners sent there by England; the misfits and malcontents of British society. (I suspect a very large percentage were ADD Hunters who couldn't succeed as the Industrial Revolution "Farmer-ized" the British labor market and culture.)

ADD also appears to be a condition that's relatively rare among Japanese whose ancestors have lived in a purely agricultural society for at least 6,000 years.

A final postscript: Some people have objected to the words Hunter and Farmer. Hunter, some say, has negative connotations: killer, predator, a threat in the night. Farmer is equally negative, in that it implies a boring, passive sort of person, and many Farmers (as described in this book) are far from either.

If it makes you more comfortable, perhaps an alternate set of words would be Lookout and Cultivator. *Both are necessary for the common good:* Where would the cultivator be without the lookout, and vice versa?

Worse, think what a disaster it would be to put either in the other's job. The Cultivator doesn't catch the little signs of the impending invasion, and the Lookout can't pay attention long enough to weed the garden.

Yet that's precisely what happens to most ADD Lookouts in today's classrooms and offices. If they look out the window (as their instincts demand), they're scolded for not being good, attentive Farmers.

A more successful approach might be to recognize and speak to the skills inherent in the fast-moving Lookout frame of mind. This may require a shift in viewpoint, but it's not difficult once you see the difference between Hunters and Farmers.

Chapter Five

Could Someone With ADD Have Survived in a Primitive Hunting Society?

Insanity in individuals is something rare—but in groups, parties and nations, and epochs it is the rule.
— Nietzsche, *Beyond Good and Evil*

Many thoughtful people on all sides of the ADD issue have asked me this question. One of the most articulate put it quite succinctly when he said that if he'd been alive 10,000 years ago he would have been doomed because "I'd forget to take my spear with me when we left for the hunt!"

Others have taken pains to point out to me the necessity of organized cooperative action for most primitive hunting parties. The ideal of a hyperactive loner going through the woods looking for dinner doesn't at all characterize how most anthropologists describe primitive (or today's) hunter/gatherer methods.

At first glance, it would appear that these considerations blow a hole in the hypothesis that modern people with ADD are carrying around a remnant of hunter/gatherer genetic material. It lends credibility to the notion that ADD is, in fact, a "disease" or at least "not normal," and may not have ever been "normal" in human history.

But that overlooks a critical issue: cultural context, the effect of what we learn to believe about ourselves as we're growing up.

Cultural anthropologists are quick to point out that it's extremely difficult for any one culture to clearly view another. We instinctively assume when observing their behaviors that they're motivated in the same ways we are, that they behave the way they do for the same reasons we would if we were in their situation, and that they share our assumptions about how the world works and humanity's role in the world.

This is a dangerous error, which even tripped up Margaret Mead when she was writing *Coming of Age in Samoa.* Since her well-intentioned but well-publicized error, few anthropologists would make this mistake. But it's easy for somebody untrained in the field.

The problem, essentially, is that most people, when thinking of "primitive times," imagine *themselves* running around in the woods wearing animal skins and carrying a spear. In their mind's eye, they transport a twentieth century person back into a fantasy past. But these "Connecticut Yankees in King Arthur's Court" don't represent what it was like to grow up in those times; they arrive in a different era complete with all our acculturation, carrying along all the damage done to them by our culture. They haul along the preparations we've received for a Farmers/Industrialists life, but utterly lacking preparation for a Hunters/Gatherers life.

The fact of the matter is that people in hunter/gatherer tribes live very different lives than we do, and therefore grow up to be very different persons from us.

ADDERS ARE DAMAGED BY GROWING UP IN OUR SOCIETY, NOT IN HUNTING CULTURES

Cultural anthropologist Jay Fikes pointed this out to me when we first discussed the idea of hunters and farmers as an explanation for many modern psychological differences among people. His research showed that individuals living among the historically agricultural Native Americans, such as the Hopi and other Pueblo Indians, are relatively sedate and risk-averse. On the other hand, Fikes said, members of the hunting tribes such as the Navajo are "constantly scanning their environment and are more immediately sensitive to nuances. They're also the ultimate risk takers. They and the Apaches were great raiders and warriors."

Navajo children grow up in a society of Navajo hunter and warrior adults (at least they did before we conquered them, destroyed their culture, shattered their religions, stole their land, and murdered most of their citizens). The Navajo raised their children as hunters and warriors. Until we arrived with horses and guns, they were extraordinarily successful, and had survived as an intact culture for thousands of years longer than we have.

But we today are not a society of hunters, raiders, and warriors. We are farmers, office- and factory-workers. Therefore, we punish and discourage hunter and warrior behavior in our children and adults.

When people grow up being punished for being the way they are, they become damaged. They think of themselves as misfits and incompetents. They lose their own personal power, become shaken and fearful, and develop a variety of compensating behaviors—many of which are less than useful.

What you—the parent, teacher, counselor, or physician—tell the ADD child about himself can have a decisive effect. Children respond very differently to being told "This is how your brain works" instead of "Your brain just don't work right."

To think that these modern ADD people—damaged, shaken, hurt, and weakened by growing up in the wrong time and culture—could somehow solve all their problems by simply transporting themselves back to some mythical prehistoric hunting era is a fantasy. It wouldn't work. They weren't raised and trained to survive in that environment; they weren't taught to channel their energies into being hunters and warriors. Instead, they were spanked and slapped, told to shut up and given detention, and—the ultimate insult—told that they are damaged goods and have a brain disease worthy of the labels "deficit" and "disorder."

HUNTERS ARE BOTH BORN AND MADE

Every type of culture puts enormous amounts of effort into educating and inculcating cultural values into their citizens. That's how it becomes a culture.

In hundreds of ways, we are daily taught and reminded of what is expected of us, what the limits and boundaries are, and what are appropriate and inappropriate goals and behaviors. Most of this teaching is so subtle we're totally unaware of it—a glance from a stranger when we talk too loud in a restaurant, for example—but our days are filled with it. It shapes us and molds our beliefs, our assumptions, and ultimately our reality.

We come face-to-face with these differences when we encounter other cultures. I remember my shock and dismay at discovering, the first time I was in Japan negotiating on behalf of my company, that I had committed dozens of major cultural blunders in my interactions. Even more shocking confrontations occur when we meet people from far disparate tribes: I remember how odd I felt when, deep in the jungle of central Uganda, I stood in a village of people who were mostly naked. My jeans, shoes, shirt, and carried jacket seemed an oddity to them, and began to seem that way to me after a few hours.

And so we train our young. We reinforce and strengthen in them those behaviors, assumptions, and beliefs that we find useful as a society, and we discourage or crush in them those that are not useful or even counterproductive to the orderly flow of our culture and its work.

Farming societies teach their young how to be good farmers. Hunting societies train their children in the ways of the hunt. Industrial societies raise their children to be good factory workers. Warrior cultures teach warfare to their children.

By the time a young man in the Ugandan Ik hunter/gatherer tribe is ready to go out on a hunt with the men, he has been trained his entire life for that moment. He's played at it virtually from birth. He's had a personal mentor for half his lifetime, an adult who has taught him the lore of the jungle and the prey. He's practiced for thousands of hours. He may be high-energy, impulsive, distractible, and a risk-taker, but he is also a brilliant and proficient hunter, a master killing machine. He has been trained from his first steps to focus and concentrate that wild energy on this one task, and to exploit and use his scanning and quick-thinking and love of adventure to cooperate with the other men in the jungle to bring home dinner.

In this context, you can see how naïve it is to ask if a "person with ADD" (which is, after all, a "disorder" defined only by, and unique to, our culture) could succeed in a hunting/gathering society.

There's little doubt that a child who's had his ego bashed from thirty different directions since he was little, who's spent his life being told "don't be that way" and "sit down and shut up," whose only well-honed hunting skill is finding MTV with his remote control, would fail in the jungle. Anyone who's always been told they're no good will lack confidence and will fail to perform.

This was perfectly illustrated by a story in *Newsweek* in 1994. It was an account of an ongoing study of a group of now-adults with ADD who were diagnosed as having ADD in elementary school in the 1960s: some had significantly lower outcomes in life than people not diagnosed with ADD.

But nowhere in the study, or the article, was it mentioned that only the ADD subjects were told they were "disordered" and required to take drugs for their "mind sickness" while still children.

For the study to have statistical validity, a matching population of non-ADD children would have to have been treated the same way, and their outcome would have to be compared against the ADD population.

Of course no ethical researcher would dare take a perfectly ordinary child and tell him such things: too many past studies in the field of psychology have shown how destructive the outcome could be. But that's exactly what we've been doing with our ADD children.

If that same child with the bashed ego had been born into a hunting tribe, so that his traits were developed instead of being beaten out of him, he may well have turned out to be the mightiest of their warriors, the most brilliant of their hunters, the wisest of their elders.

Chapter Six

How to Turn a "Disorder" Back into a Skill (A Survival Guide for ADD Adults)

Nearly every man who develops an idea works it up to the point where it looks impossible, and then he gets discouraged. That's not the place to become discouraged.
—Thomas Edison

If you've read this far with an open mind, I hope you've accepted the notion that ADD is neither a deficit nor a disorder. It is, instead, an inherited set of skills, abilities, and personality tendencies which would enable a Hunter or warrior or lookout to be eminently successful—and would condemn a Farmer or an accountant to certain disaster. So how did this powerful set of Hunter skills come to be labeled as a disorder?

Historically, societies have viewed people whose behaviors they didn't understand, or which weren't "the norm," as inferior. Certainly the debates of the seventeenth, eighteenth, and nineteenth centuries here in the United States about whether Native Americans and African slaves were human highlights the extremes to which people are willing to take notions of culturalism. People who are seen as different are often lumped into a "not-quite-human" category, as were Japanese-Americans during World War II or physically disabled Americans in present times.

The following quotation serves as example to this phenomenon: *"I am not, nor ever have been, in favor of bringing about in any way the social and political equality of the white and black races ... I am not nor ever have been in favor of making voters or jurors of Negroes, nor of qualifying them to hold office, nor to intermarry with white people; and I will say in addition to this that there is a physical difference between the races which I believe will for ever forbid the two races living together on terms of social and political equality."* (—Abraham Lincoln)

Therefore, when Hunter-type children were put into Farmer-model schools and failed, it was a logical next step to "find out what's wrong with them." Clearly, the logic went, it couldn't be the school that was at fault—some children were graduating with honors. That demonstrated the viability of the traditional, modern, (underfunded, overworked) school system.

Unfortunately, it doesn't necessarily hold true, as educators from Horace Mann to Rudolph Steiner have historically pointed out.

Very few pure Hunter societies remain on the planet, and none of them thrive as a primary culture within the industrialized world. Most modern jobs require a Farmer mentality—show up for work at a certain time, do a task for a certain number of hours, and end the day in time to rest and prepare for the next day. Put this bolt on that wheel, over and over. Meet with these people, understand that concept, move this paper from desk A to desk B and then back.

Our schools, too, are set up along Farmer lines. Sit quietly at the desk, children are told, while the teacher talks and points to pages in the book. Ignore that child next to you who's sniffling; don't rattle your papers; don't look ahead in the book.

To a smart Hunter with a low boredom threshold, this is torture! It's a prescription for failure.

And, as our schools continue to suffer from a lack of funding and classrooms continue to increase in size, so do the number of distractions. In a 15-child classroom, an ADD child may have few problems that can't be dealt with directly by the teacher. But as our schools are placed under the increasing burden of underfunding and teacher-overload/overwork, Hunter children are increasingly being noticed. As a result there seems to be a rather sudden "epidemic" of ADD.

So the kids are doing poorly in school, they're bored and acting out. The teacher figures there must be something wrong with the children. Along come the diagnostic Farmers of the psychological industry, and—presto—a new "disorder" is discovered!

This is not to say that Hunters don't have short attention spans. Far from it—they certainly do. But they have any number of compensating characteristics, such as voracious curiosity, continual scanning of the environment, and broad-based interest. If our schools and jobs were structured to allow for the expression of these characteristics, ADD might become as irrelevant a medical classification as is its reciprocal, the extreme Farmer end of the bell curve. (In a later chapter we refer to the latter as TSDD or "task-switching deficit disorder"; it's classified in medical literature as the "overfocusing syndrome.")

Unfortunately, such a utopian notion is extremely unlikely. Employers aren't about to change businesses to accommodate the Hunters in our society (although there are many jobs ideally suited, as they stand, for Hunters). And it's equally unlikely that America's schools will quickly change the structure of classrooms—despite the fact that more than 3 million American schoolchildren are on Ritalin (often at the urging of teachers) to medicate Hunters into behaving like Farmers.

So, what's an adult Hunter to do in a Farmer's world?

The easiest, most obvious, and least stressful solution is to find a Hunter job that makes use of hunting skills. Police officers, private detectives, freelance writers, reporters, airplane pilots, spies (hopefully for our side), military combat personnel, disc jockeys, salespeople, consultants, and the thousands of varieties of entrepreneurs—all have a very high percentage of Hunters among their ranks. One of the happiest Hunters I ever knew was an old man who lived in the woods of northern Michigan and made his living as...a hunter. Five wives had come and gone, but the "Old Man" as we all called him (and he called himself) would never divorce himself from his traps and guns.

If one is capable and willing to sit through the years of school necessary to get the professional credentials, there are many opportunities for Hunters among the professions, as well. Trial lawyers are often Hunters (and usually have a good, solid Farmer as a research assistant). In medicine, the areas of surgery and trauma care seem to draw the excitement- and challenge-craving Hunters. In business, when hooked up with a supportive Farmer assistant, Hunters often make excellent senior executives (read the biographies of William Randolph Hearst or Malcolm Forbes, for examples), particularly when their position requires a large reservoir of creativity and willingness to take risks—two of the cardinal characteristics of Hunters. For these same reasons, we see many politicians who are apparently Hunters (JFK is a probable example), and William F. Buckley's autobiography, *Overdrive*, is a wonderful description of the life experience of a man who, while he may not be a Hunter, certainly embodies the energy level and love of stimulation and new experience common to Hunters:

> *(I have the whole morning clear, which is good because there is a speech right after lunch at the Waldorf, which has to be thought through, as the occasion doesn't permit a regular lecture. I am to speak for only twenty minutes. I look at the assignment and calculate the time it will take to prepare for it—say a half hour, leaning on familiar material. I have found that one can work with special concentration when hard up against that kind of a deadline. I have time left to attack the briefcase.* —page 100 of Buckley's *Overdrive*)

If you're a Hunter stuck with a Farmer job, there are simple behavioral changes you can make, in order to increase your probability for success in a Farmer's world:

❖ **Organize your time around tasks.** Hunters tend to do well with short bursts of high-quality effort and attention. So, taking large jobs and breaking them into small components is a useful first step. "Pigeonhole" your jobs. (More detail about this in the next chapter.)

❖ **Train your attention span.** Techniques like meditation have been around forever, and Hunters are often drawn to them. They enjoy silence—in little chunks—because it turns off the distractions for a few minutes and allows them to relax. While many Farmers crave continual stimulation—the radio is on at the office while they're doing their work—such distractions make it almost impossible for many Hunters to work productively.

While Hunters will probably never be able to train themselves to totally ignore distractions (it's a survival skill that's hard-wired into Hunters), experience demonstrates that it is possible to learn to more powerfully direct their attention to a single item, task, or time. The literature of Transcendental Meditation is full of such studies, and many Hunters report that, while meditation was difficult at first, it became an important component of their lives once they made a habit of it.

There are many books and courses on meditation, both religious and non-religious, and many Hunters find them useful. Ask any Catholic who's performed the Rosary "meditation" at least ten minutes a day for a week or two about their experience. The ones I've interviewed say that it gave them vivid new insights into how their mind and attentional mechanisms worked, and strengthened their ability to focus on other things.

A technique taught by Tibetan Buddhist monks is called Vipassana, or mindfulness. Basically, it means you watch your own mind, and catch yourself when your attention wanders. Sit for ten minutes a day, focusing your eyes on a point on the wall or a distant tree or whatever, and, whenever you notice yourself thinking, simply say to yourself, "thinking ." By "noticing" your wandering attention, you'll bring your attention back on track more powerfully than any will-power or brute-force techniques. After a few weeks of daily practice, Hunters report that they can bring this skill of mindfulness into their work and daily lives.

Another facet of this training involves learning to convert words into pictures. The auditory-processing problem mentioned earlier is often a serious difficulty for Hunters, but is also one Hunters can train themselves to overcome. Practice making visual pictures of things while having conversations; create mental images of lists of things to do; visualize yourself doing things you commit to. And practice paying attention when people talk to you. Listen carefully.

❖ **Break your work (or home) responsibilities into specific "goal units."** Hunters tend to be task- or goal- oriented. Once a goal is reached, they go on to another one, with renewed enthusiasm and vigor. So, instead of viewing work as a life-long "if-I-can-just-get-through-this" ordeal, break each task into a set of short-term goals.

This week, write the marketing plan. Break it into pieces, and do each one a bit at a time. "Hunt" for success on a project-by-project basis, viewing each new item on your "to do" list as something to complete, scratch off, and leave behind.

Don't worry about next week, or the week after that. Break all your goals into short-term projects, and simply knock them down, one after another. At the end of the year, you'll discover that you reached your yearly goals and hardly noticed it.

❖ **Create "distraction-free zones."** Henry David Thoreau was so desperate to escape distraction in order to do his writing that he moved himself off to isolated Walden Pond. Organize your work space and time so you can create your own "Walden Pond." Close the door, turn off the radio, tell people to hold your calls, and work on one thing at a time. An hour a day in a "distraction-free zone" like this will often help a Hunter to literally double the output of work he or she could otherwise produce.

Because Hunters crave stimulation and thrive on distraction, this may seem like an alien concept at first. Moreover, some people are afraid that others will think they're just taking an hour to goof off. But those Hunters in the business world who have tried this (and there are many) report that it quickly becomes a powerful and regular habit, and that their peers are not generally bothered by it.

One ADD adult reported that, when in law school, he would rent a hotel room every Saturday in order to have a distraction-free place to "binge" his week's homework. This worked great to get him through school, but when he began to practice law, the distractions of the office made it impossible for him to accomplish anything meaningful. A secretary in a distant office dropping a pen would take his attention away from the work on which he was trying to concentrate. While this particular individual chose Ritalin as a way of shutting down his Lookout/Hunter ability, another option would have been to demand a private office and close the door. Unfortunately, in some workplaces, this is discouraged because it's interpreted as an effort to create "goofing-off time."

Another variation on creating a distraction-free

zone is to clean your desk at the end of every day, and to keep your living areas clean and organized. This is a survival skill that many Hunters have developed, because a messy desk or home represents such a multitude of distractions, it's nearly impossible to keep on a single task. Every time you start on one project, you notice out of the corner of your eye another thing on the desktop that needs attention ... and wander off-task.

It's interesting that most (but not all) adult Hunters I've interviewed report that they can only do "concentration" work when the room is absolutely silent or, if they're listening to music with no (distracting) words to it. This demand that the music be purely instrumental baffles many Farmer spouses or co-workers, but Hunters instantly recognize it as a sign of their personality type.

❖ **Exercise daily.** "If I don't run at least four times a week, I can't focus my attention worth a damn," a sales executive for an advertising agency told me recently. He is one of several Hunter adults who've reported that a half-hour to an hour of aerobic exercise "tunes" their brains nearly as well as Ritalin.

While there has been no research done on this particular area, the anecdotal evidence seems to support the notion that daily exercise—briskly walking a few miles, for example—increases blood flow to the brain, or somehow otherwise alters body chemistry in a way that increases focusing ability for Hunters. After all, if Hunters are biologically designed to hunt, then the daily "run after the prey" may well be a stimulant, or cause the release of hormones or neurotransmitters necessary for a Hunter's brain to work more smoothly.

❖ **Know what you do well, and stick to it—avoid Farmer tasks.** In over fifteen years of working periodically as a consultant to other businesses, I've met many Farmers who were successful entrepreneurs—but the majority were Hunters. It seems that the very definition of an entrepreneur is that of a Hunter.

On the other hand, I've also met many, many frustrated Hunter/entrepreneurs. The normal cycle seems to run like this:

1. The Hunter/entrepreneur comes up with a great business idea, and throws months or years into developing it. A business is produced, grows, and begins to prosper.

2. After a few years, the business reaches a size where the entrepreneur's responsibilities must shift from the "jump-start" phase (doing a little bit of everything, knowing all facets of the business, meddling in everybody's work), to the "middle management" phase. This is when an entrepreneurial venture becomes a company, usually when the organization expands to between six and fifteen employees.

At this point in the growth of a company, the Hunter skills that started the company become a liability in the head person. What the company needs now is solid, steady, carefully planned management—skills that are intrinsically unavailable to a Hunter. As a result, the company begins to falter, employees grow angry because they're not well-managed and their needs aren't being met, and the company gets jerked from new idea to new idea, with none ever becoming grounded in reality and solidified.

This is the point where most small businesses die. The reason is simple: Hunters can start companies, but they generally can't do a particularly good job of running them.

It's tragic that so many Hunters make the mistake

of trying to continue to run the businesses they started, when the appropriate thing at that stage in the life of a company is to bring in a competent Farmer as middle management, and turn the management of the business over to that Farmer. In this model, the Hunter/entrepreneur then becomes a "creative consultant" to the business, fills some traditional Hunter role in the company (such as sales), becomes the "chairperson" or overall "leader," or goes on to a new project.

I've seen some companies which have successfully navigated this hump point in the life of a business because the business was started as a partnership, where one partner was a Hunter and the other a Farmer. Often it's a husband-wife team, and after a few years one spouse ends up running the business, because he or she was the slow-and-steady Farmer, and those skills were needed at that point in the life of the business.

Hunters who are entrepreneurs must learn, if they want to be successful over the long term, to hire good Farmers, delegate both responsibility and authority to them, and not meddle. It's difficult and seems counter-intuitive, but can produce solid success.

Some companies also intentionally pair up Hunters and Farmers as a team, particularly in the arena of sales. The Hunter goes out and gets the business, the Farmer does the paperwork and follow-through. And, of course, there is the classic model of the Hunter executive who would be totally lost without his or her Farmer secretary.

When preparing this manuscript I shared this chapter with a good friend, a Hunter who is a successful entrepreneur and consultant. He replied to me via electronic mail:

> *I betcha many Hunters, while excellent at their work, are terrible at management–I'm one. If my life depended on it, I doubt I could be good at the Farmer aspects of doing a budget, doing personnel reviews, or nurturing a department of dependable Farmers. I know. I tried for years, with a very good teacher. I wanted to succeed, I worked hard at it, but I hated it and failed and felt terrible as a result.*
>
> *Being skilled but lacking the capacity to manage is enormously frustrating in a company where you can only move up by managing larger groups. In contrast, a few companies now recognize that some employees may be excellent at certain things without being good at (or interested in) managing or running a group. These companies identify a set of jobs that permit employees to advance to very high and respected positions without having to supervise.*

Andrew Carnegie, a Hunter who came to America over 100 years ago with less than two dollars in his pocket and died one of the richest men in America, wrote for himself an epitaph which says: "Here lies one who knew how to get around him men who were cleverer than himself."

Chapter Seven

The Hunter's Struggle: Impulse and Its Control

I can resist everything except temptation.
—Oscar Wilde, *Lady Windermere's Fan* (1892)

There are two characteristics of ADD which can seriously challenge a Hunter who is trying to be successful in life and society. They are *impulsivity* and *craving.*

These two characteristics are, in moderation, what make some Hunters incredibly successful in our society. Under control, these "driving forces" lead to the creation of institutions and businesses, to the writing of books and creation of art, to creative brainstorms that lead countries, companies, and lives in wholly new and wonderful directions.

When out of control, impulsivity and craving can drive a Hunter to self-destruction or prison. The two characteristics are closely interrelated.

❖ **Impulsivity** first manifests as the ability to make a quick decision, to sort through a lot of data quickly and arrive at a conclusion. The problem is that the same burst of energy that a Hunter can bring to the hunt is brought to an impulsive decision. "Wow, yeah, let's do that!" which may lead to success in simple situations like a hunt in the woods, often leads to disaster in more complex worlds such as those of business. And, since the decision is usually followed by a burst of energy (designed by nature to help finish the hunt), Hunters often charge off in new, sometimes dangerous, directions.

Some Hunters create work environments for themselves where their impulsiveness is an asset. Thomas Edison had total control of his own time and work directions. And, it is said, he went off in more than 10,000 directions to try to make a light bulb which would work. Many professional writers, a common occupation of successful Hunters, have told me that they need the flexibility of controlling their own schedule so they can "burst work" when an inspiration or idea hits them.

On the other hand, for a Hunter in a Farmer job or school, impulsivity can lead to problems. Well-thought-out decisions are required in the work or business arenas, and impulsivity doesn't lend itself well to the thinking-out process. Successful Hunters get around impulsivity by several techniques:

❖ **Partner with a Farmer.** The combination of a Hunter and a Farmer can be frustrating for both, if neither is aware of the fundamental difference between the two in their world views and ways of working. Yet such a partnership is often a solid prescription for success if both *are* aware of their differences.

The Hunter is usually the "front man," the person who's most visible, fueling the business with creative genius and new ideas, trying innovative ways of doing things, and testing new directions. The Farmer has the dual job of "reality testing" the Hunter's ideas, and keeping the Hunter on track and on task. If both are committed to the process and can recognize the strengths and weaknesses of the other, such a partnership or team can be very successful.

Unfortunately, Hunters are often drawn to other Hunters, rather than to Farmers. Two Hunters will understand each other, and, sharing mutual energy, can work each other up into an impulsive frenzy with a new idea or concept. However, without a Farmer to provide the slow, steady, supportive personality necessary to keep projects on track, Hunter/Hunter partnerships often spin out of control, crashing and burning in spectacular and often very public blazes.

Partnerships of two or more Farmers, on the other hand, sometimes seem to get nowhere. The entrepreneurial landscape is littered with companies which got started, but never had the necessary spark to move ahead and ultimately died out. Both parties were too careful, methodical, and evaluative. Everything was well thought out—but nothing ever "caught fire."

❖ **Postpone every decision by a day.** If a Hunter doesn't have a nearby Farmer to slow and balance the Hunter's impulsiveness, it's possible to create an "internal Farmer" by adopting a simple technique: wait a day. The guidelines of Alcoholics Anonymous and other 12-step types of programs seem custom-made for dysfunctional Hunters, and one of the first and fundamental techniques a recovering alcoholic or substance abuser learns is to wait—for just one day. That's about how long it takes for a "weak impulse" to fade away, and if a Hunter gets in the habit of simply postponing for a day that final snap decision, many of those decisions will melt into the fabric of time.

In other words: learn to procrastinate.

It's curious that this natural characteristic of the hard-core Farmer—to postpone decisions and procrastinate in the name of "thinking things through"—is one of the most upsetting things to a Hunter. Nonetheless, it's a useful trait to cultivate.

Write the idea or decision down, and then wait until tomorrow to do something about it.

One Hunter tells the story of how, when in college, he would always place a letter to his then-girlfriend in the drawer overnight before mailing it. Viewed the next day, the impulsive thoughts expressed in the letter often seemed in need of toning down, which minimized the chance of relationship disasters.

❖ **Break jobs into little pieces.** One of the big complaints that Farmers have about Hunters is that "they start a million things, but never finish any of them." This problem derives from impulsivity—the new project is started on an impulse, then a new impulse drives the Hunter to abandon it for another new project. So how can a Hunter achieve the persistence necessary to accomplish anything of importance?

Some years ago, I was at the home of an old friend who's a successful novelist—and a classic Hunter. This fellow had held dozens of jobs in his life, most very successfully for a short time before he "burned out" and quit to try something else. He'd been through several wives and probably twenty apartments and houses. But, years earlier, he'd started writing and was now making a good living at it.

I looked at the three-inch-thick stack of paper on his desk, a manuscript for a new novel ready to go off to a publisher, and said, "How do you do that? How can you maintain the energy to write 500 pages?"

Expecting to hear something about the wonders of Chinese Ginseng or wheat germ, I was surprised when he said, "Five pages a day."

"What?" I said, amazed by the simplicity of his answer and wondering if he was making a joke.

"It's simple," he said. "If I write five pages a day, at the end of a hundred days, or about three months, I've written a novel. I do my re-write at the rate of fifteen pages a day, so that takes another month. That means I can predictably turn out three novels a year."

"How long does it take you to write five pages?" I asked.

He turned his hand palm-side up, then over again. "It varies. I start writing when I get up in the morning. Sometimes I'm done by 10 a.m. and I can have breakfast and spend the day reading or playing. Sometimes I'm not finished with those five pages until midnight. But I've taught myself to never go to sleep until that day's five pages are finished."

Since that conversation, I've heard many other successful writers, all to some degree Hunters, say much the same thing. Edison and Tesla followed that dictum when producing their world-changing inventions. Many businesspeople use the principle to get large jobs done. "Break a large job into smaller components and then tackle them one at a time," is one of the basic rules that Dale Carnegie put forth, and it's as useful a bit of advice now as it was in 1944, particularly for Hunters.

❖ **Craving** is the other side of the coin of impulsivity. Hunters often describe strong urges and desires, be they for sweets, sex, excitement, drugs, alcohol, success, or toys. Some Farmers hear these descriptions of a Hunter's cravings and simply cannot understand them: the only time they'd experience a desire that strong might be moments before orgasm. Yet many Hunters live with daily cravings that drive them through life, often in self-destructive directions.

The high percentage of Hunters in our prisons attests to the dangerous power of cravings mixed with impulsivity. Particularly as children, Hunters sometimes totally disregard the long-term consequences of their behavior, so strong is the urge to "get" whatever they want or "do it now." This is probably related to the elasticity of time experienced by Hunters—if they have to wait for gratification, it seems like *forever*. To a person who's profoundly affected with the Hunter gene, it often seems as if there simply never will be a future to contemplate, so why worry about the consequences of today's actions? This, of course, can lead to disaster.

In the sales arena, there's an old maxim about how the easiest people to sell something to are other salespeople. It's generally true, and the reason is that sales is a natural profession for a Hunter. And all you have to do to get a Hunter to buy something is to stimulate his desire, his *craving*, for it. Hunters are the original impulse buyers.

Hunters are more likely than Farmers, particularly as adolescents, to engage in risky behavior. They're more likely to try drugs, tobacco, and alcohol—and more likely to become addicted to them. They're more likely to jump out of airplanes, off bridges with bungee cords attached to them, and to hop into bed with somebody they don't know particularly well.

It's almost as if some Hunters have a constant

yearning for something; a yearning that can't ever be satisfied for more than a brief time. They have passionate affairs that burn out rapidly. They're always experimenting with themselves and the world.

The dangers of a Hunter letting his cravings mix with his impulsivity are obvious. Having discussed how to get control of impulsivity, here are the three techniques a Hunter can use to redirect his or her cravings:

❖ **Wait for it to pass.** Some decisions are just plain wrong, yet the craving is strong. However, if they resist the craving—be it for food, sex, or a new toy (like a cellular phone or a new car)—for even a few hours it'll often pass.

❖ **Redirect the craving.** Freud talked about the "free-floating libido." While we think that the object of our love is the only person we'll ever love, in fact it's love itself that we're experiencing and the person on the other end of it is only a vehicle for us to experience our own love. In other words, the desire is internal, not external, and can be attached to something other than the one thing to which we think it's attached. So, for the Hunter with more than one goal (and often Hunters have multiple "irons in the fire," or goals that they're trying to achieve at the same time), simply concentrating on Item B, when the craving for Item A comes along, will give time to diminish the craving for Item A to the point where it can be ignored long enough for it to go away.

In other words, if fighting a craving is difficult for you, don't say no to it, but, instead, say yes to something else for a while. Often the original desire will pass.

Chapter Eight

How to Work with a Hunter: Practical Advice for Managers, Parents, and Teachers

Great works are performed, not by strength, but by perseverance. He that shall walk, with vigor, three hours a day will pass, in seven years, a space equal to the circumference of the globe. —Samuel Johnson

IN THE WORKPLACE—MANAGING A HUNTER

I once served as a consultant to a large chain of retail stores and, when discussing their employment policies, was told by an executive, "We look at a person's job history. If they're job hoppers, we don't consider them for employment. We avoid people who can't stay with a job for at least four years."

This perspective is common sense for a retailer who recognizes that training staff is a significant expense—and has no use for the skills that a Hunter can bring to the workplace. A store clerk is not expected to do much more than ring up a sale. Creativity and personal initiative are unnecessary.

On the other hand, when I was conducting training for a large travel agency in New York State, the owner told me, "We expect our outside salespeople to last about two years; that seems to be about the average. While our inside people, the reservations agents, usually stay with us for five years or more, for some reason, the outside salespeople go off to other things in about two years."

Oddly, she saw it less as a problem and more as a basic reality. Certainly difficulties were involved in bringing new salespeople on board, training them, and getting them up to speed. But good salespeople were so solidly capable of repaying that learning curve that this business owner willingly paid the price every two years or so.

These two examples illustrate the importance of matching job function with personality type. Farmers make excellent store clerks; Hunters are better salespeople. And while a Hunter may not stick with a job for his or her entire career, an employer can often wring enough job performance out of that Hunter to easily pay for the learning curve of the replacement Hunter. (Many sales-driven organizations base their business plans on the assumption that there will be high turnover among their salespeople.)

Hunters do, however, need an extraordinary amount of structure in the workplace. Here are a few quick guidelines:

❖ **Define expectations in measurable, single, short-term goals.** This helps Hunters break large jobs into smaller parts and bring their extraordinary powers of short-term focus to bear on them. Rather than saying, for example, "We want to increase sales by 10 percent this month," try saying, "I want you to be making ten cold-calls a day." The more specific, definable, and measurable the goals, the more likely they'll be reached. And, when possible, give them only one priority at a time.

❖ **Build in daily evaluation systems.** Since their time sense is quite different from Farmers, a day is a long time in the life of a Hunter. By meeting with a Hunter daily, or having a Hunter fill out a daily report, the odds are greatly increased that the Hunter will meet or exceed his or her goals.

❖ **Offer short-term, rather than long-term, rewards.** While a Farmer may be able to visualize the vacation she'll earn if her two-year performance exceeds her goals, this payoff is too distant for a Hunter. A $100 bill pinned to the wall if he meets his goal this week is much more likely to motivate a Hunter.

This is not to say that long-term goals and rewards shouldn't be defined or offered to Hunters: they should. But history shows us that short-term rewards and measurable short-term results are far more relevant to a Hunter than their long-term counterparts.

❖ **Create systems-driven, rather than people-driven, work, home and school environments.** Hunters are often chronically disorganized, and a properly structured work system will help keep them in line and on task. Such systems should include daily definitions of job, performance, goals, and self-measurements. For example, for a salesperson, you may require a form which asks, on a daily basis, how many cold-calls were made, how many follow-up calls, how many client service calls. The salesperson fills it in as the day goes along, keeping him- or herself on track. And the "template," which defines the sales job, might say, "You're expected to make at least ten cold-calls every day to try to bring in new clients. Each existing client is to be called once a month."

IN SCHOOL AND AT HOME—TEACHING OR PARENTING A HUNTER

Over the years, our school systems have experimented with numerous programs to meet the needs of "special" children. Some addressed the boredom and need for stimulation often experienced by very bright students. Others looked at ways to motivate the seemingly unmotivated child. Still others sought to compensate for the behavioral disruptions of "problem" children.

To date, though, few programs outside of the mainstream classroom model have attempted to deal with the ADD or Hunter-type child. Since ADD has been viewed as a "disorder" or a "disease," its logical treatment has been drugs or medicine.

Therefore, millions of Hunter children are sitting today in Farmer classrooms—on drugs. (Testimony before the US Senate in 1975 put the number of children taking medication for hyperactivity at over 2 million. In the nearly two decades since that time, most experts believe the number has more than doubled, and a fourfold increase is not inconceivable.)

Because many Hunter-type children are also above average in intelligence, they're often able to fake it, making their way through school paying attention only 20 to 30 percent of the time. Sometimes their ADD isn't noticed or diagnosed until they reach junior or senior high school, where the increased demands for organization and persistence exceed their ability to use their usual coping strategies or outfox the system with their raw intelligence.

A variety of systems can easily be implemented to keep Hunters on task. More importantly, special educational programs targeted toward "bright" children shouldn't be unavailable to ADD Hunters simply because they haven't succeeded in Farmer-oriented classrooms. Because many of the "gifted children's" special classes are project- and experience-based, providing more opportunities for creativity or shorter "bites" of information, special classes may be a place where a failing Hunter could excel.

Here are a few other simple systems which will help Hunter children succeed in school:

❖ **Create a weekly performance template and check it daily.** Each Hunter child should have a single weekly grid with classes on the vertical axis and the days of the week on the horizontal axis. Each day, the child's performance (both positive and negative—turned in his or her homework or failed to turn in the homework, etc.) is charted both by teacher *and* parent. Creating a larger-than-the-child system will help keep ADD children on task and on time.

❖ **Encourage special projects for extra credit.** Hunter kids do well with special projects (for reasons already cited). These give them an opportunity to learn in a mode that's appropriate to their disposition, and provide them a chance to maintain high grade point averages even if they're not always consistent in doing their "boring" homework.

❖ **Label them as Hunters or Lookouts, not as "Disordered."** Labels are powerful things. They create for us paradigms through which we see ourselves, the world, and our place in it. For children (who struggle far more with issues of "who am I?" and "where do I fit in?" than do adults), applying a label that says "you have a deficit and a disorder" may be more destructive than useful.

This book puts forth a new model to view ADD, a new paradigm which is not pejorative and won't diminish a child's view of his or her own self-worth and potential.

To say, "You have a disorder," is to tell a child that he or she has less potential than others; that he or she will be trouble or cause problems; that he or she has an excuse on which to blame his or her failures. None of these messages are constructive, particularly since ADD can be so easily characterized in a way that leaves self-esteem intact: as a collection of adaptive mechanisms and personality traits that are more suited to some societies and tasks than others.

To tell a child that his or her personality is well adapted to some areas, and that he or she may experience difficulties in others—and to offer ways around those difficulties—usually enhances self-esteem. There's often something very positive about the Hunters in our society, as this book points out. The positive aspects of their uniqueness should therefore be stressed to Hunter children so they can nurture and develop personality traits which may make them successful in later life.

❖ **Reconsider our programs for "gifted" children.** In an Atlanta-area school, there is a program for the "smart" kids called Target. In the Target program, the children's work is more project-oriented than classroom-oriented. They take field trips. They do experiments to learn the principles they're studying. The program emphasizes *doing* rather than simply sitting in a chair and *listening*.

It's a perfect model for Hunter/ADD children.

The irony of the situation is that there are a number of very bright Hunter children who can't get into the Target program, because the criterion for entrance is grades. And their grades, in the "normal" Farmer classroom system, generally aren't good.

A double irony is that some of the good Farmer children who excel in a normal classroom end up struggling in the Target program. They aren't "wired" for experience-based learning. They work best in the Farmer-style classroom where they were doing so well. The simple truth is that different people learn differently.

So the Farmers who excel in the Farmer classrooms get put into the Hunter classroom, whereas the Hunters can't get into the Hunter Target program because they aren't successful in the Farmer classroom.

The solution, of course, is to determine a child's appropriateness for experience-based learning situations by considering *how they learn*, not how well they're currently doing academically. Children who learn well in a traditional classroom situation should remain there. Children who need a high level of stimulation, smaller classes, and an experience-based learning environment should be placed in programs targeted to those styles of learning.

❖ **Think twice about medication, but don't discard it as an option.** Medicating ADD Hunter children is very problematic. There's the issue of the mixed message it sends to those people who are most at risk to be substance abusers in later life.

And there is a very real and legitimate concern

about the long-term side effects of the drugs themselves. All drugs used to treat ADD modify the levels of neurotransmitters in the brain, particularly serotonin and dopamine. There is some evidence (cited in the chapter *Hunters on Drugs*) that these different levels of neurotransmitters may trigger a compensating mechanism whereby the brain grows new neuroreceptors, or adjusts its own level of neurotransmitter production to compensate against the drug-induced "abnormal" levels.

Since later-life conditions such as Parkinson's and Alzheimer's disease are neurotransmitter-level-related, some of the medical literature expresses concern that children who are medicated for ADD may be more at-risk for such conditions in later life. Additional concerns exist over rebound effect, addiction, and cravings for other drugs that long-term use of stimulants or tranquilizers may cause.

On the other hand, in the absence of support systems or special classrooms to meet his or her special needs, not medicating an ADD Hunter child may also lead to problems. Without extraordinary compensatory intelligence, many of these children will simply fail to make it through high school, often being a disruptive element in the school until they finally give up and drop out. Viewed in this context, the relatively unknown long-term risks of drug therapy may be more than offset by the short-term benefits of improved classroom performance.

It's interesting to note that parents report many children who were diagnosed as ADD and failed in the public schools sometimes excel in private schools. Smaller classrooms, more individual attention with specific goal-setting, project-based learning, and other methods discussed earlier are quite common in private elementary and secondary schools.

These systems have demonstrated that ADD/Hunter children don't necessarily need drugs to succeed in school.

The unfortunate reality, though, is that most public schools don't have the resources to replicate the private school environment for ADD Hunter children, although as more information about the scope of the "ADD problem" filters down to the taxpaying general public, to parents, and through school administrations, this situation may change. The cost to schools and, particularly, to society (through lost potential as ADD Hunter children fail in school, and then in life), is greater if nothing is done than if proactive programs were instituted.

A new view of ADD, as a natural adaptive trait

Trait as it appears in the "Disorder" view	How it appears in the "Hunter" view: they're...	Opposite "Farmer" trait: they're...
Distractable.	Constantly monitoring their environment.	Not easily distracted from the task at hand.
Attention span is short, but can become intensely focused for long periods of time.	Able to throw themselves into the chase on a moment's notice.	Able to sustain a steady, dependable effort.
Poor planner: disorganized and impulsive (makes snap decisions).	Flexible; ready to change strategy quickly.	Organized, purposeful. They have a long term strategy and they stick to it.
Distorted sense of time: unaware of how long it will take to do something.	Tireless: capable of sustained drives, but only when "hot on the trail" of some goal.	Conscious of time and timing. They get things done in time, pace themselves, have good "staying power."
Impatient.	Results oriented. Acutely aware of whether the goal is getting closer *now*.	Patient. Aware that good things take time; willing to wait.
Doesn't convert words into concepts adeptly, and vice versa. May or may not have a reading disability.	Visual/concrete thinker, clearly seeing a tangible goal even if there are no words for it.	Much better able to seek goals that aren't easy to see at the moment.
Has difficulty following directions.	Independent.	Team player.
Daydreamer.	Bored by mundane tasks; enjoy new ideas, excitement, "the hunt," being hot on the trail.	Focused. Good at follow-through, tending to details, "taking care of business."
Acts without considering consequences.	Willing and able to take risks and face danger.	Careful, "look before you leap."
Lacking in the social graces.	"No time for niceties when there are decisions to be made!"	Nurturing; creates and supports community values; attuned to whether something will last.

Attention Deficit Disorder: A Different Perception, by Thom Hartmann

Chapter Nine

Creativity and ADD: A Brilliant and Flexible Mind

The genius of poetry must work out its own salvation in a man; it cannot be matured by law and precept, but by sensation and watchfulness in itself. That which is creative must create itself.

In "Endymion," I leaped headlong into the sea, and thereby have become better acquainted with the soundings, the quicksands, and the rocks, than if I had stayed upon the green shore, and piped a silly pipe, and took tea and comfortable advice.

–John Keats (Letter to James Hessey, October 9, 1818)

Many teachers, psychiatrists, psychologists, and others who work with ADD children and adults have observed a correlation between creativity and ADD.

Experts define the following personality characteristics as most necessary for creativity:

❖ **The willingness to engage in risk-taking.** Daring to step out into unknown territory is almost by definition a creative effort. Picasso, Dali, Warhol, Salinger, Hemingway, and Poe all struck out in profoundly new and original directions—and were first criticized for their efforts. It's a risk to be original, to try something new. Yet risk-taking is essential to the creative process, and is one of the classic characteristics of the Hunter.

❖ **Intrinsic motivation.** Creative people, while often not motivated by extrinsic factors such as a teacher's expectations or a job's demands, usually have powerful intrinsic motivation. When they're "on a job" that's important to them personally, they're tenacious and unyielding. Parents of ADD children often report the apparent incongruity between their ADD child's apparent inability to stick to his homework for more than fifteen minutes, and his ability to easily spend two hours practicing his guitar, absorbed in a novel, or rebuilding his motorcycle.

❖ **Independent belief in one's own goals.** Creative people, often in the face of derision and obstacles (look at Sartre or Picasso, both ridiculed for their early ideas), believe in their own ideas and abilities. When allowed to pursue those things which they find interesting (their intrinsic motivations), they can be tenacious for years at a time, often producing brilliant work.

❖ **Tolerance for ambiguity.** While Farmers generally prefer things to be ordered and structured, and think in a linear, step-by-step fashion, creative Hunters often have a high tolerance for ambiguity. Because their attention wanders easily, they can often see a situation from several directions, noticing facets or solutions which may not have been obvious to "normal" people. Einstein, who flunked out of school because "his attention wandered off," often pointed out that the theory of relativity didn't come to him as the result of tedious mathematical equations. Rather, the theory was a flash of insight that struck when he was considering the apparently ambiguous nature of the various natural forces. He pointed out that "The whole of science is nothing more than a refinement of everyday thinking" (*Physics and Reality*, 1936). Similarly, Carl Jung, when talking about the ability of creative people to let their minds wander among seemingly ambiguous paths, said, "Without this playing with fantasy, no creative work has ever yet come to birth. The debt we owe to the play of imagination is incalculable" (Psychological Types, 1923).

❖ **Willingness to overcome obstacles.** Creative people are often described as those who "when given a lemon, make lemonade." Thousands of businesses and inventions originated with this ability of creative people, often after dozens of different tries. There's an old model of "horizontal" and "vertical" problem-solving: When a person who's a vertical problem-solver comes to a door that's stuck or locked, he will push harder and harder, banging on it, knocking on it, and, ultimately, kicking it in. Conversely, a horizontal problem solver would look for other ways to enter the house, trying windows or other doors. While this is a simplistic view of different problem-solving methods, it does demonstrate the difference between "linear" and "random" ways of viewing the world. Creative individuals more often tend to fall into the latter category. They're usually the ones who devise new ways to do old tasks or to overcome old problems.

❖ **Insight skills.** Creative people can make links between seemingly unrelated events in the past, to develop new solutions for current problems. This apparently relates to the ability to think in more random, rather than linear, ways—one of the cardinal characteristics of the typical ADD thought processes.

❖ **The ability to redefine a problem.** Rather than thinking of a problem in the same fashion, creative people often reframe it entirely. This enables them to find within the problem itself the seeds of a solution. Often, they discover that what was viewed as a problem in the past is, in fact, a solution to something else altogether. (The notion of viewing ADD as a Hunter trait might be considered an example of this "reframing" process.)

NURTURING CREATIVITY IN THE HUNTER

When you look through this list of creative characteristics, it reads almost like a recompilation of the American Psychological Association's assessment criteria for diagnosing ADHD. And, reviewing the biographies of some of history's most creative individuals (see the chapter *Hunters Who Have Changed the World*), we discover that they have much in common with ADD Hunters, and, in fact, were most likely people who were "afflicted" with ADD.

A creative Hunter adult describes the experience this way: "The Hunter trait of a constantly shifting point of view is a fabulous asset here. It's what lets you see unexpected things where others see only the obvious. It's like looking for one elusive piece of a jigsaw puzzle, picking something up, and discovering you don't have what you sought but you found something even better instead—it fits somewhere unexpected."

Unfortunately, the risk-taking so necessary to creativity is often pummeled out of our children in school.

Robert J. Sternberg, the author of numerous books and articles on the creative process, points out that risk-taking is often discouraged, or even punished, in a school situation.

Sternberg suggests that our schools, which are largely staffed by earnest non-risk-takers and Farmers, are sometimes unintentionally organized in such a fashion as to discourage both creative people and the learning of creative skills. Similarly, many jobs demand that people not innovate. There are risks in coming up with something new which may not work, so risk-taking is generally frowned upon in corporate America. These anti-creative models are also, probably not by coincidence, anti-ADD/anti-Hunter models.

An educational model that's more experience-based will better preserve and nurture the creativity of the Hunter personality. This is not to suggest that the basics of education can or should be ignored; instead, we should consider establishing public-school classrooms and systems which encourage activities which will bring out the creativity that's wired into the brains of so many Hunter children.

In the workplace, Hunters may want to consider career or position changes into areas where creativity is encouraged, rather than punished. In my years as an entrepreneur in the advertising and marketing industry, I've noticed a very high percentage of Hunters who are drawn to that business.

Hewlett Packard was famous in the 1960s for its workplace model that encouraged engineers to pursue areas of independent research, following their own "intrinsic motivations." In *In Search of Excellence*, Tom Peters points out that Hewlett Packard had a policy of "open lab stock," actually encouraging engineers to take things home for their own personal use and experimentation. Two of their engineers, Steve Jobs and Steven Wozniak, came up with an idea for a computer which Hewlett Packard rejected, which Jobs and Wozniak built in their garage: it was the first Apple computer. Bell Labs, too, has historically offered their engineers a similar wide latitude in pursuing creative impulses. The transistor, the integrated circuit, and superconductivity are the result, revolutionizing our world.

An interesting footnote to this discussion about creativity and the Hunter personality: I've spoken with numerous ADD-diagnosed writers, artists, and public speakers about their experience with Ritalin and other anti-ADD drugs. Many report that, while their lives become more organized and their workdays easier when taking the drugs, their creativity seems to dry up. One novelist told me that he uses Ritalin when doing the tedious work of proofreading, but drinks coffee instead when he's writing. "Coffee lends itself to flights of fancy; it seems to make me even more ADD, which allows my wandering mind to explore new ideas, to free-associate. Ritalin brings me to a single point of concentration, which is useless when I'm trying to find that random spark of inspiration about how my character is going to extricate himself from a snake pit in India, or escape a horde of Mongols."

A professional speaker told me, "I made the mistake once of taking Ritalin before giving a three-hour speech to a group of about 100 editors in Washington, DC. Normally when speaking, I'm thinking ahead about what I'm going to say next, formulating concepts into pictures in my mind, dropping in examples before I say them, and continually scanning the audience for cues that my words are either boring or exciting them. But with the Ritalin in my bloodstream, I found myself having to refer back to my notes for that speech—something I haven't done in years. It was a painful and embarrassing experience, and convinced me that Hunters make great public speakers, whereas Farmers, while probably well-organized in their material and presentations, are often boring to an audience because they're not continually scanning their environment."

A writer in the *New York Times Magazine*, describing his diagnosis at age thirty of ADD and subsequent successes with Ritalin, also commented on how much he enjoyed those days when he didn't take his medication. He found that the Ritalin, while smoothing out his emotional swings, stabilizing his time-sense, and giving him the ability to concentrate on his work, also took away a bit of his spontaneity, humor, and sense of the absurd, which he enjoyed.

Reflecting on the dozens of successful public speakers, actors, magicians, other performers, and writers I've worked with and known over the years, I'd guess that many, many of them are ADD adults*.

* One Hunter adult suggested, as a title for this book, "I'm not inattentive, you're just boring."

Chapter Ten

Hunters on Drugs

Surely this is the stuff heaven is made of.
—Ralph Waldo Emerson (describing nitrous oxide)

Could it be that drugs are the "cure" for attention deficit disorder?

Sir Arthur Conan Doyle's famous novel *The Sign of the Four* opens with a theme that any fan of Sherlock Holmes will recognize:

> Sherlock Holmes took his bottle from the corner of the mantelpiece and his hypodermic syringe from its neat morocco case. With his long, white, nervous fingers he adjusted the delicate needle, and rolled back his left shirt-cuff. For some little time his eyes rested thoughtfully upon the sinewy forearm and wrist, all dotted and scarred with innumerable puncture-marks. Finally he thrust the sharp point home, pressed down the tiny piston, and sunk back into the velvet-lined armchair with a long sigh of satisfaction....
>
> "Which is it today?" I asked. "Morphine or cocaine?"

> He raised his eyes languidly from the old black-letter volume which he had opened. "It is cocaine," he said; "a seven percent solution. Would you care to try it?"
>
> "No, indeed," I answered, brusquely. "My constitution has not got over the Afghan campaign yet. I cannot afford to throw any extra strain upon it."
>
> He smiled at my vehemence. "Perhaps you are right, Watson," he said. "I suppose that its influence is physically a bad one. I find it, however, so transcendently stimulating and clarifying to the mind that its secondary action is a matter of small moment."

When Watson continued his protest at Holmes' use of cocaine, Holmes replied a few paragraphs later:

> "My mind," he said, "rebels at stagnation. Give me problems, give me work, give me the most abstruse cryptogram, or the most intricate analysis, and I am in my own proper atmosphere, I can dispense then with artificial stimulants. But I abhor the dull routine of existence. I crave for mental exaltation. That is why I have chosen my own particular profession...."

(If there's a literary archetype of the ADD Hunter, it's certainly Sherlock Holmes, who notices everything around him, and leaps from thought to thought with the grace of a gazelle.)

I recently visited an adult ADD support group meeting in a major American city. The speaker, a psychiatrist, asked for a show of hands:

"How many of you have been diagnosed as ADD?" About half the room raised their hands. (There were many newcomers that night, the result of a recent television show about ADD and this particular support group.)

"How many of you are on medication for your ADD?" Virtually all the adults who had raised their hands for the "diagnosed" question raised their hands.

"How many of you, at one time or another in your life, have self-medicated?" More than four-fifths of the room raised their hands. Those who didn't looked around self-consciously, and the thought struck me that most likely they had, but were afraid to admit it.

The psychiatrist continued with the story of how he, himself, had survived medical school. "Black Beauties (an illegal form of 'street amphetamine') were what got me through," he said. "They heightened my ability to concentrate and study, and many of my friends in medical school were taking them, too."

DRUG USE IN HISTORY

Taking drugs to make it through a difficult job requiring great concentration is nothing new: during "Operation Desert Storm," the United Nations operation against Iraq in 1991, a news report by Cable News Network revealed that United States Air Force fighter and bomber pilots routinely took amphetamines to keep them alert during their flights and have been since before World War II. (The practice was officially discontinued in April 1992, apparently because of the CNN report and other adverse publicity in the midst of the administration's "war on drugs.") Records also show that John F. Kennedy often took methamphetamine, a drug similar to Ritalin, while he was President of the United States.

Sigmund Freud, for several years during his practice of psychology, was of the opinion that cocaine was a wonder drug which would unlock the doors of the unconscious and restore "functional ability" to "dysfunctional" people. Freud, who himself used cocaine, even composed a poem in praise of the drug, and suggested that *every* patient in therapy should be given cocaine. It wasn't until years later, when some of his patients began to overdose on the drug or show signs of drug abuse and addiction, that he reversed his position and suggested that drugs in therapy should be administered carefully, on a case-by-case basis.

Here in America, an Atlanta, Georgia, pharmacist named John Pemberton came up with a formula for a "cure-all" tonic in 1886. He claimed it would cure depression, lack of concentration, headaches, and a host of minor ailments. The tonic formula was purchased five years later by Asa Candler, another pharmacist, and added to carbonated water, producing a soda-fountain drink. By the turn of the century, Coca-Cola could be purchased in virtually every city in America, Hawaii, Canada, and Mexico, and contained as its main active ingredient the substance after which it was named: cocaine. It wasn't until the second decade of the twentieth century that the cocaine was replaced by another powerful stimulant drug, caffeine.

Drug use has been with us for a long, long time. Evidence of the use of fermentation-produced alcohol is well documented in the Bible, and some archaeologists claim that early cave men used the drug. Other cultures have chosen opium, coca, tobacco, or marijuana as their drug of choice. Psychiatrist Andrew Weil postulates that the "urge to alter consciousness" is a basic human drive, just like the drives for food, sex, and security, and he points to children's games where kids spin around in circles until they're dizzy, and animals which will seek out fermented fruit or psychoactive plants, as examples of this instinct.

When Dexedrine was first marketed in 1938, its promoter, Dr. Bradley, hailed it as a "miracle mathematics pill" for its ability to help students perform difficult math projects. Nancy Reagan, while making public pronouncements that people should "Just Say No" to drugs, was herself taking psychoactive drugs, albeit with a doctor's prescription. And it was confirmed in 1992 by the White House that President George Bush and Secretary of State James Baker both occasionally used Halcion, a controversial and powerful tranquilizer in the Valium family, most often prescribed as a sleep aid.

Who among us doesn't drink an occasional cup of caffeine-containing coffee, tea, or cola? And anybody who's been to an Alcoholics Anonymous (AA) meeting knows full well that a majority of the attendees are not living drug-free lives: they consume coffee in prodigious quantities, often smoke tobacco, and some are on prescription drugs which include tranquilizers or stimulants. (This is not to minimize the extraordinary benefits of participation in AA, or the incredibly destructive effects of alcohol addiction; clearly it's one of the most dangerous drugs available, and consumption of it by an alcoholic is tantamount to suicide. AA has probably saved more lives, both directly and indirectly, than any other organization in America.)

Given the pervasiveness of drug use in human history, and the way that over-the-counter drugs are promoted on television as quick cures for everything from arthritis to the common cold, it shouldn't surprise anyone that a first response of our culture to the "disorder" of ADD would be to administer drugs.

DRUGS FOR ADD

Stories of Hunter adults who drink ten to sixty cups of coffee a day just to make it through their unpleasant Farmer jobs are standard fare at any meeting of ADD adults or psychiatrists who specialize in ADD. Replacing these massive, and often ineffective, amounts of caffeine with a small dose of Ritalin or Dexedrine often produces an amazing transformation, "curing" the attention deficit disorder so long as the person is on the drug.

It doesn't work for everyone, but it does produce results for many. Wives tell stories of their newly medicated husbands "paying attention to me, really sitting in one place and listening to me for a half hour, for the first time in years." Relationships improve, people are more functional in the workplace, entrepreneurs become managers, children in trouble become good students and view their former trouble-making peers with disdain. Even some alcoholics and drug addicts (most likely, the ADD Hunters among that sub-population), who claim that their initial attraction to alcohol or drugs was to "stop the boredom" or "turn off all the inputs," find that their craving for alcohol and/or drugs drops off dramatically when they begin Ritalin therapy. There's also growing anecdotal evidence that impulse-control problems, such as sexual promiscuity (and possibly even rape, crimes of violence, etc.), are controllable when the ADD person is medicated with Ritalin or other substances routinely prescribed for ADD.

Sitting in the back row of the Adult ADD Support Group, listening to people tell stories about how Ritalin or Dexedrine had saved their lives, made me wonder if I would have heard similar stories from Arthur Conan Doyle, who claimed that cocaine gave him the genius to write the Sherlock Holmes stories. Would a group of Freud's cocaine-taking patients have offered the same reports? Or a ladies' group in the nineteenth century who all imbibed Lydia Pynkham's Tonic, one of the dozens of over-the-counter tonics containing cocaine, opium, or both, that were sold for over 150 years in America, and consumed by such respectable people as senators, presidents, and their wives? Heroin, too, was first introduced to the market as a cough syrup, and was available for years in corner markets and pharmacies without a prescription; many people reported that it cured more than just their coughs, and use of the "elixir" became quite popular among the "educated classes."

So, again, the question: could it be that drugs *are* the "cure" for attention deficit disorder?

Certainly there is a huge body of medical and anecdotal evidence that says "Yes." Ask any teacher: Ritalin is so pervasive in our schools now that it's almost impossible to find a teacher who can't tell Jekyll and Hyde stories about troublesome or troubled children who became "A" or "B" students when they started taking Ritalin.

And when we look at our prison populations, with their huge percentage of ADD adults as inmates, one is forced to wonder how these people would have turned out if they were given access to such medication when they were young. Statistics indicate that ADD is far more a "disease" of middle-class white children than of poor blacks or other minority groups; yet many argue that instead of this representing a genetic difference, this only reflects the difference in access to medical care and diagnostic resources between these two groups.

It's also interesting to note that the vast majority of prisoners have experimented with, used, or abused drugs long-term prior to incarceration. (Many continue to abuse drugs while in prison, but that's another story.) Could these be attempts to self-medicate as a way of "curing" ADD? Might they be attempts to solve a medical "dysfunction," a "malfunctioning of the brain," with the corner pusher playing the role that a psychiatrist would fill for a more affluent person?

DRUG-FREE ALTERNATIVES

Viewed in this context, Ritalin therapy for ADD seems like an appropriate, and possibly even conservative, step. And it may well be, particularly for those Hunters who are stuck in Farmer life-situations and have no way out of them, or whose impulsivity is a threat to themselves or others.

But a different view may say:

1. People use drugs to deal with the difficulty of being a Hunter in a Farmer's society; and,
2. The solution is not to change or increase the frequency of medication, but to find Hunter jobs, school situations, and life situations for these people, and teach them the basic life skills mentioned in previous chapters which can enable them to be successful as *Hunters*.

One particularly poignant moment occurred at an Adult ADD support group meeting I attended when a man who had been on Ritalin for nine months, with dramatic and positive results, stood up and said, "What I'm having to deal with now is my anger. My anger over the fact that I'm forty years old and have wasted my life. If I'd known about ADD when I was in high school, and had had Ritalin then, I may have made it through. I might have graduated from college as an honors student. I might be a successful professional now, instead of somebody who's had ten jobs in twenty years. I feel like my life has been totally wasted, and there's no way I can go back and recover those lost years." He had tears in his eyes as he spoke those words.

The paradigm he presented was: "I've been sick and defective all these years and didn't know why. Now I'm cured by taking Ritalin, but I've wasted all those years when I didn't know what my sickness was." And, of course, he's angry about that wasted time—angry with himself, angry with the doctors who didn't diagnose him, angry with the schools who just called him a troublemaker.

But an alternate paradigm might be: "I've been a Hunter all these years, with a set of skills ideally suited to being an entrepreneur, or a writer, or a detective. Instead, I spent twenty years trying to be a Farmer, in jobs that required an entire day's concentration at one desk on one task, and it was a disaster. I wish I could have realized years ago that I was a Hunter, and enrolled in a Hunter school system, and found Hunter jobs."

Probably the practical reality is somewhere in between the two. I've talked with many non-ADD people who have experimented with drugs, including Ritalin, and found them useful when working on a task or project. It may be, as Dr. Bradley said of Dexedrine in 1938, or Freud first believed of cocaine, that *everybody* would gain some benefit from Ritalin. That's what television tells us about the other stimulant drug so commonly used in our culture: coffee.

But, as the legion of coffee-habituates are so quick

to point out, there's a down side to stimulant drugs. People who have used coffee or cola drinks for years often report severe withdrawal symptoms when they stop using them: headaches, lethargy, constipation, even migraine attacks.

There are several chemicals which control or regulate activity of and in the brain (neurotransmitters) which are affected by taking methylphenidate (Ritalin) and most other stimulants. The principal neurotransmitters are dopamine, norepinephrine, and serotonin, along with the chemicals into which they break down (their metabolites). Increased levels of these three neurotransmitters affect the part of the brain which controls our ability to shift from a focused state to an open state of awareness (the frontal lobes). They also affect the part of the brain which controls our sense of time (the basal ganglia, corpus striatum).

[Note: Nearly everybody, Hunter, Farmer, or in-between, has experienced the fluidity of time in their life. For Hunters, it's an everyday occurrence. For Farmers, it's usually brought on by a crisis, such as a car accident. The flood of adrenaline releases massive amounts of various neurotransmitters, causing time to seem to slow down. Countless eyewitnesses to accidents or violent crimes have reported that events occurred "as if they were in slow-motion."]

While being highly focused and not bored (not having the sense that time is passing slowly) may be desirable in a classroom or office setting, these states of consciousness may not be best if a person were, for example, walking through a forest or driving a car, where attention to many details all around them is important. One ADD adult on Ritalin told me the story of nearly causing an auto accident because he was so focused on the car in front of him while changing lanes that he didn't notice the car beside him. "When I'm not on Ritalin," he said, "I notice everything. I walk through the house and turn off lights, pick up lint, and constantly scan my environment. When I'm on Ritalin, I tend to do one thing at a time, very focused."

Everybody innately has the ability to shift between these two different states of consciousness. Even ADD-diagnosed children and adults are able to focus their attention and speed up their time sense when working on a project that interests them. There's also considerable evidence that people can train themselves to shift between open and focused consciousness. When they accomplish this shift, PET scans show that the levels of chemical activity change in the brain. (Although "extreme Hunters" are most often in the open state, and "extreme Farmers" are most often in the focused state.)

So, the first downside of using drugs to control ADD is that a person begins losing their ability to turn on and off a state of consciousness.

The second downside is more a possibility than a certainty: long-lasting changes in brain chemistry may result from the long-term use of medication.

Chlorpromazine, sold as Thorazine, is a tranquilizer which functionally reduces levels of serotonin in the brain (a dopaminergic antagonist). Years ago it was routinely prescribed for schizophrenia. Unfortunately, it was also extensively used inappropriately to control psychiatric patients, because it made them so passive.

In an article for *The Journal of Orthomolecular Psychiatry* in 1981, I reported on a twelve-year-old boy who was referred to a residential treatment facility of which I was the Executive Director. This child had been in the state mental hospital for two years, and was on Thorazine nearly the entire time. We took him off the drug, but for three years after that he experienced periodic seizures known as tardive dyskinesia.

The tardive dyskinesia seizures were caused by the brain's response to the Thorazine. Sensing that serotonin levels were abnormally low, the brain actually grew new serotonin receptors to try to get more serotonin. When the Thorazine was withdrawn, the brain was overloaded with its own serotonin, and the seizures resulted. (We also learned later that the boy had no mental illness and was of above-average intelligence; he'd been "dumped" in the mental hospital because of abuse in his home and a lack of foster homes. Living without drugs, but with extensive therapy for his ADD and other emotional problems, he graduated from high school with honors.)

The same process has been well-documented in dozens of opiate studies over the past 100 years: people who use narcotics for long periods of time actually become more sensitive to pain, because the body's production of endorphins has been permanently decreased, and/or the number or sensitivity of pain receptors has been increased. Similar permanent changes have been observed in the numbers of receptor sites, or levels of neurotransmitters, in the brains of laboratory animals given marijuana or cocaine for extended periods of time.

Some researchers assert that ADHD is the result of low levels of dopamine in the brain. Ritalin and other stimulants increase dopamine levels, which appears to be how they "cure" ADHD/ADD. If the brain reacts to the increased levels of stimulant-induced dopamine the same way it does to serotonin level changes induced by Thorazine, or endorphin level changes induced by opiates, then the result of long-term use of stimulants would be that, when they were discontinued, the patient would be *more* ADD than before the beginning of the therapy. Normal levels of dopamine would be lower, as a result of having taken the drug, because the brain's "compensating mechanism" would have kicked in to try to get rid of the extra dopamine. It's important to emphasize that, while this effect has been documented with two other major families of drugs, and research indicates long-term and possibly permanent changes in brain chemistry from extended use of cocaine, no studies have been done which document (or refute) the possibility of this happening with Ritalin.

Since dopamine disorders in old age are at the root of Parkinson's disease, and methylphenidate (Ritalin) affects dopamine levels, there has been some concern expressed that use of this drug over years may have negative side effects in old age.

There's also the concern that tolerance to Ritalin and other stimulants may develop, indicating long-term changes in the brain. One group of researchers, using the language of their trade, reported that after a three-week regime with methylphenidate "desensitization of cortisol and prolactin response [namely, suppression] to methylphenidate rechallenge might indicate development of sub-sensitivity of post-synaptic dopamine receptors following long-term dopamine agonistic activity of methylphenidate." (Translation: "Over three weeks people became progressively less sensitive to methylphenidate in their bloodstream, and this may indicate that changes are taking place in the parts of the brain that react to the drug.")

Animal studies have also demonstrated a cross-tolerance between methylphenidate, cocaine, and amphetamines, indicating that all three of these substances affect the brain in similar fashions.

Other side effects to the use of stimulants include increases in blood pressure, weight loss, and occasional hair loss. Fortunately, none of these seem to be particularly widespread or problematic when dosages are carefully controlled. Some experts have expressed concern about methylphenidate affecting the growth of children, but these studies are too new to be considered conclusive; for now the evidence is marginal. Production of Human Growth Hormone (HGH) by the pituitary gland appears to occur mostly during times of sleep, and at these times methylphenidate levels are lowest in the bloodstream.

In the 1980s a group affiliated with the Church of Scientology launched an aggressive campaign against the psychiatric profession's use of Ritalin with children, raising many of these concerns. Psychiatrists refer to that time as the "Ritalin scare," and often dismiss the concerns raised by this group because of the Church of Scientology's well-known disdain for the psychiatric profession.

Neither side of this issue, however, has been demonstrated as a medical certainty. While Ritalin has been in use since the 1950s, has a relatively short half-life in the body, and is considered relatively safe (I recently heard a psychiatrist publicly refer to it as "safer than aspirin"), no long-term well-controlled studies have been done on its affects among people who use it from childhood through adulthood and into old age. Since it's only in the past ten years or so that adult ADD has even been recognized by the psychiatric profession in general, no long-term studies of Ritalin usage among adults have yet been conducted.

On the other hand, there is little evidence that Ritalin poses a serious risk of the problems postulated earlier. Since no controlled studies have been done on either side of the issue, it's difficult to truly assess its risk. Considering how powerful the withdrawal from caffeine, tobacco, and alcohol can be, however, Ritalin may ultimately be viewed as rather benign when compared to these "normal, recreational" drugs of our culture.

The final question, particularly for schoolchildren, is whether Ritalin is an aid to learning, or merely a way of compensating for behavior difficulties which make learning difficult in a school environment.

Certainly, numerous studies show that many children's grades improve when they take Ritalin. But, again, this doesn't prove that Ritalin is helping learning. It may only be compensating for deficiencies in the classroom which otherwise make learning difficult for ADD children.

Some authorities believe that people learn fastest and best when they are constantly shifting between a focused and an open state of awareness—taking in information in focused detail, then free-associating openly with that information and hooking it onto various memory pegs in the brain. If this is true, then Ritalin (or other drugs which tend to lock the brain into a single attentional state) may do little to aid learning, or may even reduce pure learning ability.

On the other hand, how much can a child learn when he's disrupting the class, regardless of his state of awareness? With many children, if the school is incapable of meeting their Hunter-personality needs through an "action-oriented, project-based" curriculum, Ritalin may be the only option to provide a learning opportunity. Again, though, many educators would argue that this is not the failure of the child, nor is it due to a "deficiency" or "disorder" that the child has; it is, instead, the inability of the school to fund and structure programs appropriate to the needs of Hunter children, thus requiring the child be medicated in order to conform to the school's Farmer systems of teaching/learning.

At the institution I directed, and in numerous private schools around the country, it has been repeatedly demonstrated that ADD Hunter children are not incapable of learning. They do, however, often need a different structure than that provided in the typically overcrowded, underfunded classroom of the 1990s. Smaller classes, information presented in segments of twenty to thirty minutes instead of one hour, visual aids, instruction in visualization (teaching auditory processing, as mentioned earlier), enforced "quiet times" when disruption is not allowed while children are doing homework, and lots of hands-on experiential work, can all combine to provide a powerful learning environment for ADD Hunter children, even in the absence of Ritalin or other drugs.

For Hunter adults—who are more self-aware than children and more likely to know when it's appropriate to take, or not to take, a drug—the availability of Ritalin or Dexedrine may well be analogous to the availability of coffee or alcohol. The vast majority of adults self-medicate with coffee and alcohol in order to achieve specific purposes. A Hunter who must function in a Farmer job may find that occasional use of Ritalin is a useful thing. If it doesn't impair his or her performance in other arenas, doesn't produce negative side effects, and can be set aside during times of vacation, weekends, or when such "focused" awareness is not absolutely necessary, it actually may be a useful psychopharmacological tool.

THE "PERIODIC DRUG USE" OPTION

Another option would be to use Ritalin or Norpramin for three to twelve months in order to develop new patterns of behavior, and then to drop the use of the drug, or reduce it drastically. Several ADD adults who tried Ritalin or Norpramin have reported to me, "what a shock it was to think like that—I never knew other people could concentrate that way." Over time, many have successfully taught themselves concentration skills that could be carried over into drug-free intervals.

It is helpful to point out to people on drugs the apparent differences in their pre- and post-drug states of consciousness and concentration. This awareness may help them learn to develop the "Ritalin/Farmer-concentration" behaviors during times when they are not using drugs. An analogy would be the use of training wheels on a bicycle: a child uses them until he or she has learned the skills necessary to ride the bicycle without them. Once those skills become second nature, the training wheels can safely be discarded.

The important step in this process is to help the child (or adult) to identify his or her behavior on medication. This must be followed by a conscious effort to transfer those behaviors to non-medicated periods. This process may provide a useful middle-ground between the two opposing camps of "always medicate" and "never medicate."

Ultimately, the use of drugs is a decision which each individual or parent must make for him- or herself but should never be viewed as the only way for a Hunter to develop Farmer skills.

ALTERNATIVE THERAPIES

Debate about non-pharmaceutical treatments for ADD has recently moved from the "fringe" health-food publications into "mainstream" magazines and newspapers. Articles about herbs, homeopathy, vitamins, and EEG Neurofeedback as methods of treating ADD are appearing in the popular press in increasing numbers. Many people are experimenting with these non-traditional therapies. While none can match Ritalin's substantial body of supporting scientific research, it is nonetheless important to touch on these subjects since their popularity is growing and many Hunters or parents of Hunter children may consider them as a therapeutic option, now or in the future.

❖ Herbal treatments for ADD usually focus on the "nervine" category of herbs—those which contain an active ingredient traditionally regarded as "relaxing" or "healing" to the nervous system. These include skullcap (Scutelleria lateriflora), valerian (Valeriana officinalis), hops (Humulus lupus), blue cohosh (Caulophyllum thalictroides), black cohosh (Cimicifuga racemosa), chamomile (Anthemis nobilis) and lady's slipper (Cypripedium pubescens). Occasionally, herbalists will recommend stimulant herbs, such as ginger root (Zingiberis officinale) or licorice (Glycyrrhiza glabra) for ADD.

It should be emphasized that herbs contain active ingredients which may be toxic in high doses or have side effects. So far, none have been subjected to the rigorous double-blind, peer-review studies which would demonstrate their viability as a therapy for ADD.

❖ **Homeopathy** presents fewer risks of side effects than herbs, because homeopathic remedies work through the "vital force" or "life essence" of a medication.

Homeopaths maintain that the homeopathic substances, when properly triturated, are invested with a subtle power which science has not yet learned to measure, but which, nonetheless, works. Pointing to the fact that science has yet to produce an explanation for the dual wave/particle nature of electricity, and therefore cannot explain how electricity works, homeopaths suggest that their remedies work with these same types of now-inexplicable subtle energies.

Homeopathic remedies suggested for treatment of ADD include Tarentula hispanica, Nux vomica, Lycopodium, Stramonium, Chamomila, Tuberculinum, and Veratrum album. Of course, these remedies should be administered under the care of a licensed homeopath.

❖ **Vitamins** and nutritional supplements have been the subject of medical claims since 1912 when biochemists Casimir Funk and Frederick G. Hopkins developed the vitamin theory of deficiency disease and named the substances "vital amines."

The food supplement that has generated the most interest in the context of ADD is choline. Choline is one of the few nutrients which can penetrate the blood-brain barrier. It is converted into the neurotransmitter acetylcholine directly in the brain. Several recent studies link high levels of acetylcholine to improved memory function, and imply benefits for attention span.

Choline is available as a nutritional supplement, and is found in highest concentrations in egg yolks, wheat germ, whole grains, legumes, spinach, sweet potatoes, and lecithin.

❖ **EEG Neurofeedback** involves the use of a rather complex machine, which sells for between $10,000 and $30,000. The device is a modified electroencephalogram, which monitors the relative strengths of various brain-waves. By sitting in front of a monitor or computer screen attached to the EEG device, with the EEG electrodes on your head, you can see your brain-waves and, so the theory goes, train your brain to increase levels of the "focused-awareness" brain-waves while decreasing the power of the "distracted-awareness" brain-waves.

EEG Neurofeedback devices are principally used by health care professionals, although there are home-use units now coming onto the market in the under-$3000 price range. Those initial studies which claim that the technology can "train away" many of the deficits associated with ADD behavior indicate that thirty to fifty half-hour to one-hour sessions may be required.

While there is little interest within the traditional scientific community about the efficacy of herbs, vitamins, and homeopathy (some would argue because there's little profit to be made selling them), EEG Neurofeedback machines are currently the subject of several scientific studies. As of this writing the results look promising. If these devices actually are successful at helping people train their brains to behave in a non-ADD-like fashion, the question is then raised: could the training occur without the machine?

When the final verdict is in on EEG Neurofeedback, it may simply be a validation of the meditation and concentration techniques discussed elsewhere in this book.

In summary, given the recent "discovery" of ADD, it's difficult to claim total success for any one therapy. Drugs such as Ritalin, Norpramin, and Dextroamphetamine have their proponents, just as there are people who claim to benefit from herbs, homeopathy, vitamins, diet, meditation, chiropractic or EEG Neurofeedback.

In my opinion it is important to recognize and understand the strengths and weaknesses intrinsic to an inborn Hunter mindset. Knowing this, we can modify our behavior and create new life situations which compensate for or accommodate our "Hunterness."

Chapter Eleven

Can Parents' Smoking Cause Childhood Behavior Problems?

What unknown power governs men? On what feeble causes do their destinies hinge!

Voltaire, Semiramis

The question first popped into my mind as I sat in a pub in rural England with four parents of severely hyperactive ADD children. As the parents each lit their cigarettes, they proceeded to tell me absolute horror stories about how their children had kicked in doors, smashed windows, punched and even stabbed their siblings, and violently attacked their parents and their teachers. These kids were out of control with a ferocity I'd rarely seen among middle-class ADD/ADHD children in the United States.

Why would this be? I wondered. Why did it seem that there was so much more violent childhood behavior among the children of England's middle class, as compared with America's?

Sometimes we don't notice what's right in front of us because we're so used to it. I'd heard similar stories from parents all over the UK, in Germany, and, particularly in poorer neighborhoods and on Indian reservations, in the United States.

As my lungs screamed in pain from all the cigarette smoke around me, my mind raced back over the many stories and the parents who'd told them to me. I looked at the smoke in the air, and recalled how many other times parents had sat with a cigarette in their hand and told me about their off-the-wall children.

Could it be?

How many, I wondered, of those parents of the "most violent" children were smokers? My mind began to race through the list. By my recollection, it seemed as if it were a majority, but then memory is often a highly variable thing. Maybe it was just the pain cigarette smoke causes me that was coloring my perceptions.

But the question persisted: Could there be a relationship between parental smoking and childhood violence?

And, if so, what was the mechanism? Was it that parents who smoke are more likely to come from lower socioeconomic classes, where hitting a child as a form of discipline is more accepted? Or could it be that the children had become addicted to the nicotine in the passive smoke and were acting out a craving or withdrawal when they didn't have it?

Sitting in that pub, these questions raced through my mind. I was beginning to feel restless, my nose and lungs on fire, my heart racing as I inhaled their heart-stimulating drug.

At that time, I knew that nicotine is the most addictive drug currently known to man. It's more addictive than heroin (by one measure it's five times more addictive), more addictive than crack cocaine, and far more addictive than alcohol (as you can see from all the smokers at any AA meeting). Inhaling nicotine in smoke causes it to hit the bloodstream and the brain twice as fast as injecting it, so smokers get a more rapid "rush" than heroin users (which is why they're often so resistant to using nicotine gum, which eliminates the craving but doesn't give the "high" because it hits the bloodstream hundreds of times more slowly).

I also knew that nicotine is one of the most powerful drugs we know of to affect the central nervous system (CNS). It's wildly more powerful than amphetamine or Ritalin, for example.

It's such a powerful CNS drug that the tobacco plant produces it as an insecticide to kill predatory bugs. Nicotine is purified from tobacco and used as an insecticide in some countries and it's incredibly effective, leaving virtually any insect in its path twitching and convulsing in massive CNS overload. The main reason it's not more widely used on crops, in fact, is because it's so dangerous to humans: three drops of pure nicotine will kill a full-grown man in less than ten minutes.

Wondering if there may be a connection between childhood behavior and parental smoking, I did a bit of research.

The first article I found was in the July 15, 1992 issue of the *American Journal of Medicine* ("Nicotine and the central nervous system: biobehavioral effects of cigarette smoking"). In it, researchers pointed out that nicotine is a "neuroregulatory" drug, which profoundly adjusts and modifies the state of the entire central nervous system. When nicotine is absorbed (by smoking or inhaling others' smoke), "dose-dependent neurotransmitter and neuroendocrine effects occur," including increases in blood levels of norepinephrine and epinephrine (two hormone/neurotransmitters involved in the "fight-or-flight" response), and brain levels of dopamine (one of the neurotransmitters some researchers think is off-balance in children with ADD) are altered. Other hormones and neurotransmitters that flood the brain as a result of exposure to nicotine include arginine, vasopressin, Beta-endorphin, adrenocorticotropic hormone, and cortisol (the violence-enhancing hormone released when a person is under stress). Several of these neurochemicals are so highly psychoactive that they modify behavior at a "limbic brain level" in a way which is beyond the conscious control of the individual ... as any smoker who's tried to quit will tell you.

This was an interesting beginning, but I narrowed the search to specifically look for a correlation between "bad behavior" (not just ADD but disruptive or violent behaviors) and parental smoking.

What I found then was shocking.

It began in 1979, when a national survey was done by Harvard Medical School and the University of Rochester, polling 12,000 young people between the ages of fourteen and twenty two, to determine their smoking and childbearing behaviors. Follow-up interviews were conducted annually, and by 1986 it was found that 2256 children, ranging in age from four to eleven years old, had been produced by this group. At that point, the children of these parents were rated as to their behaviors, and it was found that children of smokers were "40-50% more likely" to be extremely disruptive than children born of or living in the homes of non-smokers. Researcher Barry Zuckerman published the results of this multi-year, large-population study in the September, 1992 edition of the well-known *Child Health Alert* publication for physicians.

Interestingly, Zuckerman's epidemiological data found that smoking during pregnancy wasn't nearly as likely to cause extreme behaviors among children as was smoking in the house where the children were living. Passive smoke, according to this study, was a clear candidate for the role of "cause" for the extreme behaviors of many of these children.

Another report discussing this study, published in the *Pediatric Report's Child Health Newsletter* in 1992, pointed out that the researchers had been so meticulous as to even determine that there was a "dose dependent" correlation between how much nicotine the children inhaled in the home environment and how severe their behavior was. They pointed out that children of mothers who smoked more than a pack of cigarettes a day were twice as likely (that's 100% more likely!) as other mothers to have children with highly disturbed behavior, whereas mothers who smoked less than a pack a day were only 1.4 times as likely to produce these types of children.

At first, reading this, I wondered if it might just be that people who smoke generally (particularly in the USA) are more likely to come from lower income groups. In the upper-middle-class suburbs of Atlanta where I've lived for the past decade, I don't know of a single parent who smokes: it's seen as a sign of low class. In England and the rest of Europe, however, that distinction has not yet hit the masses, and smoking is widely accepted. And in England I also found many, many more highly disruptive children than I've found in America among the children of people showing up for ADD support groups. So I wondered, could it be a class or income issue?

"No," was the unequivocal answer of this study's authors. They'd carefully factored out issues of class, income, lifestyle, use of other drugs, and even diet from their study. This was smoking around the kids, and only smoking around the kids, that predicted violent and disruptive behavior.

Since that time, I was amazed to discover, numerous studies have been done which corroborated the conclusions of this early Harvard study. One was published in the prestigious medical journal *Pediatrics* in 1992. In that study, Weitzman and his colleagues found a clear correlation between how much Mom smoked and how off-the-wall (my term, not theirs) her child was. They wrote that the connection was "highly statistically significant," which is researcher jargon for "This looks like a very strong connection!!"

That study's publication was followed by the publication of another, a year later and also in Pediatrics, this time by David Fergusson and two other scientists. They spent twelve years studying children of mothers in New Zealand who smoked, compared to a carefully selected group of similar class/income/lifestyle non-smokers. In this study of 1,265 children, they methodically removed from consideration other possible causes of (or variables affecting) poor conduct, including gender, ethnicity, family size, maternal age, maternal education, socioeconomic status, standard of living, maternal emotional responsiveness, avoidance of punishment, number of schools attended, life events, changes of parents, parental discord, parental history of drug use, and parental history of criminal offense.

Having pulled out every possible factor which could contribute to a child becoming violent, acting out, or engaging in antisocial behavior, only one factor was left, and it was staring them right in the face. Their research found a clear and obvious association between mothers smoking during pregnancy and both poor conduct and attention deficit disorders (their phrase).

Other studies have corroborated these. They include studies done by Fried & Watkinson (*Neurotoxicology & Teratology*, 1988), McCartney ("Central auditory processing in school-age children prenatally exposed to cigarette smoke," *Neurotoxicology & Teratology*, 1994), Richardson and Tizabi ("Hyperactivity in the offspring of nicotine-treated rats: Role of the mesolimbic and nigostriatal dopaminergic pathways," *Pharmacology and Biochemistry of Behavior,* 1994), Sexton & Fox ("Prenatal exposure to tobacco: Ill effects on cognitive functioning at age three," *International Journal of Epidemiology,* 1990), Wakschlag & Lahey, et al ("Maternal smoking during pregnancy associated with increased risk for conduct disorder in male offspring," manuscript submitted for publication), Weitzman & Gortmaker, et al ("Maternal smoking and behavior problems of children," *Pediatrics*, 1992), Bertolini & Bernardi ("Effects of prenatal exposure to cigarette smoke and nicotine on pregnancy, offspring development, and avoidance behavior in rats," *Neurobehavorial Toxicology*, 1982), Cotton ("Smoking cigarettes may do developing fetuses more harm than ingesting cocaine," *Journal of the American Medical As-*

sociation, 1994), and Fried & Gray ("A follow-up study of attentional behavior in six year old children exposed prenatally to cigarettes," *Neurotoxicology & Teratology*, 1992).

These studies not only corroborated the earlier ones, but also showed that this effect could be seen in rats and other animals (which rules out the socioeconomic factors theory). In rats and dogs, researchers have found that "passive" exposure to smoke "alters neurotransmitter functioning" (Cotton, 1994; Slotkin, 1992), increases hyperactivity and motor activity (Richardson & Tizabi, 1994), and decreases learning efficiency and ability (Bertolini, et al., 1982). In humans, they showed that nicotine exposure could do profound damage to the cognitive (thinking) abilities of children from birth right through the teenage years, and that the longer and more severe the exposure was, the more visible and serious was the damage. Several of these studies focused specifically on conduct disorders, and the results were consistent: exposure to passive cigarette smoke in the home correlates with violent behavior in children.

The mechanism by which this effect takes place is, at this moment, unknown. It is known, however, that cigarette smoke stimulates at least two different parts of the brain at the same time. It stimulates the production of cortisol, the "stress hormone," which leads to large releases of adrenaline, epinephrine, and other "rage" and "fight-or-flight" hormones and neurotransmitters, and, in the high doses that a smoker inhales, also stimulates the production of endorphins, the naturally-occurring opiates of the brain which produce the "high" smokers experience (along with the cortisol stimulation).

But while smokers are getting both parts of their brain stimulated, children inhaling their smoke are only getting enough nicotine to stimulate the cortisol mechanism: the dose isn't high enough to produce endorphins.

This is intuitive knowledge to any smoker—ask him how he'd feel if he could only smoke one or two cigarettes a day, instead of the twenty or forty he normally smokes. He'll describe how easily upset, on-edge, irritable, and filled with anxiety he'd feel at such a low dose of nicotine—which is the sort of dose his children are receiving as second-hand smoke.

Reading these studies, and many others that I came across in the course of my research, I was amazed that the issue of cigarette smoking around children hadn't gotten more coverage in the popular media. Certainly if a child were exposed to, for example, marijuana smoke at home, there would be considerable concern among the authorities about the child's absorption of THC, the active drug in that plant. And the same would be true of parents who smoked crack cocaine. But nicotine?

Then I remembered my days working as a writer and contributing editor to numerous magazines. Nearly all took hundreds of thousands, sometimes millions, of dollars a year from the tobacco companies in exchange for advertising. Who would bite that hand?

Only medical journals, like *Pediatrics*, which don't carry advertisements for cigarettes....

Chapter Twelve

Halfway to the Stars: How Unrealized ADD Can Limit an Apparently Successful Life

If thou follow thy star, thou canst not fail of a glorious haven.

—Dante Alighieri, *The Divine Comedy* (1310)

Movies and literature are rife with stories of people who overcame seemingly insurmountable odds to arrive at a level of success even the "average" person would hardly consider attainable. Examples include Terry Fox, the one-legged man who ran coast-to-coast to publicize the fight against cancer; Martin Luther King, Jr., the obscure African-American preacher who nonviolently freed a nation from the burden of segregation; Helen Keller, the woman born blind and deaf who wrote inspiring literature and revolutionized the world's view of "handicapped" people; and Pete Gray, the one-armed ball player who played in the major leagues.

Just as these people overcame handicaps to reach their goals, many adult Hunters have also overcome the limitations of their baseline attention spans and succeeded in the world and in society. Some are such geniuses to begin with that, like Thomas Edison, they're able to push through, past, around, or over their short attention spans.

Many, however, would describe themselves as the walking wounded.

They've succeeded, using many of their Hunter talents, but also often *in spite of* their Hunter instincts. Just like with the one-armed athlete, they are confronting a personal obstacle in the world of business or education, yet they're still apparently "successful."

When such individuals, who may to all outward appearances be "normal," read this book (or others) and recognize themselves as an ADD adult, they may seek professional help—and run straight into a wall.

Disorders and dysfunctions, by definition, mean that a person cannot function well—they're somehow impaired. So when a successful person walks into the office of a physician or psychiatrist and says "I think I have attention deficit disorder" (and, particularly, if they're asking for Ritalin or other drugs for it), the response of the physician may be, "You seem successful enough; what could possibly be wrong with you?" The result is that people who are functional may be misdiagnosed as not having ADD.

The irony here is the frequent failure of teachers, parents, employers, and professionals to see the invisible handicap that the ADD person must work around. And many Hunters who have sufficiently high intelligence to develop adaptive coping strategies through the course of their lives are even able to "fool" attention tests (which are largely designed for children), and "test out as normal."

These people have the potential, the talents, and the raw intelligence to reach the stars—but as a Hunter in this Farmer's world, they'll often only get halfway there.

"YOU'RE DOING WELL ENOUGH ALREADY"

At a recent support group meeting for parents of ADD children, several parents stood up to tell stories of children they believed were ADD, but whom physicians wouldn't treat because, "The kid is doing okay in school; what's the problem?"

The problem, in the eyes of these parents, is that their children are capable of doing *extraordinary* work, and "okay" just isn't a true reflection of their child's intelligence, nor a realization of his or her potential. One parent told the story of taking his son from a public school with an average classroom size of thirty-five children, placing him in a private school with a classroom size of sixteen children, and watching his grades go from Cs to As. The child had native intelligence which would qualify him as a genius, but this genius was not being realized or used because his Hunter characteristics got in the way of his learning ability in a Farmer public school setting.

Brad, who graduated from MIT and was, by all appearances, successful in the world with his various business ventures, realized that he was a Hunter and thought that Ritalin might help him become more successful in dealing with detailed projects that required long hours of concentration. When he visited a local psychiatrist, the doctor told him that he didn't show any symptoms of "minimal brain dysfunction," and implied that Brad was just trying to hustle drugs. At Brad's insistence, the psychiatrist performed a battery of attention and memory tests, and Brad scored "average." His success in passing the tests was because he'd trained himself, over the years, in ways to get around his short attention span. Using some of Harry Lorayne's classic memory techniques, Brad would create absurd pictures in his mind, or organize lists of things into specific categories. It gave him an edge on the test, allowing his very poor attention span to test out as average, just as his extremely high IQ occasionally tested out as average when he became bored with tests while in school.

Because psychological and medical professionals are largely trained to look for problems, if a person's life isn't in total disarray, he or she is often dismissed as not being in need of help. This is particularly true if the physician is under pressure to limit patient visits (as in a health maintenance organization or HMO), or is worried about pressure from government authorities for excessively prescribing controlled substances such as Ritalin or Dexedrine.

NEEDLESS LIMITATIONS ARE INDEED A PROBLEM

The Civil Rights and Women's Movements have sensitized most of us to the notion that a person may have tremendous potential, but be prevented from realizing that potential because of subtle impediments built into the fabric of our society. "Glass ceilings" and "invisible barriers" are common phrases used to describe these situations. If not for the efforts of heroic people like Martin Luther King, Jr. and Gloria Steinem, our society of the 1990s would be as blissfully ignorant of the subtle barriers blacks and women face as we were in the 1950s, when the United States government worked so hard to maintain segregation of schools, restaurants, and other public facilities in the face of "growing restiveness among the Negroes."

ADD is just now beginning to be recognized by government and educational agencies as a barrier to success in public school classrooms and the workforce. Treatments, including special educational programs designed for Hunter children, are occasionally now included in the range of services some schools offer. The United States Department of Education is also under increasing pressure to address the issue. (For more information or details, write to: The Assistant Secretary, Office of Special Education and Rehabilitative Services, United States Department of Education, 400 Maryland Avenue SW, Washington, DC 20202-2500.)

Unrealized potential, in addition to producing human casualties, is also a loss to our society. How many of us have met a taxi driver or construction worker or ex-con who's so articulate and well-informed that you ask yourself, "What's this guy doing driving a cab?"

In jobs such as cab-driving or being a cowboy, Hunter skills are actually a benefit. Unfortunately, many of these people, although sensing their own innate potential, gave up on ever trying to reach beyond cab driving because of all the obstacles they encountered. If they could either: a) pair with a Farmer, or, b) learn new coping skills (possibly including medication) specific to their areas of weakness, they might instead end up as brilliant statesmen, trial lawyers, entrepreneurs, consultants, salespeople, or detectives.

An ADD adult discussing this situation with me (the difficulty of diagnosis, the confusion about the condition, the variety of options for treatment, and, most importantly, the unfortunate circumstances of those who are ADD but whose pleas for help are ignored or rebuffed) shared this very articulate perspective on the situation, gleaned from his own experience:

Successful ADD-copers (especially adults) already have a lifetime of experience at outfoxing their own short attention. They've learned to get by, to get things done—even though sometimes it ain't pretty to watch.

Picture, if you will, three people taking the same test. You have to watch a long, boring series of numbers flashing on the screen, and punch a button when a certain number pops up. The idea is that people with an attention problem will drift away, won't notice the number, and will get a low score.

The first subject is a typical, non-ADD adult. As he watches, he just plain notices when the number appears and punches the button.

The second subject is the opposite: a severely ADD person. No matter how hard she tries, she just can't pay attention. Score: low. This person is likely to have all the everyday coping problems that come from being unable to focus your attention.

The third person, though, has ADD but has learned to cope. First, he knows he's being tested, and over the years of schooling, he's learned how to get through tests. (Otherwise he wouldn't have had the good grades to be successful!) So he starts by putting himself in the "test-me" frame of mind.

As the numbers start to go by, he notices his attention drifting away, and catches himself—just like a bike rider who notices he's falling, and jerks himself back upright.

But still, despite his best conscious efforts to pay attention and do well on this test, he still drops off and misses one. What happens? The examiner reaches out and makes a mark on the score sheet—and the distraction instantly "wakes up" the constantly-scanning subject.

Notice the difference here: the first and third people are getting similar scores, but their experience is very different. The first one just does it; the third one is constantly coping with a tendency to "fall over," and is getting a similar score by a very different process.

And to cap it off, after he's told he has no attention problem, person number three mentions to the receptionist that he has to stop at the dry cleaner's two blocks away, then he gets in his car and drives right past it.

So there you have it: the absent-minded professor, the disorderly genius, the mathematical wizard who can't keep his checks from bouncing. Thousands of people who might achieve greatness have settled for just getting by. People with rapid-fire, quick-connect minds that hop readily from subject to subject.

People who have adjusted have the same underlying problem. But we've spun a web of tricks that helps us "stay afloat" from day to day. We may do things in a mad flurry at deadline time; we may be expert at blaming problems on others; we may have self-medicated our brains with caffeine, nicotine, and endless busy rituals. And, behind it all, we may feel complete hopelessness about ever getting our lives under control.

I sincerely hope that healthcare professionals will open their eyes to the traits of this form of attention problem. The signs are easy enough to spot. If treatment programs can reduce all the time and effort devoted to simply coping, and direct it instead to success strategies, vast amounts of human potential will be unlocked. The person who's already made it halfway to the stars just might go all the way....

Chapter Thirteen

A Disorganized Collection of "Hunter in a Farmer's World" Anecdotes

Education is not the filling of a pail but the lighting of a fire.

—W. B. Yeats

Many books about ADD, particularly scholarly tomes, contain a few case histories which purport to give clinical examples of the condition. Rather than boring the many Hunter readers of this book with detailed case histories, this chapter offers a collection of anecdotes, each designed to give a brief glimpse into the worlds of other Hunters. Hunters will recognize many of these stories, and Farmers may get a new insight into the world of their Hunter friends, spouses, and co-workers.

A few of these stories are sad, some are encouraging, and many demonstrate how knowledge of their own instincts can help Hunters cope with life in this largely Farmer's society and culture. Hunters have inherited a frame of mind, a way of responding to the world, which has a very sensible heritage. They are not weak, bad, or inconsiderate people. But being a Hunter without realizing it has disabled many people in their work and relationships, while learning to manage their Hunter tendencies has brought many others back into the functional world.

Some of the following anecdotes are from interviews by the author. Some are the author's distillation of a Hunter's story—a "factual" retelling of what may have been a long or convoluted conversation or quote. Others are from public statements made by Hunters, or are summaries of "on-line" conversations on a computer bulletin board service.

Each illustrates a common facet of the unique Hunter personality.

A million projects started, but none ever finished

"Until I met my second wife, I never finished anything. I didn't finish high school, the apartment was always littered with half-completed woodworking projects, I had a dozen different hobbies, and dropped out of three different vocational schools. I dropped out of my first marriage after a year.

"I could never finish a book, and don't think I've ever read a magazine all the way through in my life. I knew I was smart, but always ended up in dead-end jobs and have never had what 'normal' people might call a career.

"When I married my second wife, she pushed me to complete things, and I resented her terribly for it. I often accused her of being a bitch and a nag, whether she was urging me to stay with my job or pick up my socks. But somehow we stayed together for a few years, and she kept me at the same job, too.

"It wasn't until after I realized I have ADD, and that she and I see the world differently, that I began to finish things and pay attention to details. Now I realize what a pain in the butt I must have been to live with all those years."

Single with children

"I'm a working, single mother. It's damn hard. The house is always a mess. I start to clean up the kitchen, and then get distracted by finding something and go off on some other tangent. Or one of the kids will interrupt me, and it'll totally blow whatever I'm trying to do.

"I sometimes get so angry with my children that I treat them very poorly. I've hit them a few times, I get so angry. All I want is a little peace and quiet, but they're always in my face, always wanting this or that, and it makes it impossible for me to do anything.

"As if my being ADD isn't bad enough, two of my kids have it, too.

"Every night when I go to bed, I pray to God for the strength to not get upset or out of control again the next day. And every day, it seems, I blow it again."

A day in the office, going to the water cooler

"I started out sitting at my desk, knowing that I had to review this contract. There was a sound outside, and I looked up and out the window—there was a minor fender-bender on the street. As I was looking back toward the contract, I noticed my vitamin bottle, and that reminded me that I hadn't taken my vitamin today. I looked for the glass of water I keep on my desk, but the cleaning people must have emptied it and left it in the office break room. So, I got up to go to the break room to get my glass.

"In the break room, I noticed that the water cooler was almost out of water. I went into the storage area to get a new 5-gallon jug, and there noticed that the little red light on the phone system's music-on-hold radio was flickering. I punched up the music-on-hold, and heard that the radio station was fading in and out, so I began to tune the radio into a stronger station.

"At that point, my partner came into the storage room. 'How's the contract coming?' she asked, glaring at me as I fiddled with the radio. 'And why's the door propped open with this water bottle?'

"You know the ironic part? I never did remember to take that vitamin."

Misdiagnosed as manic-depressive, bipolar

"I could just never get a handle on life, it seemed. I fell in love with dozens of men, but nothing ever seemed to last; after a few months I'd lose interest in them. I could fall in love with somebody from across the room—just catch that one particular, long look, and, bang, you know that this is it—for a few weeks.

"Anyhow, when I hit thirty, I started getting really depressed about it. I'd changed jobs a dozen times, been through probably a hundred or more men, and often wondered if I was alcoholic because I drank a lot. I never got plastered drunk, you know, but I was drinking two or three drinks almost every night. Living alone, it got me to sleep.

"So I went to see this psychiatrist, who told me that I was manic-depressive, and gave me lithium. Two days later I fell asleep while driving home from work, and woke up in the hospital. My car had run off the road and into the highway guard rail. Thank God I didn't hit anybody else.

"So they began dropping my dosage, more and more, until I was taking almost nothing at all, and it was still putting me to sleep, and I was still depressed. So he gave me Valium, and then another tranquilizer, Prozac. None of it seemed to help.

"It wasn't until I saw a television show about ADD and realized, 'Hey, that's me!' that I knew what was wrong with me.

"But when I went back to my doctor, he said that only children get ADD, and then it's almost always boys. 'You outgrow it,' he says. 'Women don't get it.'

"So I went through three shrinks before I found one who said, 'Yeah, adults can have ADD, and lots of women have it, too.' That validation, and the new insights, therapies, and strategies that came with it, have completely turned my life around."

The Interrupter

"All my life, my mother called me 'the interrupter.'

"'You constantly interrupt everybody,' she used to say. And it was true.

"What she didn't realize was that I *had* to interrupt them. If I didn't interrupt, by the time they were done with their sentence I would have forgotten what I was going to say. I would have been distracted by something else they were saying, and my mind would have gone onto something else, and I never would have made my point.

"When I got into college, I learned how to take notes. And so now, in business, whenever I have a meeting, I always take notes, so I don't have to interrupt people. I can just look back at my notes, at the things I was thinking about. It's hard to do in a social situation, though. Sometimes, with my girlfriend, I'll take notes when we talk. It helps.

"Other ADD people tell me that they're interrupters, too. Or, if they're shy, that they want to be. That they have these raging conversations going on inside their heads. I guess it's part of ADD, because Farmer people I know tell me that they don't need to interrupt, that they can remember a thought for a few minutes at a time, and they let me finish my sentences."

Just get your wife pregnant; she'll stop bothering you

"Before I was diagnosed as being ADD and started working on that as 'my' problem, my wife and I were having terrible difficulties. She felt like I didn't love her, because I'd forget her birthday, or get up and walk off while she was in the middle of a sentence. 'You never pay attention to me,' she'd always complain. I'd just try to tell her that she was being needy and neurotic, but she'd insist that there was something wrong with me.

"So we went to see this marriage counselor. Explained the whole thing to him. You know what his solution was? 'Get her pregnant,' he said. 'That'll give her something else to focus her attention on, and she won't hassle you so much.'

"She wasn't ready for that one, so we tried another counselor who told us that I was ADD and sent me to a psychiatrist, who gave me Ritalin. Now I actually sit and talk with her, sometimes for more than an hour, which is something I don't think I've ever done with anybody else in my entire life. And our marriage is better than either of us ever thought possible."

Applying new skills to the job

"I had a very good computer-technical-support day today, at a major national magazine.

"I realized on the drive home from San Francisco that I successfully handled this situation differently from my usual response, simply by being aware of my ADD tendencies and how I'm different from the mid-road masses. See, typically, while grokking all the stuff about how a client's system is and isn't working, I'll notice a bazillion things that need to be tweaked, each a simple little change. I make the changes in the little slices of time between steps of the main task.

"But people get unsettled by these changes after I'm gone. So this time I took the changes back out. Result: I changed only what needed to be changed to respond to the customer's reported need. Less to keep track of, less to document, less to debug. Less effort, more results.

"A positive change in my behavior, an increase in my effectiveness, without medication, just by being aware of the Hunter versus Farmer perspectives. See, it *can* be done. Didn't even take effort on my part—just by being aware of it, I saw the situation differently."

I've always felt like a fraud and a phony

"A lot of people in my life have commented on how smart I am, and I'm successful as a saleswoman—very successful. But I had a heck of a time with school, and I could never really memorize things, or understand anything like physics that really required concentration. Although I'd done well until then, I almost flunked out in my senior year of high school. So, I never thought I was as smart as everybody always said I was, because I couldn't handle anything that really required concentrating and intense learning.

"All my life, I've felt like a phony. It wasn't until I

learned that I have ADD that I realized it's possible to be both smart and incapable of concentrating long enough to understand physics ...."

Dancing with the stars (an online transcript)

CompuServe Message: #201867
Date: Sat, Apr 11, 1992 5:26:12 AM
Subject: #201735–attention deficit disorder
From: Marsha
To: Robert

I, too, have never felt ADD is a disorder. My son has a gift (and my sister). Their minds can go places mine cannot, and I'm envious of that. Unfortunately, all gifts have a price—and theirs is a lack of attention to detail. Small price to pay for being able to dance among the heavens during the course of your day, don't you think?

–*Marsha*

CompuServe Message: #201884
Date: Sat, Apr 11, 1992 7:01:15 AM
Subject: #201867–attention deficit disorder
From: Robert
To: Marsha

Well, m'dear, *you* may call it dancing among the heavens, and *you* may call it a small price. If that's so, then I can tell ya, heaven has lotsa sharp, pointy things to bump into.

The tough thing, for some kids, must be getting treated as "not right" when science is just now beginning to discover how they actually work. The "bad" news is that these discoveries didn't happen in the nineteenth century. The good news is that these discoveries didn't have to wait for the twenty-first century!

In fact, in the long history of such kids, I'd say the ones born 1975-1995 are in a rare, pivotal position.

They are the first, I'd guess, to have a chance to be viewed in the new way. They're pioneers; their contributions to our knowledge will benefit people forever—especially their own descendants (and, therefore, yours).

Do you feel good to be making a contribution to this, right now? (smile) —*Robert*

CompuServe Message: #202429
Date: Mon, Apr 13, 1992 6:21:09 AM
Subject: #201884—attention deficit disorder
From: Marsha
To: Robert

When I said, "dancing among the heavens" I was referring to the ability to grasp abstract (heavenly) concepts. People who have this ability don't realize what a struggle abstractions are for some of us. For example, I was a great math student up until calculus. I made decent grades in calculus, too, but strictly by memorization. I never really understood it—too much abstraction. My son, however, struggles with the routine, "easy" stuff, and finds the abstract concepts instinctual.

I know life is full of sharp points for ADD people—believe me, I know. But I still think, as time passes, we'll come to view this "affliction" as a "side-effect" (if you will) of creative, abstract thought.

And yes, I do think this generation is on the cusp. In fact, I often tell my son it will be *his* generation—the first to make it through school in large numbers—who will truly change things for the next one.

—*Marsha*

He's speedy, I'm not ... and we're both ADD

"When my husband was diagnosed as having ADD, I thought, sure, this is it. He's hyperactive. He's always on the go, always doing something new, always looking for a different challenge. It makes sense that he's one of those hyperactive people, those ADD people.

"But then I took the test, and realized that I'm ADD, too. I forget things constantly. I'll drive all the way to the store, only to realize when I get there that I forgot what I was intending to buy. While people are talking, I'm thinking a million miles an hour, about this and that, thoughts that go shooting off in some direction because of something they said. And then, a few minutes later, I realize I'm not paying attention at all.

"I'm not hyperactive, I'm pretty quiet, in fact, but I'm ADD. I never thought it was possible."

The "Dingbat Blonde"

"I'm the blonde they make the jokes about. Except it's not a joke.

"I'm smart and I know I'm smart. But before I realized I was ADD and learned the memory and organization exercises, I always played the dumb blonde role and nobody but me knew I *was* smart.

"Being a dingbat was an easy part for me to play, because I could never concentrate on anything, and it was a socially acceptable stereotype. I'd forget a shopping list with three things on it. I can't tell you how many times I've killed the battery on my car because I left the lights on. Somebody will say something that'll trigger a thought, and, poof, I'm off. And then they say, 'There went Debby. The lights are on, but no one's home.'

"Nobody's calling me a dumb blonde anymore, though. I'm even thinking of getting my hair dyed brunette."

Working around ADD

"Here's a tip (before I forget) to ADDers: constantly

losing things? Eliminate ambiguity. Always put things in one place, or at most one of two.

"My wallet is always either in my right hip pocket or on my dresser.

"My plane tickets, when I travel, are always inside my left coat pocket.

"My keys are always on the kitchen wall hook or in my pocket.

"When I travel (I used to lose things in hotels), everything that comes out of my pockets goes on top of the television. This vastly diminishes my confusion in the mornings!

"My personal life is now organized by a small calendar/phone book. The important thing here is that it's tiny and it doesn't have an ouchy spiral binding, so it lives in my left hip pocket. It's always there.

"With this constant predictability, if something's not where it's supposed to be, I know right away that I have to look for it—there's no chance it might be in a dozen different places."

Suicidal adolescents with ADD

"As a teacher, I can tell you that almost every time I've come across a suicidal adolescent, it's been a very bright, or gifted, or genius child with ADD. They can't handle the dichotomy of knowing that they're brilliant, yet unable to do their schoolwork. And the distortions of time-sense with ADD cause their lows to seem so very painfully low that they get suicidal."

An alcoholic who found relief

"When I was seventeen I finally found something that would turn off the constant grinding of the gears in my brain: alcohol. By the time I was twenty-three, I was a full-blown, down-and-out drunk. I hit bottom, and made it back with the help of God and Alcoholics Anonymous.

"But it wasn't until I was thirty and started on EEG Neurofeedback that the constant chatter in my head, the persistent distractions from every direction, stopped. Then, for the first time, I could smell the flowers. I could experience life. I could actually listen to other people, and understand what they were saying.

"And I have gone from fighting the urge to drink, to no longer having the urge to drink."

Cleaning the desk with my Farmer-wife

"This morning my extremely stable Farmer-partner-wife sat patiently with me and took papers off the huge pile on my desk, one by one, and 'brought them to my attention' by sticking them in my hand. Each was disposed of immediately: filed appropriately, put in the Bills To Pay or Expenses Folder, discarded, and so on. An hour into this I got out my briefcase (for a very good reason of course) and started looking for something important; found something else and remembered I needed to send someone a message about something three weeks old. So I sat down to my computer to send an e-mail ... Alarm! She says 'Am I losing you?'

"We've done this 'hand me each paper' thing a few times in the past but I've always felt terrible about having to be babysat. She's been rather disgusted too, and *really* disgusted when she'd start to 'lose' me. 'Hell,' she thinks, 'if I'm gonna babysit him like this, the *least* he can do is not ignore me! If he's not gonna pay attention, I'm leaving!'

"But this time when she said 'Am I losing you?' I shortened the e-mail, shortened the briefcase task, and sat right back down in the 'next-paper-please' chair.

"The desk is now clear for the first time in months. (There are still other piles to be sorted through, but the desk is clear!)

"What a gift it is to have a Farmer-partner who's willing to assist, and for us both to now understand the differences between Hunters and Farmers."

Chapter Fourteen

The Edison Trait: Hunters Who Have Changed the World

I represent a party which does not yet exist: the party of revolution, civilization.

This party will make the twentieth century.

There will issue from it first the United States of Europe, then the United States of the World.

—On the wall of Victor Hugo's room when he died in Paris, 1885

Hunters sometimes have difficulty answering the question "What do you do for a living?" It's not that there isn't an answer; it's that there are too many answers. Hunters of above-average or genius intelligence often have resumés which are startling in their diversity and accomplishment, even though they may have struggled to simply finish high school.

Similarly, the stereotype of the "eccentric genius" or "loony, creative type" is often applied to Hunter inventors, artists, writers, and designers. At many ad agencies, the "creative types" are allowed (or even encouraged) to have an eccentric appearance, with flowered shirts, long hair, jeans, etc.

As the chapter on ADD and creativity pointed out, the ability to think innovatively is intrinsically tied to the ability to fall into an open (and therefore distractible) state of consciousness. Conversely, to make use of the "inspirations" gained from such typical Hunter free-association, there must be a compensating burst of focused energy, in order to bring these concepts into reality. Learning to channel these bursts is the challenge of every Hunter.

When Hunters fail in life it is often because their self-image was distorted at an early age when they were labeled as a "problem". Their assets are also neglected if they plug into a job or a segment of society which requires Farmer, rather than Hunter, skills.

But let's look at some successful Hunters in history who have demonstrated tremendous powers of transformation, vitality and dynamic energy, and whose biographies appear to conform to the American Psychiatric Association's DSM criteria of ADHD. While it is impossible for us to reach back to historic figures and ask them to answer the questions which might lead to a medically supportable diagnosis of ADD, their life stories very often give us those answers in a rather overt fashion. Consider the following:

The life of **Thomas Alva Edison** has been an inspiration to Hunter boys for nearly a century. Born in the Midwest before the Civil War, Edison wrote, "I remember I used never to be able to get along at school. I was always at the foot of the class. I used to feel that the teachers did not sympathize with me, and that my father thought I was stupid...."

Edison complained about the distractions of the other children in his school, and the fact that learning was "abstract" and not "real." To be able to actually *do* something, to test a theory or discover a fact through *experience* (he wrote in his diary) "for one instant, was better than learning about something he had never seen for two hours."

Believing her son had potential, Edison's mother took over his schooling. Instead of requiring her son to learn a particular curriculum by rote, she instead encouraged him to explore things he found interesting; he soon became a voracious reader and consumed a huge body of knowledge on a wide variety of subjects.

Edison left home at age twelve and started a long procession of short-lived jobs. The year he was seventeen, he held four different jobs, being fired from each one because of his inattentiveness to the duties or routine of the job. When he was fifteen, he had a job as a railroad signalman during the night, and had to clock in via telegraph every hour. He was fired when his superiors learned that his punctual check-in signal was actually transmitted by a simple invention he'd created from an alarm clock, which would send the Morse Code signal on the hour. That invention led to his developing the first automatic telegraph, and then the first stock ticker, although he held a dozen more jobs before he received $40,000 for his stock ticker, at age twenty-one, and was able to establish a laboratory where he could devote himself to inventing.

Being a classic Hunter, Edison usually worked on many projects at the same time. In the year of 1877, for example, we know that he had more than 40 inventions in process in his laboratory—concurrently. He kept his own hours, often working through the night. When he became bored or saturated with one invention, he would quickly hop to another.

Edison credited his *inability* to stick to one task for a long time as being the power of his creative efforts. He said, "Look, I start here with the intention of going there" (drawing an imaginary line) "in an experiment, say, to increase the speed of the Atlantic cable; but when I have arrived part way in my straight line, I meet with a phenomenon and it leads me off in another direction—to something totally unexpected."

Thomas Edison transformed the twentieth century with his invention of the electric light bulb, the central power generating station, the phonograph, the flexible celluloid film and movie projector, the alkaline storage battery, and the microphone (merely a few among the more than 1,000 major patents he registered before his death in 1931).

Benjamin Franklin flunked out of George Brownell's Academy after only two years of formal education. It was said that he was "slow at doing sums," and he utterly failed in arithmetic; his teacher complained that he would never pay attention to his lessons. He spent two years as an apprentice candlemaker to his father, but his father's frustrations with young Ben were legion: the boy was always slipping off to explore the town, the salt marshes, the incoming ships.

Having demonstrated his Hunter inability to be a scholar in the formal Farmer schools of the day, Franklin went on to become one of the most well-educated (in terms of practical abilities) men in American history. Although he couldn't stick with a single job, Franklin is now celebrated for his accomplishments in *dozens* of roles: he was a printer, moralist, civic leader, essayist, inventor, scientist, diplomat, publisher, statesman, postmaster, candlemaker, mechanic, and philosopher, among others.

His impulsive streak, which was partly responsible for the creation of an independent United States of America, showed itself early when, at age sixteen, he wrote several articles for *The Courant*, a Boston newspaper, making fun of Boston's authorities and society figures. His persistence in writing such articles led to the imprisonment of his brother, James, who published the paper. After running the paper until James got out of jail, Ben left his job with *The Courant*.

Taking a huge risk, a penniless Ben Franklin left for England in 1724, where he soon became a master printer and writer. Two years later, upon returning to Philadelphia, he began publishing his own newspaper, the *Pennsylvania Gazette*, and also started, wrote, edited, designed, printed, and distributed a periodical titled *Poor Richard's Almanack*.

Once these two publishing endeavors were up and running well, Franklin, now bored and looking for a new challenge, created a network of printers throughout the colonies to do the government's printing. During this time he also opened a book shop, then became clerk of the Pennsylvania Assembly, and the first postmaster of Philadelphia.

With his businesses doing well and his income assured, he turned over management of his publishing business, book store, and other endeavors to trusted Farmer-types, and went off in search of other challenges, sustained for more than twenty years by the income from these early startups. He founded the Junto Society, which created one of America's first libraries (1731), Philadelphia's first fire station (1736), the University of Pennsylvania (1749), and—in one year—both an insurance company and a hospital (1751). He also organized Philadelphia's first public works department, supervising the lighting, paving, and cleaning of the streets, and organizing a volunteer militia. In 1763, Franklin took on the job of reorganizing the entire American postal system.

During this time of his "retirement," Franklin also pursued many private interests. He invented the Franklin Stove in 1740, which still heats millions of American homes. In 1752 he proposed that lightning was a form of electricity and, with characteristically impulsive abandon, risked flying a kite in a thunderstorm to prove his thesis. His scientific theories and discoveries made him world famous and, in 1756, he was elected to the Royal Society, which numbers among its members Newton, Einstein, and Hawking. He was inducted into the French Academy of Sciences in 1772. He was the first man to measure the Gulf Stream. He pioneered the science of tracking storm paths (which led to modern predictive meteorology). He designed sailing ships, and invented the bifocal lens for glasses. A man who was thrown out of the third grade, he was granted honorary degrees from St. Andrews (1759) and Oxford (1762).

In 1751, Franklin ran for and was elected to the Pennsylvania Assembly. In 1754, he presented a plan to the Albany Congress for partial self-government of the American colonies. Not content to simply sit back in a legislative mode, Franklin himself led an expedition of military men into the Lehigh Valley, fighting both the French and the Indians and building forts there to protect the frontiersmen.

Franklin's personal life reflected the occasionally reckless streak seen in so many ADD adults. He had an illegitimate son, a wife in Philadelphia, a mistress in London, and there were rumors of several other women who kept his company over the years, particularly during the time he spent in Paris where his nickname was *le Bonhomme Richard.*

At the age of seventy, in 1776, Franklin signed the Declaration of Independence that he'd helped draft. That same year, he also served in the Continental Congress, proposed a new constitution for Pennsylvania, and wrote the Articles of Confederation for the United Colonies, soon to become the United States of America. Ten years later, after returning from France, he became president of Pennsylvania and attended the Constitutional Convention of 1787, where the final draft of our Constitution was written with his help.

Sir Richard Francis Burton, not to be confused with the late Welsh actor and husband of Elizabeth Taylor, is perhaps one of the most fascinating Hunters of recent history.

In his early childhood Burton, born in 1821, was described by those who knew him as a "terror." Once when his mother was taking him through town, at age seven, he broke a shop window to get at a pastry she told him he couldn't have. He regularly terrorized nannies, and was a total failure at school, constantly fighting with the other boys and describing his teacher as "no more fit to be a schoolmaster than the Grand Cham of Tartary."

Eventually, Burton made it through to Oxford University, but then dropped out to purchase a commission in the Bombay Native Infantry in 1843. He was a soldier, for the next five years, in what is now Pakistan.

Following his brief career as a soldier, Burton became a world-famous explorer. He disguised himself as a Muslim, "Sheik Abdullah," and became the first Westerner to ever visit Mecca and Medina for the Haj, the holy Muslim holiday. Had he been revealed as a non-Muslim during this trip, he most surely would have been put to death. Following that success, which was widely reported in England, he made an equally dangerous foray to the Ethiopian forbidden city of Harar.

His greatest exploration, and the one that thrilled the world of European society, was his 1857 exploration of Tanzania. He became, in 1858, the first white ever to view Lake Tanganyika. Having explored Africa, he later crossed the American continent to Salt Lake City, and then mapped the territory to Panama.

Following this flurry of exploratory success, Burton was named British consul at Fernando Po, off the coast of Nigeria, was the first white to visit Benin (then called Dahomey), and was one of the first whites to ever travel up the Congo River. Later, he served Britain as consul in Damascus, Trieste, and Santos, Brazil.

If his explorations weren't enough to establish Burton's reputation, he also wrote twenty-one books that still remain (his wife burned a number of his manuscripts—perhaps as many as fifty—upon his death), including tales of his travels, books on falconry, and an esoteric tome on swordsmanship (of which he was a master). He was a brilliant linguist, and was the first European to translate the *Tales of the Arabian Nights* from Arabic into English, as well as secretly translating a number of Eastern manuals about sexual positions and perversions. During the times of his writing, his easy distractibility caused him to seek rooms in distant monasteries, mountain retreats, and other places where he could work for days or weeks in total isolation.

Burton had an impulsive streak that nearly killed him several times. He was involved in a number of duels and fights-to-the-death as a result of remarks he made without first thinking through their consequences. Although married, he had numerous mistresses all around the world, and publicly advocated polygamy.

Burton's interests ranged from the rational to the spiritual to the bizarre. He became a world-respected authority on reptiles, mining, and mountain climbing. He wrote extensively about slavery, religion, and odd sexual practices. He was fascinated by different cultures, and brought back from his trips to Africa numerous illustrations which shocked and amazed Western anthropologists.

His biographer, Byron Farwell, pointing out the breadth of Burton's career and his astounding range of interests, called him "one of the rarest personalities ever seen on Earth."

When he died in 1890, Burton had made and lost several fortunes, held dozens of jobs and posts, written at least fifty books, changed the western world's perspective on archaeology and African anthropology, and become one of the most respected—and vilified—men of his day.

Ernest Hemingway struggled to make his way through school, finally graduating from Petoskey, Michigan's Oak Park High in 1917. His unpleasant school experiences, the result of his short attention span and "boredom," convinced him that college would be a wasted effort. He instead took a job as a cub reporter for the *Kansas City Star.* After only seven months on the job, Hemingway became restless and tried to enlist in the U.S. Army so he could fight in World War I. When the Army rejected him because of weak eyesight, his desire to take risks and his craving for stimulation propelled him to join the Red Cross as a volunteer ambulance driver and he was shipped off to Italy.

After a severe injury from shrapnel and a brief recuperation in Milan, Hemingway returned to North America and got a part-time job as a feature writer for the *Toronto Star.* Within a year he tired of that, and moved on to a job in 1920 as a contributing editor of a trade journal in Chicago, where he met and married, in a whirlwind romance, his first wife. They traveled to France on their honeymoon, where Hemingway decided to stay, and arranged to be a "foreign correspondent" for his old employer, the *Toronto Star.* In 1923, Hemingway moved to Toronto (where his son John was born) to try to work a regular job at the Star, but the routine and many distractions of the news office drove him to quit his job and, on an impulse, return to Paris, jobless, where he intended to launch a career as a serious and financially successful writer.

It took four years for Hemingway to reach his goal. His first American publication was a small volume of short stories, *In Our Time*, that was published in 1925 (although two small chapbooks of prose and poetry were published in Paris in 1923 and 1924). By 1927, Hemingway had established his reputation as a writer (and was actually making a living at it). He'd published *The Torrents of Spring, The Sun Also Rises*, and *Men Without Women.* He also divorced his first wife that year, and married Pauline Pfeiffer.

Hemingway's ADD-restlessness caught up with him again in 1928. He moved to Key West with Pauline, then began a series of world travels, from dude-ranching in Wyoming, to deep-sea fishing in Cuba, to extensive travels through Europe and Africa, where he enjoyed big-game hunting.

By 1940, his second marriage had disintegrated, and Hemingway, seeking to get away from the constant stream of visitors that distracted him from his work, married his third wife, Martha Gellhorn, and moved to a remote farm outside Havana, Cuba. The next year, they flew to China to report on the Japanese attacks on China. When the United States entered World War II, Hemingway armed his cabin cruiser, "Pilar," and cruised around the Caribbean for the next two years, hunting German submarines.

Just before the Allied invasion of Normandy, a new impulse drove Hemingway to London, where he met Mary Welsh, his fourth wife. He joined the Fourth Infantry Division in the summer and fall of 1944, pursued fleeing Nazi forces during the liberation of Paris, and fought in the Battle of the Bulge.

After the war, Hemingway retired again to Cuba, where he alternated between streaks of brilliant writing and wild drinking in his remote hideaway. So great was his need for solitude in order to concentrate, he often shot at visitors who arrived looking for autographs or wanting to meet the "great writer." On other occasions, if he was drinking instead of writing, he might welcome visitors with open arms and engage in all-night drinking and talking sessions, providing wonderful entertainment with his free-associations and wandering stories of his life. (This is a pattern which several ADD alcoholics have reported to me from their own lives.)

Finally unable to reconcile his impulsiveness, his alcoholism, and his easy distractibility which, compounded by the fame which followed his winning the

Nobel Prize for Literature in 1954, led to severe difficulties in writing, Hemingway followed in his father's footsteps and killed himself in 1960.

Thomas Carlyle, whose quote opens the preface to this book, was born about 200 years ago in Scotland to a sternly Calvinist family of peasants. He was described as a skeptic and an empiricist, and, like many ADD adults, struggled through many different attempts at building a career. He started in law, then went to journalism, the ministry, teaching, and mathematics, before deciding, in 1821, to become a writer. He was forty-two years old when his first published work, *The French Revolution*, brought him out of poverty and into the world of published writers. Many of his works such as *Latter Day Pamphlets* (1850) and *Niagra And After?* (1867) were essentially tirades about modern society—a Farmer society which his Hunter's low threshold for frustration and high distractibility had, in his view, kept him from success. Carlyle's work is alternately described by his biographers as "uneven," "rhetorically audacious," and "full of energy."

(Certainly there are many modern people who are both successful and Hunters. A famous, high-energy comedian and actor is often mentioned in informal discussions of ADD, as is the brilliant founder of a major television network. However, since ADD or ADHD is currently classified as a mental illnesses by the psychiatric profession, it would be uncharitable at best, and risky at worst, to reveal or speculate on the mental state of living persons.)

Chapter Fifteen

Baseline States of Consciousness

The secondary imagination...dissolves, diffuses, dissipates, in order to re-create; or where this process is rendered impossible, yet still at all events it struggles to idealize and to unify. It is essentially vital, even as all objects (as objects) are essentially fixed and dead....

The fancy is indeed no other than a mode of memory emancipated from the order of time and space.

—Samuel Taylor Coleridge (*Biographia Literaria*, 1817)

This chapter speculates on the nature of various states of consciousness, how they evolved, and how we can best utilize them. What are the differences between Hunters and Farmers in terms of how they experience the world? How different are their realities? Is one state of consciousness "better" than the other in some global sense, or are they merely "separate but equal"? Might other "variations" of consciousness also be adaptive mechanisms left over from more primitive societies?

And might there be an opposite disorder to ADD, where the individual cannot *stop* focusing?

TASK-SWITCHING DEFICIT DISORDER (TSDD)

Many modern microcomputers are capable of doing more than one thing at the same time. On DOS-based personal computers it's called "multi-tasking," whereas on a Macintosh computer it's the difference between the "Finder" and "MultiFinder." It works by causing the computer to perform a few hundred calculations on one job or in one program, then shift to the next job or program and perform a few hundred calculations there. Shifting back and forth between two different programs or jobs, one in "foreground" and the other in "background," the computer seems to actually do two things at the same time.

In actual point of fact, though, the computer is only doing one thing at a time. It just switches from that one thing to another and back again so fast (often in a ten-millionth of a second!) that it seems to be performing parallel tasks.

ADD Hunters often report that they consider the ability to do several things at once as one of their "special skills." Betty is most in her element when she has a job printing from one computer, is performing backup onto another computer, and she's doing design work on a third. She reports getting a special satisfaction from her unique ability to do three things at once, when the other computer-based designers with whom she works must plod along on one job at a time.

Conversely, non-ADD Farmers are often irritated by their Hunter-peers' tendency to go shooting off in new directions in the middle of a conversation. "I was talking and Bill just pulled out a piece of paper and started writing," said John indignantly. "I know he couldn't have been listening to me; he was writing."

Bill, however, is emphatic that he could both write down his idea and listen to John at the same time. He couldn't understand why John would get so upset, just because he didn't "seem focused on the entire conversation, every minute."

While John's perception—that Bill was ignoring him as he was writing—may have been correct, it may also be that John was simply judging Bill, using his own abilities as a reference. John, being solidly a Farmer, couldn't imagine trying to do two things at once, because neither would get done well! But to Bill it just seemed normal for people to pay attention to two things at the same time.

Perhaps Bill is capable of task-switching, just like the computers which are performing multi-tasking functions. What if ADD Hunters are capable of doing more than one thing at a time—that it's hard-wired into them—and is part of those "alert in the woods" survival skills: walk, listen to sounds, sniff the air, scan between the trees, prepare the weapon, all at the same time?

If Bill and Betty (the Hunters) are capable of easily switching tasks like multi-tasking computers do and we call this attention deficit disorder, then perhaps John (the Farmer) is suffering from a Task-Switching Deficit Disorder (TSDD).

Consider the case of Frederick, who's apparently afflicted with TSDD:

He sat down at his home desk to begin writing a marketing manual for a client. It was just after dinner, and he planned to work for an hour or so. "It was two in the morning when I suddenly realized that I'd been writing for seven hours straight," Frederick said. "My wife and kids had gone to bed, and I hadn't even noticed."

Frederick also claims that he can't work in a quiet place. "I must have a radio or television on when I'm working, otherwise I actually get nervous. I need the stimulation, or I vanish into the job I'm working on and can't climb out for hours."

The problem for Frederick isn't that he can concentrate too much or too easily, but that he can't easily control his concentration. His normal, baseline state of concentration is focused, and he has difficulty turning it off.

Many Hunters describe this same phenomenon—the ability to totally escape into a particular area of focused concentration—but they report it as an *abnormal* or episodic state of consciousness. It's a state some Hunters describe as "being on." (One Hunter adult told me he'd always thought of that state as being "on the jazz," but had never before shared that phrase with anybody else.) There also appear to be subtle differences between the way Hunters and Farmers experience focused consciousness.

Here's how one Hunter described it: "When I'm 'on,' it's not just one thing, it's three! Today was one of those days: from 1:00 p.m. to 6:00 p.m., I was putting together a complex application for a client in Minnesota, writing the documentation for it, creating and running alpha test files on a new printer and writing the alpha report for another client in New Hampshire, and regularly interacting with people via CompuServe. This is a very familiar situation—doing three things at once on different computers. It actually feels physically satisfying, I must say. I remember this feeling way back in '75 working for a big typesetting company. I'd love being there alone at night because I could get all the machines humming at once.

"So perhaps I shift states rather thoroughly. When I get working, time becomes immaterial and I can spin and juggle without difficulty. When I'm 'on,' it is most definitely what you describe as focused, but it's not just one task, it's multi-tasking. All those sounds do blend into a gray shroud, but the bright light illuminates the *mix* of tasks."

(Adult Hunters who take Ritalin report that the drug gives them the ability to "switch on" the focused state with little effort, but that the Ritalin-focused state is not a multi-tasking focused state: attention is directed to one single thing. Many describe this as being the first time in their lives they could control this state of consciousness, or enter a single-point focused state for more than a few minutes at a time—which probably accounts for the common reports of life-transforming experiences as a result of using this drug. The literature of Transcendental Meditation (available from that group nationwide), which teaches how to switch on a focused state without drugs, is similarly filled with studies documenting how people transformed their working and/or personal lives by learning how to activate single-task focused consciousness at will.)

Some Farmers, similarly, are capable of experiencing open consciousness and multi-tasking. For extreme Farmers, though—those suffering from TSDD—this is as difficult as the challenge of remaining in a focused state for an hour is to an ADD Hunter.

Ralph, another TSDD victim and a respected psychotherapist, reports difficulty driving and talking at the same time. When driving and in conversation, he's likely to unthinkingly swerve out of his lane when trying to make an important point, or when mentally struggling with a complex concept. "I'm terrible that way," he reports. "I'm simply constitutionally incapable of doing two things at one time, and my wife won't drive with me because of it."

It's interesting to note that both Frederick and Ralph are married to women whom they describe as "highly distractible." Frederick reports that his wife, who's a surgeon, can't stand to have the radio or television on unless she's directly watching or listening to it; she craves silence when she wants to concentrate or relax. Ralph says the same of his wife; when she's working, she goes into her home office, closes, and sometimes even locks the door so he won't be tempted to distract her.

Ralph and Frederick, on the other hand, both prefer music in the background, or a television on in the room, regardless of what they're doing. Conversely, many Hunters report that the only music they can tolerate (if any) when working is music without words (although this is certainly not a universal comment, and is in no way a diagnostic criterion).

Many ADD/TSDD couples report this incompatibility. While they often support each other's "disorders" by the ADD person bringing excitement and variety to the relationship and the TSDD person supplying patience and stability, their ways of relaxing and working are totally different. Until they realize that one is a Hunter and the other a Farmer—that there are definite differences in the way they use and experience their consciousness—each may simply think the other is being eccentric or difficult. "Why can't he drive while he's talking?" Ralph's wife asks. "Why does my wife get so upset when I want the television on and nobody's watching it?" Frederick asks.

If there's a bell curve to behaviors as postulated earlier, with extreme ADD Hunters on one end, it should be no surprise that severely TSDD Farmers should inhabit the other end. Fortunately for the Farmers, the problems that come out of TSDD are rarely as socially or educationally destructive as those of ADD. Farmers with TSDD may burn-out their working companions with their ability to engage in lengthy meetings on a single subject, or may seem "boring" or "obsessed," but TSDD seems to be a condition better suited to successfully completing school and plugging into the corporate world.

Pediatric neurologist Marcel Kinsbourne, M.D., in his landmark work *Overfocusing: An Apparent Subtype of Attention Deficit-Hyperactivity Disorder*, detailed the characteristics of what this book calls TSDD. In this article, and a previous book published by Little, Brown in 1979 called *Children's Learning and Attention Problem*, Dr. Kinsbourne referred to the condition as "overfocusing." He also gave several examples of the condition and the way it affects the lives of sufferers. Suggesting that ADD may be, in some environments, an adaptive behavior, Dr. Kinsbourne points out that the overfocused state which he has observed in numerous patients is probably the other end of the curve of hereditary behaviors, both of which, *in this society and culture*, are no longer adaptive but, rather, maladaptive.

CULTURAL TRAINING OF OPEN AND FOCUSED AWARENESS

There are apparently two distinctly different positional states into which we can direct normal waking consciousness: *open* and *focused*.

With focused consciousness, a person is totally on

a task, absolutely absorbed in it. The ticking of the clock, the droning of the television, the sounds from the street or the next office all vanish into a gray background, as the bright light of consciousness illuminates only the single task.

Open consciousness, on the other hand, is diffused. The mind wanders from thing to thing, touching one after another lightly, keeping what's interesting, discarding the rest, then wandering to another input. Attention touches the ticking of the clock, which triggers a childhood memory of Uncle Ralph's grandfather clock, which makes you think of those odd ties Uncle Ralph used to wear. That thought's interrupted by the sound of a truck rumbling by on the street outside, which reminds you of the time your father took you for a ride in the truck he'd rented to move household items to a new neighborhood when you were a child.

Everybody has experienced both open and focused awareness. The difference between Farmers and Hunters seems to be the *baseline* state, or the state of consciousness to which the person automatically reverts, when he or she is not trying to maintain one state or the other. Farmers naturally relax into the focused state; Hunters relax into the open state.

An interesting historical anecdote here pertains to the different ways that cultures have trained their members to shift states from open to focused or vice-versa:

The agricultural farmers of Tibet, China, and Japan developed variations on the meditation technique mentioned earlier in the book called Vipassana or *mindfulness.* With this technique, the meditator seeks to empty his or her mind, touching thoughts when they bubble up so that they'll be released and not become a "focus of attention." This technique, practiced for thousands of years in Buddhist monasteries, is a way of training a normally focused person to develop a highly fine-tuned, purely open state of consciousness.

The hunting and warrior cultures of medieval Europe, on the other hand, developed a form of meditation which involved bringing the mind to a single focus, training it to stay with one thought. Passing beads between one's fingers to serve as "reminders" to bring the thought back to the prayer, the meditator would repeat: "Hail Mary, full of grace, the Lord is with Thee..." Similarly, the warrior caste of India developed a meditation technique called Mantra Yoga, which involves repeating a single sound over and over in the mind, for hours at a time, drawing the mind to a single point of focus. (The most famous of these sounds is "Om.")

It's interesting to see how different individuals gravitate to one or the other of these two meditation techniques. Farmers find the Focusing techniques of Mantra Yoga to be easy but, in my experience, they don't stick with them for years at a time. Perhaps this is because they're merely practicing bringing about a state of consciousness which is already pretty routine for them; there's no powerful new insight or experience.

But the sure-and-steady Farmer personality-types seem to predominate at the American, Chinese, and Japanese Buddhist monasteries I've visited. It's almost as if they know the value of training themselves to drop into an open state of consciousness, and enjoy or crave the experience because it's so unique to them.

And, as one might expect, the reverse is true for

people committed to mantra or rosary meditation: they seem more often to be Hunters, who enjoy and/or need the periodic disciplined excursion into the realm of focused consciousness.

Discussing this subject with a senior executive of a major Japanese company in America (he's also native Japanese, who's lived in the United States for about four years), he observed:

"Japan has historically been a farming culture. It was important that everybody show up for planting on the right day at the right time, when the moon and weather were perfect. Each person would have his line of rice to plant, and each sprout had to be placed in the right row, in the right way, at the right time. The survival of our people depended on our being able to perform as a group, with no deviations, and with attention totally concentrated on that one task."

He went on to point out that, in his experience, ADD-type behaviors were very rare in Japan, and told me that there's currently a best-selling book in Japan about how the Japanese culture has evolved as the natural product of an agricultural society. Without extensive research, it's impossible to know if the low reported incidence of ADD in Japan is the result of a lack of awareness of the condition, or of a lack of ADD-genes (except, perhaps, among the descendants of the Samurai?). Or if culture is such a powerful shaping influence that Hunter and Farmer, ADD and TSDD, behaviors are, to a lesser or greater extent, also the result of the societal conditioning.

Some researchers believe that the recent explosion in ADD diagnoses is a result of an increased sensitivity to the condition coinciding with a deterioration in our public schools' ability to deal with ADD children (largely because underfunding has increased class sizes). Others argue that technology drives culture, and that our *society* is now more likely to produce ADD-type people because of technological changes in the past forty years.

Marie Winn, in her book *The Plug-In Drug*, argues that an inability to concentrate is the natural result of the proliferation of television. She points out that fifty years ago children spent much of their lifetimes practicing the focused process of reading for entertainment. Today, they frequently spend hours every day watching television, which rarely maintains an image or a concept for more than a few moments, which, she claims, "trains" a short attention span. Home video games may have a similar effect.

PHYSICAL VERSUS MENTAL EVOLUTIONARY ADAPTIVE CHANGES

There is considerable evidence that Tay-Sachs, sickle-cell anemia, and even the dreaded cystic fibrosis are genetic conditions which developed as survival mechanisms in response to specific times and conditions. Hereditary size aids survival in a primitive society, where the biggest warrior lives to pass on his genetic code, or where the small man consumes fewer calories during a famine, or can hide more easily in the jungle or forest. While child-onset diabetes is usually caused by a destructive infection of cells in the pancreas, there's some evidence that adult-onset diabetes is an inherited condition and (perhaps like the genetic predisposition to obesity) may play some part in surviving episodic famines.

Much has been written over the years about *physical* dysfunctions representing the natural evolution of survival mechanisms. But what about *mental* dysfunctions? There's a very close link between mind and body. If the same evolutionary variation takes place in the brain, then perhaps some abnormal mental states had a valid historical use. Just as the Hunter state equips a person for a particular kind of survival, perhaps other mental states let the brain "tune in" to perceptions that aren't accessible to most of us.

It seems strange that the breakdown of normal consciousness could be accompanied by accurate insights, but it happens. I personally knew a woman who (as she entered schizophrenia) had some startling insights. And I sat with some old men from a primitive culture as they recited facts they had no apparent way of knowing—while they engaged in a bizarre ritual. Here are those stories.

DEBBY THE VISIONARY ARTIST

Debby was a wonderful woman and a good friend. I'll never forget the evening she came to my apartment, while we were both in college, to tell me that the moon was revealing the future of the world to her. We walked outside and sat on the cool grass all night discussing the fate of mankind, the nature of creativity, and the voices she was hearing within her head whenever she performed a secret and magical series of hand motions. The moon was warning us, she said, that man was poisoning the earth. All the killing in Vietnam (this was in 1968) was creating a pain in the collective human psyche which would echo through generations. A hole would be burned in the sky by our toxic chemicals, one day making the planet unlivable. The great world power that we needed to worry about was not the Soviet Union, but Germany, where the Nazis would rise again before the end of the twentieth century. And Bill, our friend who played the guitar so beautifully, would be dead one day soon (he died a year later).

Assuming that Debby had taken some of the then-omnipresent LSD, I baby-sat my friend through her trip, listening to her often-profound insights into the human condition, the future of the world, the history of ancient man, and intelligence among the stars. Frequently, she lapsed into long, rambling episodes, whose logic was so buried in meaning only accessible to her mind, layer within layer, that I was totally lost. But I nodded, or agreed, or held her hand when her insights struck her with an occasional terror.

Debby was a brilliant artist and writer. That night she composed some short poetry and created some sketches (now, alas, forever lost) which, to my young mind, rivaled T.S. Eliot and Salvador Dali. Her work was brilliant—rich in subtle meaning, filled with details that became profound when Debby explained them.

The next day, Debby did not "come down." Sometime during the night before, she'd called her mother to share one particularly powerful "insight," and her mother had called a psychiatrist. Within a day, Debby was in a psychiatric hospital, diagnosed as schizophrenic. (It turned out she had never taken the LSD that I'd assumed was driving her behavior.) Medicated to a thick docility, she'd lost both the joy and the terror of her voices and insights, and begged me to finish one of her poems, a job I worked on for a week with little success. It was *her* glimpse into another world that the poem sought to recreate, which I could only blandly describe.

It took about five years of Thorazine and lithium and various other drugs for Debby to "come back to normal." The diagnosis of schizophrenia was confirmed several times and, it was found, the disease apparently ran in her family. With medication, she now has a child and teaches art in an elementary school, and no longer hears the voice of the moon.

THE UGANDAN "TOUCHED BY THE GODS"

In 1980, James Mbutu (an Episcopal priest and member of the interim cabinet of the Ugandan government) and I traveled in an old taxi (missing a windshield and right-hand door, the trunk and back seat filled with cans of gasoline and boxes of wheat), through central Uganda, past the mouth of the Nile River at Lake Victoria, and up to the famine-ravaged Karamoja region. When Idi Amin and his 20,000 soldiers fled the region a few months earlier (they were driven from the country by the then-occupying Tanzanians), they'd passed this way, robbing, raping, and killing. Particularly hard-hit were the simple nomadic people of the extreme north, the Karamajong, who lived by drinking blood and milk from the cows they herded in the desert-like scrub land, a thousand-mile strip separating the jungle of Uganda to the south from the desert and mountains of Ethiopia and Sudan to the north.

At one refugee camp just north of Jinja, James and I visited a gathering of the elders, a group of old men who had somehow escaped the slaughter of Amin's troops (the pattern had been kill the men, rape the women, steal the food). The sun was setting and a bitter smoke cut into my nose from the many tiny campfires; the air was about 50 degrees, and women and children everywhere were huddled under tarps or blankets to escape the cold. The obvious tuberculosis and cholera victims were segregated in the corners of the camp under the watchful eye of an Irish woman from the Red Cross. (Her name was Ann, and she was killed by a sniper's bullet a month later. I've never met a braver or more compassionate person.) And, in the morning, an old Ethiopian priest led us in the task of digging mass graves and burying the bodies of those who had died of disease or starvation during the night.

But that first night I witnessed an extraordinary event. I was one of only seventeen whites in the entire nation (Amin had run all "foreigners" out two years earlier in a "purge"), and the old men of the tribe asked James to invite me to their evening ceremony. About a dozen ancient, withered, toothless men sat in a circle around a large gourd filled with a milky, fermented liquid. One man, bizarre images painted onto his face with charcoal and plant dye, walked from person to person with a ten-foot bamboo straw, giving us drinks from the gourd, which James said was a fermented mixture made by chewing a local root, then spitting the chewed mixture into the pot, where it was left in the sun to brew into a potent alcoholic mixture. Other herbs from the jungle were added in, and, James said, "the effect can be rather powerful."

A few minutes later, the medicine man walked around the circle and waved a burning bundle of herbs in each of our faces. He then sat and rambled for an hour or two in Swahili and broken English about Idi Amin, looking into the "spirit world" to tell us where Amin was and what he was doing. Amin would live like a king in Saudi Arabia, the man said, and a plague would befall Uganda. He held conversations with invisible spirits, occasionally jumping up and screaming, dancing around the circle.

Remembering my friend Debby, I turned to James,

who held a masters degree in psychology as part of his divinity studies. "Schizophrenic?" I asked.

James shrugged. "He throws bones. Sees the future. Heals people. Here, they would say he has been touched by the gods."

In medieval Europe, I thought, they would have said he was touched by a demon and burned him at the stake. The Native Americans of the Southwest might have elevated him to greatness as a medicine man. If he could write, in another culture he might be called a Nostradamus; if he could paint, a Van Gogh. Here, then, is another trait that is occasionally adaptive and furthers a culture, but more often is maladaptive and destroys the individual.

Several psychiatrists have mentioned the popular notion that ADD is a dopamine deficiency in the frontal lobes of the brain. It's popular, particularly in books which are trying to destigmatize the condition for children, to use diabetes and insulin therapy as an analogy.

This analogy, of course, presupposes some sort of desirable norm. Had Edison, Franklin, Nostradamus, Handel, Dali, Ford, Mozart, Hemingway, or Van Gogh been medicated back to "normal," the world might well be a very different and far less interesting place. On the other hand, had such normalizing medication been available during childhood to the huge percentage of ADD adults in our prisons, much human suffering might been eliminated, lives saved, and our society might well be a safer and more comfortable place to live.

THE "DRUG ABUSE/ALCOHOLISM/ADD GENE"

The United States of America, a country that some cultural anthropologists could argue was most recently conquered by ADD-gene-carrying northern Europeans, recently surpassed South Africa as having the highest per-capita prison population in the world. A significant majority of these crimes are drug-related, which brings us back to the original question posed: Are Hunters mental diabetics? Are ADD people actually genetically deficient in dopamine and/or other essential brain chemicals, or the receptors to them? And, if so, does this mean that the simple act of administering widespread medication to Hunters will, ultimately, cure many of our social ills? Might it also provide a cure for that significant subpopulation of alcoholics and drug addicts who resist any form of group or individual therapy for their addiction?

David E. Comings, M.D., et al., found a specific gene which appears to have a relationship to alcoholism, drug abuse, Tourette's Syndrome, and ADD. This gene, the A1 variant of the D2 dopamine receptor gene, appears more than twice as often in people with ADD as it does in "normal" individuals, and controls the ability of certain cells in the brain, called receptor sites, to be sensitive to dopamine (producing the effect of a deficiency of dopamine). Among Tourette's Syndrome sufferers, the ratio of the presence of this gene is almost four-to-one compared to the general population. Interestingly, among alcoholics and severe drug abusers, prevalence of this gene variant is over eight-to-one.

This returns us to the difficult notion of how to view, treat, and, perhaps most important, how to present to children, the concept of ADD. Many books on the subject, particularly those written for children, treat it as a purely medical condition. They discuss kids' questions like "How did I catch ADD?" and "Can other people catch ADD from me?" which serve to reinforce in the child's mind the notion that she or he is somehow diseased or defective. Since most of this literature is written by medical professionals, it shouldn't be surprising that any condition or deviation from the norm would be viewed in the medical-model context as a disease. Many parents, and some therapists, however, are uncomfortable telling a child that she or he has a mental disease, and must, therefore, take drugs, perhaps for the rest of his or her life.

On the other hand, drug intervention for ADD Hunters, like that for schizophrenics (who, in another culture, may have been saints or mystics), can sometimes be life-saving. Particularly for those Hunters who have spent much of their life in fruitless, dangerous, and often illegal attempts at self-medication, appropriate therapeutic, pharmacological intervention may be a huge relief.

Some books on the subject have now taken the diabetes/insulin approach to describing ADD, rather than the mental-illness/take-a-drug model. This is certainly more constructive for a child trying to understand the nature of his difference from his peers, but it still raises troubling societal questions—particularly when one remembers the graphed incidence of the A1 variant dopamine receptor gene, and its correlative frequency of drug abuse. If the desire for drugs is genetic, is it ultimately impossible to stop drug abuse? And while Van Gogh's mental and emotional agony, leading him to cut off an ear and ultimately commit suicide, may have been eliminated by proper medication, would we all really be the better for his having been "normalized?"

Answering questions about the appropriateness of drug decriminalization, or getting into the political/religious arena of determinism versus free choice when discussing the actions of addicts, compulsives, or offenders, is beyond the scope of this book. But it is indeed thought-provoking to take a detailed look at the statistics which suggest a genetic basis to ADD, its apparent statistical correlation to a craving for drugs or alcohol, and the significant numbers of people with ADD who are either in prison or, alternately, are among the most famous of our society's creative, political, or business leaders.

In the context of a discussion of ADD, however, the important point of this chapter is the notion of baseline states of consciousness.

If one were to imagine a 12-inch ruler balanced on a finger at the 6-inch point as representing the spectrum of consciousness, then extremely focused consciousness may appear at the 2-inch area. Extremely open consciousness is represented by the 10-inch area. At 6 inches is the center point, into which the "average" person falls when relaxing. A Hunter may relax into the 7- or 8-inch area as a norm, whereas a Farmer may relax into the 5- or 4-inch area. And, some have speculated, an autistic person may be at the 1-inch area, or a schizophrenic may be stuck at 12 inches.

While this is extremely simplistic and doesn't take into account the variety of overlapping levels of genetic predispositions, neurotransmitter levels, etc. (particularly when discussing autism and schizophrenia), it's still a useful model for viewing ADD and task-switching deficit disorder.

This paradigm also gives us a model to appreciate and even celebrate the diversity of the human family, rather than immediately labeling the differences between people in a socially pejorative fashion. Learning to focus, or learning to open up, takes on a new meaning when viewed in this context. It suggests that non-drug methods, such as meditation or the restriction of access to television for children, can be therapeutic without side effects, cost, or particular difficulty. It also shows us how those who choose to use drugs to make themselves more Farmer-like are not necessarily "mentally ill."

By reframing the entire discussion of ADD and ADHD from one of mental illness to one of normal, explainable human differences, we can provide relief and offer solutions.

Relief is due those people who know they have ADD but who are embarrassed by the current social stigma of having a "deficit" or a "disorder." They are not ill, nor are they deficient: they're Hunters, and most of the problems they encounter in modern society come from their Hunter's instincts clashing with our culture's Farmer's norms. Heirs to "the Edison Trait," as a group they retain vast potential which, in many cases, is unexploited by our society.

The solution—indeed, the salvation for children who are struggling through school or adults who cringe at the "daily grind"—is to re-set the stage.

Hunter children in our schools need Hunter-based classrooms. Smaller classes, more experience-based learning and visual aids, and fewer distractions will nurture hidden talents and, often, brilliance in children who are now failing or whose potential is stunted by the anti-Hunter systems in our schools.

For adults, the solution is to find a workplace that provides the stimulation and change they need. ADD adults need to recognize the things that they may never do particularly well, shifting their efforts, instead, to those things at which they can easily excel.

The first step is for our schools, our workplaces, and our health care professionals to view this continuum of behavioral differences from a Hunter/Farmer, "Edison Trait" perspective. Reformulating our views and systems on this basis will make millions of lives more productive, and our society as a whole will benefit from the liberation of thousands of potential Tom Edisons and Ben Franklins.

Epilogue

Older and Younger Cultures: Further Thoughts on Cultural Anthropology and Our Future

In all of my books on ADD I have pointed out that survival skills persisting from prehistoric times, when our ancestors were hunter-gatherers and scavangers, are now problems in many modern schools or workplaces. I have elaborated on this perception, which for some people depicts a history where noble Hunters have been systematically destroyed by the encroachment of ignoble Farmers.*

While it is true that there are now very few hunting societies left on the Earth, the real paradigm is deeper than just Hunters vs. Farmers.

That model does a fine job of explaining why some kids excel or fail in school, or why high-stimulation-seeking people are drawn to jobs like being an emergency

*Much of this material first appeared in my book *The Prophets Way.*

medical technician while low-stimulation-seeking people are drawn to jobs like accounting, but it misses a larger and more important point. Prophets from Jeremiah to Jesus to Nostradamus to Edgar Cayce have pointed out to us that "modern" (post-agricultural revolution, since 10,000 BCE) humankind is destroying the world in which we live.

A common explanation put forth for this is that there is a basic flaw in human nature. This concept of Original Sin is said to be depicted in the biblical story of Eve and the apple in Eden, where this defect supposedly orignated.

One problem with this concept is that there have been human societies around for hundreds of thousands of years—people not too different from you and me—who have not acted destructively. Instead, they have lived in harmony with nature.

I first encountered this understanding more than thirty years ago, reading Margaret Mead's book *Coming of Age in Samoa.* But there are good counter-arguments to her view of the noble primitive, and it seemed to me then that her Samoan "primitive" people were lacking basic and important things like advanced medical care and communications—things which would have improved their lives.

My assumption then was that our culture, what we call Western Civilization, was inherently better and more valuable than the "primitive" cultures which preceded it.

Recently I became aware of cultures exemplified by the ancient Kogi tribe who live far up in the Andes mountains. The Kogi people call themselves Elder Brothers and they have existed in harmony with the world for thousands of years. They tread lightly upon this Earth and even their architecture has not damaged the local ecosystems. In terms of the Hunter/Farmer metaphor, the Elder Brother people exhibit characteristics of Farmers. But I had been mentally blaming Farmers for much of the mess of modern civilization.

If some Farming cultures have lived peacefully and acted as caretakers of the earth, they apparently possess knowledge or wisdom which we moderns lack. But how could primitive people who survive on simple cereal crops have anything to teach civilized men and women? We have, after all, conquered the Earth. We have conquered disease, hunger, space, and even the atom.

If some ancient civilizations have lived in accord with the world as Farmers, without creating a "civilization" that (like other Farmer societies of Europe, Africa, and Asia) would ultimately lead to the death of the world, what was different about them?

How could it be that some Farmer peoples would leave behind a planet relatively unscathed, whereas others would wreak such incredible damage that it would put all life on Earth at risk?

I had similarly paradoxical questions about Hunters. Many primitive Hunting people (using my metaphor) left only gentle footprints on the planet. Elaborate cave paintings from 30,000 years ago in France, and 20,000 years ago in Australia are the remnants they have left us: not piles of nuclear waste which will be lethal for over a million years into the future.

But other Hunting people were exploitative. They burned forests to drive out animals, or, more commonly, turned their hunting efforts against their neighbors and became hunters of humans. The Mongols and Tartars, originally nomadic hunting tribes, rose to conquer most of Europe and ruled it with a brutal iron fist for centuries, every bit as cruelly as had the Roman empire which had evolved from an agricultural society.

ADD may to a large extent be something as simple as Hunter and Farmer material remnant in our genetic code. But more can be learned and finer distinctions can be made by considering the idea that cultures may be characterized as "Old" and "Young." The Old Cultures, be they agricultural or hunting/gathering, live with an intrinsic connection to the Earth. For them, the planet on which we live is itself a living organism. It has its own life, its own destiny, and, in a way that the Younger Cultures could never understand, its own consciousness. Things that run counter to the Earth's nature will (naturally) not work in the long run—although the damage may be too slow to be noticeable on the Younger Culture time scale. To tell which culture is which, we need only look at what is happening on the planet. What I have seen in my own travels is very disturbing.

The Younger Cultures view themselves as separate from the Earth, with "dominion" over it. They see the resources of Earth as things to be used and then discarded. Nature is often the enemy, not the mother, father, or brother/sister of these Younger peoples. Their disregard for it is so visceral, so intrinsic to their world-view, that many live their entire lives without ever once questioning their own cultural assumptions about man's place in the universe.

The Older peoples are so clear in their understanding of humankind's place on Earth that they often pray for the soul of an animal as they kill it for food. They may daily thank G-d for the life given them, and the life around them, all of which is viewed with reverence.

The Younger peoples, on the other hand, are so

egocentric that they have tenaciously fought—killed and tortured—to preserve their belief that our planet is at the center of all creation. They make it an article of faith to seek out and convert Older Cultures to their view of the world ... or obliterate them entirely, as was done to indigenous tribes across much of North and South America, Africa, Australia, and Europe.

Currently, Older Cultures the world over are warning Younger Cultures of the danger and stupidity of their ways. We have only to listen.

This may seem far afield of a discussion of ADD and its causes, but no one can travel in the world today with open eyes and fail to see an ongoing escalation of social and ecological destruction. Drastic solutions are called for. We need to change our way of living, or perish. Historically, necessary transformational changes in our culture have been brought about by misfits, malcontents, and dropouts—people like Thomas Edison and Benjamin Franklin. Perhaps some of our young Hunters, who we view as having difficulty in school and with adjustment to our society, will be the ones to show us new ways into a new future.

A final thought from two decades ago

"There are approximately five million children who are considered to be hyperactive children in this country. There has been a great deal of concern and interest as to the best way and means of treating these young children.

"It has been brought to the attention of the subcommittees in recent times about certain drugs that were being required to be administered to children in order for the children to go to school....

"I understand that schoolteachers are the ones who are making the decision about the need of the children to take that particular drug (methylphenidate or Ritalin). This drug is given in order for the child to be able to continue in the classroom. That is the way I read that.

"It is not a doctor who is doing the deciding (although doctors are doing the prescribing). Irrespective of what perhaps you and I believe about the overutilization of those drugs among children, it is not even a doctor, but it is a school official who requires the parent to administer that drug to the child in order to participate in the classroom.

"The question about the teachers themselves making those decisions is very interesting. I think any of us who see children, who have children or who have a lot of nieces and nephews, know they are fidgety, anxious, and maybe bored in some of their classrooms. Now we have a situation— at least in this reported area— where a schoolteacher who has some children who might not be as interested, who may be a little bored with the classroom, can require the children to take a drug in order to stay in the classroom.

"I'm not sure that that is a very hopeful or helpful sign."

– Senator Edward M. Kennedy, Chairman, in his opening remarks and discussion with Dr. Ben Feingold before the Subcommittee on Health, Committee on Labor and Public Welfare, hearings on "Examination into the Causes of Hyperactive Children. . . " 1975

A final thought from Dave deBronkart:

One hears of life passing before the eyes as death approaches, but I suspect that is not quite what is happening. Rather, we may always have all those moments of our lives available to us, but we block most of them out.

With this in mind, for decades I've had an urge to open up, to be present in all times of my life at once.

One function of consciousness may be to take the totality of all-at-once time and separate it into a string of apparently unconnected moments, so that each moment can be dealt with separately. This can be useful, but it comes at a price: to deal with a single moment, you give up being present in *all* moments.

There may be good reason for "Hunters" to have a time-sense that is different from what we think of as the norm. The goal of hunting is to bring pertinent things together at once. What matters is that the hunter and the weapon and the prey are converging, so you need the ability to synchronize all the cues. "Farmers," in contrast, need the ability to see what leads to what, in a much more distant future.

To a Hunter with an "all at once" mind, it may seem pretty silly to try to get food by putting seeds in the dirt and walking away. But for a Farmer who experiences time in a "this leads to that" sequence, it is exactly the right thing to do.

Perhaps the hunter/farmer difference is, among other things, a difference in how we experience time. The farmer's time emphasizes patience and "first things first." Many Hunters see things as "Now" (part of this time) or "Not now." And if you expand Now enough, you experience the whole of your life . . . all at once.

About the Author

by Dave deBronkart

In the opening paragraph of Chapter Thirteen, the author wrote: Hunters sometimes have difficulty answering the question *What do you do for a living?* It's not that there isn't an answer: there are too many answers.

That statement easily applies to his own life, and shows that ADD need not keep a person from success.

Thomas Hartmann has worked with hundreds of ADD and hyperactive children and adults over the past twenty years. In 1978, he and his wife Louise opened the New England Salem Children's Village (NESCV), a residential treatment facility for children on one hundred and thirty-two wooded acres on Stinson Lake in New Hampshire. The Children's Village is based on the family model of the international Salem program located in Germany.

As executive director of NESCV for five years, Hartmann worked with numerous psychologists and psychiatrists, social workers and courts, and hundreds of children and parents. He taught parenting classes, helped train child-care workers, was co-founder of the New Hampshire Group Home Association, and worked closely with that state's governor to develop programs for children in crisis.

NESCV specializes in providing previously institutionalized children with a family model, non-institutional setting, and works, usually, without drugs with children who have nearly all been in some form of drug therapy. It was the subject of three major reports on National Public Radio's *All Things Considered* afternoon news program, as well as feature articles in *Parenting, Prevention, East-West, Country Journal*, and over a dozen other national publications and newspapers.

Hartmann also worked with the international Salem program based in Europe to set up famine relief and other, similar programs in Africa, Europe, South America, and Asia, and lived with his family for a year in Germany at the international Salem headquarters. In Uganda, in 1980 (just months after Idi Amin was run out of the country), he entered a war zone and negotiated with the provisional government for land to build a hospital and refugee center, which is still operating and seeing an average of over five hundred patients a day. He has helped set up similar programs in several other countries, most recently traveling to Bogotá, Colombia.

From 1972 to 1978, and 1987 to 1991, he taught concentration and meditation techniques through a series of weekly classes, and spoke on these subjects at numerous conferences in the United States and Europe.

As a journalist, Hartmann spent seven years as a radio and television news reporter during and immediately after his college years, and has been published over two hundred times in more than fifty different national and international publications, ranging from the German version of *International Business Week* and *The Christian Science Monitor*, to *Popular Computing*, for which he wrote a monthly column for two years. At one time he was Contributing Editor to, and a columnist for, seven different national magazines, and he is the winner of the prestigious Jessie H. Neal award for excellence in reporting. His monograph about dietary intervention in the hyperactive syndrome was published in 1981 in *The Journal of Orthomolecular Psychiatry*, and one of his short stories won a national award.

Additionally, Hartmann has successfully started seven businesses, one of which made the front page of *The Wall Street Journal*. Enterprises he has started (and, with two exceptions, later sold) include an advertising agency, a newsletter/magazine publishing company, an herbal tea manufacturing company, an international travel wholesaler and travel agency, a training company presenting seminars nationwide, an electronics design and repair company, and a company which sells computer peripherals. He has written nine novels, is both a licensed pilot and a licensed private detective (neither of which he practices), and a former skydiver.

The founder of the Michigan Healing Arts Center, and a student of "alternative" medicine, he received a C.H. (Chartered Herbalist) degree from Dominion Herbal College, an M.H. (Master of Herbology) degree from Emerson College, and a Ph.D. in Homeopathic Medicine from Brantridge in England (his Ph.D. thesis was published in a national-circulation magazine in the United States, and these degrees qualify him to practice homeopathic and herbal medicine in England, Canada, India, and several other countries). He also completed a residential post-graduate course in acupuncture at the Beijing International Acupuncture Institute, the world's largest accredited acupuncture teaching hospital, in Beijing, China, in 1986.

A student of technology, he held a radio and TV station broadcast engineering license from the federal government, is a former amateur radio operator, a Certified Electronics Technician, and a former engineer/technician for RCA.

He currently holds contracts with the CompuServe Information Service to supervise and operate the Desktop Publishing and DTP Vendor Forums, Office Automation Forum, ADD Forum, International Trade Forum, and half a dozen others. In this capacity, he daily helps serve the needs of CompuServe's millions of members, and can easily be reached online at 76702,765 or www.mythical.net. His books about ADD, business and spirituality are available in bookstores nationwide.

In the marketing and advertising field (his specialty), he is the former partner in an advertising agency, the current president of three active companies including a newsletter publishing company, a consultant to hundreds of companies, and has taught seminars on advertising and marketing to over ten thousand companies and individuals in the past fifteen years. His clients include over four hundred and seventy of the Fortune 500 firms, and he has been a keynote speaker to groups ranging from a Hong Kong banker's meeting, to a forum on international travel sponsored by KLM Airlines and American Express in Amsterdam, to the California Teachers Association's annual conference. He has spoken to over 100,000 people on four continents.

An inveterate traveler and sometimes a risk-taker, Hartmann has often found himself in the world's hot spots on behalf of the Salem organization or as a writer, a situation which causes his friends to sometimes wonder aloud if he works for the CIA (he does not). He was, for example, in The Philippines when Ferdinand Marcos fled the country; in Egypt the week Anwar Sadat was shot; in Uganda during the war of liberation by Tanzania; in Hungary when the first East German refugees arrived; in Germany when the wall came down; in Peru when the Shining Path first bombed the presidential palace; in Beijing during the first student demonstrations; in Thailand when they were briefly invaded by Laos, then again when the military coup of 1991 occurred, then again when the military were thrown out in 1992; in Barbados during the recent anti-government strikes and shutdowns; in Bogotá and Medellin, Colombia, during the spate of killings of presidential candidates; in Israel, in the West Bank town of Nablus, the week the Intifada started there; on the Czech border the week Chernobyl melted down; in Kenya during the first big wave of crackdowns on dissidents; and in Venezuela during the 1991 coup attempt.

Hartmann is a certified and licensed NLP Practitioner and NLP Trainer.

Born in 1951, he is the father of three children aged sixteen to twenty-three, and has been married to the same (very patient) non-ADD wife for twenty-five years.

Bibliography

American Psychiatric Association. "Tic Disorders." *Treatments of Psychiatric Disorders*, vol. 1. Washington, DC: American Psychiatric Association, 1989.

American Psychiatric Association. *Diagnostic and Statistical Manual of Mental Disorders*. 3rd ed. Washington, D.C.: American Psychiatric Association, 1987.

Anderson, J. C., *et al.* "DSM-III Disorders in Preadolescent Children. Prevalence in a Large Sample from the General Population." *Archives of General Psychiatry*, 44 (1987), 69-76.

Barkley, R. A., *et al.* "Development of a Multimethod Clinical Protocol for Assessing Stimulant Drug Response in Children with Attention Deficit Disorder." *Journal of Clinical Child Psychology*, 17 (1988), 14-24.

_______. *Hyperactive Children: A Handbook for Diagnosis and Treatment.* New York: Guilford, 1981.

_______. "The Social Behavior of Hyperactive Children: Developmental Changes, Drug Effects, and Situational Variation." *Childhood Disorders: Behavioral-developmental Approaches.* Edited by R.J. McMahon and R.D. Peters. New York: Brunner/Mazel, 1985.

Bowen, Catherine Drinker. *The Most Dangerous Man in America: Scenes from the Life of Benjamin Franklin.* Boston: Little, Brown & Company, 1974.

Brown, Ronald T., *et al.* "Effects of Methylphenidate on Cardiovascular Responses in Attention Deficit Hyperactivity Disordered Adolescents." *Journal of Adolescent Health Care*, 10 (1989), 179-183.

Buckley, W. F., Jr. *Overdrive: A Personal Documentary.* New York: Doubleday & Company, 1983.

Burdett, Osbert. *The Two Carlyles.* 1930 repr. 1980.

Campbell, Ian. *Thomas Carlyle.* 1975.

Clubbe, John, ed. *Froude's Life of Carlyle*, 1979.

Comings, D. E., *et al.* "The Dopamine D2 Receptor Locus as a Modifying Gene in Enuropsychiatric Disorders." *Journal of the American Medical Association*, 266 (1991), 1793-1800.

_______, and Comings, B. G. "Tourette's Syndrome and Attention Deficit Disorder with Hyperactivity: Are They Genetically Related?" *Journal of the American Academy of Child Psychiatry*, 23 (1984), 138-146.

Doyle, Sir Arthur Conan. "The Sign of the Four." *Lippincott's Monthly Magazine*, London, 1890.

Einstein, Albert. *Out of My Later Years*. New York: Bonanza, 1956, 1990.

Evans, R. W., Clay, T. H., and Gualtieri, C. T. "Carbamazepine in Pediatric Psychiatry." *Journal of the American Academy of Child Psychiatry*, 26 (1987), 2-8.

Farwell, Byron. *Burton: A Biography of Sir Richard Francis Burton*. London: Penguin, 1990.

Feingold, Benjamin. *Why Your Child is Hyperactive*. New York: Random House, 1975.

Garber, *et al. If Your Child is Hyperactive, Inattentive, Impulsive, Distractible* ... New York: Villard Books, 1990.

Gittelman-Klein, R. "Pharmacotherapy of Childhood Hyperactivity: An Update." *Psychopharmacology: The Third Generation of Progress*. Edited by H. Y. Meltzer. New York: Raven, 1987.

Goyette, C. H., Conners, C. K., and Ulrich, R.F. "Normative Data on Revised Conners Parent and Teacher Rating Scales." *Journal of Abnormal Child Psychology*, 6 (1978), 221-36.

Greenhill, Laurence, *et al*. "Prolactin: Growth Hormone and Growth Responses in Boys with Attention Deficit Disorder and Hyperactivity Treated with Methylphenidate." *Journal of the American Academy of Child Psychiatry*, 23 (1984), 58-67.

Hayes, Peter L. *Ernest Hemingway*. New York: Continuum, 1990.

Henker, B., and Whalen, C.K. "The Changing Faces of Hyperactivity: Retrospect and Prospect." *Hyperactive Children: The Social Ecology of Identification and Treatment*. Edited by B. A. Henker and C. K. Whalen. New York: Academic, 1980.

Josephson, Matthew. *Edison: A Biography*. New York: John Wiley & Sons, 1959, 1992.

Kelly, Kevin L., *et al*. "Attention Deficit Disorder and Methylphenidate: A Multistep Analysis of Dose-Response Effects on Children's Cardiovascular Functioning." *International Clinical Psychopharmacology*, 3 (1988), 167-181.

Kinsbourne, M., and Caplan, P. J. *Children's Learning and Attention Problems*. Boston, MA: Little, Brown and Company, 1979.

_______. "Overfocusing: Attending to a Different Drummer." *Chadder*, 1992.

_______. "Overfocusing: An Apparent Subtype of Attention Deficit-hyperactivity Disorder." *Pediatric Neurology: Behavior and Cognition of the Child with Brain Dysfunction.* Edited by N. Amir, I. Rapin, and D. Branski. Basel: Karger, 1991.

Klein, Rachel G., *et al.* "Methylphenidate and Growth in Hyperactive Children. A Controlled Withdrawal Study." *Archives of General Psychiatry*, 45 (1988), 1127-30.

Kuczenski, R., *et al.* "Effects of Amphetamine, Methylphenidate and Apomorphine on Regional Brain Serotonin and 5-Hydroxyindole Acetic Acid." *Psychopharmacology*, 93 (1987), 329-335.

Lorayne, H., and Lucas, J. *The Memory Book*, New York: Ballantine, 1986.

McGuinness, Diane. "Attention Deficit Disorder, the Emperor's Clothes, Animal Pharm, and Other Fiction." *The Limits of Biological Treatment for Psychological Distress.* Edited by S. Fisher and R. Greenberg. New York: Erlbaum, 1989.

________. *When Children Don't Learn.* New York: Basic Books, 1985.

Mendelsohn, Robert S., M.D. *How to Raise a Healthy Child ... in Spite of Your Doctor.* Chicago: Contemporary Books, 1984.

"Methylphenidate Effects on Ultimate Height." *Archives of General Psychiatry*, 45 (1988), 1131-34.

Moss, Robert A., and Dunlap, Helen H. *Why Johnny Can't Concentrate.* New York: Bantam Books, 1990.

Murray, John B. "Psychophysiological Effects of Methylphenidate (Ritalin)." *Psychological Reports*, 61 (1987), 315-336.

Peters, T., and Waterman, R. *In Search of Excellence.* New York: Harper & Row 1982.

Rapaport, J. L., *et al.* "Dextroamphetamine: Its Cognitive and Behavioral Effects in Normal and Hyperactive Boys and Normal Men." *Archives of General Psychiatry*, 37 (1980), 933-43.

Rapport, M. D., *et al.* "Attention Deficit Disorder and Methylphenidate: A Multilevel Analysis of Dose-response Effects on Children's Impulsivity Across Settings." *Journal of the American Academy of Child Psychiatry*, 27 (1988), 60-69.

Safer, Daniel J., *et al.* "A Survey of Medication Treatment for Hyperactive/Inattentive Students." *Journal of the American Medical Association*, 260 (1988), 2256-2258.

Satterfield, J. H., Satterfield, B. T., and Schell, A. M. "Therapeutic

Interventions to Prevent Delinquency in Hyperactive Boys." *Journal of the American Academy of Child Psychiatry*, 26 (1987), 56-64.

________, *et al.* "Growth of Hyperactive Children Treated with Methylphenidate." *Archives of General Psychiatry*, 36 (1979), 212-217.

Scarnati, Richard. "An Outline of Hazardous Side Effects of Ritalin (Methylphenidate)." *The International Journal of Addictions*, 21 (1986).

Shaffer, D., *et al.* "Neurological Soft Signs: Their Relationship to Psychiatric Disorder and Intelligence in Childhood and Adolescence." *Archives of General Psychiatry*, 42 (1985), 342-51.

Sharma, Rajiv P., *et al.* "Pharmacological Effects of Methylphenidate on Plasma Homovanillic Acid and Growth Hormone." *Psychiatry Research*, 32 (1990), 9-17.

Sokol, Mae S., *et al.* "Attention Deficit Disorder with Hyperactivity and the Dopamine Hypothesis: Case Presentations with Theoretical Background." *American Academy of Child and Adolescent Psychiatry*, (1987).

Sternberg, Robert J., and Lubart, Todd L. "Creating Creative Minds." *Phi Delta Kappa*, April, 1991, pp. 608-614.

Stewart, A. "Severe Perinatal Hazards." *Developmental Neuropsychiatry*. Edited by M. Rutter. New York: Guilford, 1983.

Strauss, C. C., *et al.* "Overanxious Disorder: An Examination of Developmental Differences." *Journal of Abnormal Child Psychology*, 16 (1988), 433-43.

Swanson, J. M., and Kinsboume, M. "The Cognitive Effects of Stimulant Drugs on Hyperactive Children." *Attention and Cognitive Development*. Edited by G. A. Hale and M. Lewis. New York: Plenum, 1979.

Taylor, E., *et al.* "Which Boys Respond to Stimulant Medication? A Controlled Trial of Methylphenidate in Boys with Disruptive Behaviour." *Psychology Med*, 17 (1987), 121-43.

Ullmann, R. K., and Sleator, E. K. "Responders, Nonresponders, and Placebo Responders Among Children with Attention Deficit Disorder." *Clinical Pediatrics*, 25 (1986), 594-99.

US Congress. Senate. *Examination Into the Causes of Hyperactive Children and the Methods Used for Treating These Young Children. Joint Hearing* before a Subcommittee on Health of the Committee on Labor and Public Welfare and the Subcommittee on Administrative Practice and Procedure of the Committee on the Judiciary of the United States Senate, 94th Cong., 1st sess., September 11, 1975. US Government Printing Office.

Weiss, G., and Hechtman, L. T. *Hyperactive Children Grown Up: Empirical Findings and Theoretical Considerations*. New York: Guilford, 1986.

Weizman, Ronit, *et al*. "Effects of Acute and Chronic Methylphenidate Administration of B-Endorphin, Growth Hormone Prolactin and Cortisol in Children with Attention Deficit Disorder and Hyperactivity." *Life Sciences*, 40 (1987), 2247-2252.

Wender, P. H. *Minimal Brain Dysfunction in Children*. New York: Wiley, 1971.

Weiss, Lynn. *Attention Deficit Disorder in Adults*. Dallas: Taylor Publishing, 1992.

Whalen, C. K., *et al*. "A Social Ecology of Hyperactive Boys: Medication Effects in Structured Classroom Environments." *Journal Appl Behav Anal*, 12 (1979), 65-81.

Wilson, John. *Thomas Carlyle: The Iconoclast of Modern Shams*. 1973.

Winn, Marie. *The Plug-In Drug*. New York: Bantam, 1978.

Wolkenberg, F. "Out of a Darkness." *The New York Times Magazine*, October 11, 1987.

Recommended reading:

- ***Focus your Energy:*** *Hunting for Success in Business with Attention Deficit Disorder*. Thom Hartmann. Pocket Books, 1994
- ***ADD Success Stories:*** *A Guide to Fulfillment for Families with Attention Deficit Disorder*. Thom Hartmann, Underwood Books, September, 1995.
- ***Women with Attention Deficit Disorder:*** *Embracing Disorganization at Home and in the Workplace*. Sari Solden, Underwood Books, October, 1995.
- ***Driven To Distraction***. Edward Hallowell, MD, and John Ratey, M.D. Pantheon Press, 1994.
- ***How to Raise a Healthy Child ... In Spite of Your Doctor***. Robert S. Mendelsohn, M.D. Contemporary Books, 1984.
- ***Attention Deficit Disorder in Adults***: *Practical Help for Sufferers and their Spouses*. Lynn Weiss. Taylor Publishing, 1992.
- ***You Mean I'm not Lazy, Stupid or Crazy?!*** Kate Kelley and Peggy Remundo. Scribners, 1995

- ***Beyond ADD:*** *Hunting For Reasons In the Past & Present.* Thom Hartmann. Underwood Books, 1996.
- ***The Prophet's Way:*** *Touching the Power of Life.* Thom Hartmann. Mythical Books, 1997.

Index

THINK FAST: THE ADD EXPERIENCE

Edited by Thom Hartmann & Janie Bowman

This book gathers expert information on treatment and presents everyday experiences with ADD in a format that can be read from cover to cover or scanned for specific topics.

"A delightful smorgasboard of vital information"
—Jane B. Shumway, M.D., Behavioral Pediatrics

$12.95, Trade paper, ISBN1-887424-08-3
256pp, 6 1/4 x 9 1/4

ADD SUCCESS STORIES

A Guide to Fulfillment for Families with Attention Deficit Disorder

Thom Hartmann
Introduction by John J. Ratey, M.D.

Inspiring real-life stories that show how people with ADD can succeed in school, at work, and in relationships.

"Inspiring and validating—I recommend it highly"
—Edward Hallowell, M.D.,
co-author of *Driven to Distraction*

$11.95, Trade paper, ISBN 1-887424-03-2
$24.95, Cloth, 1-887424-04-0, 288pp, 5 1/2 x 8 1/2

WOMEN WITH ATTENTION DEFICIT DISORDER

Embracing Disorganization at Home and in the Workplace

Sari Solden, M.S., M.F.C.C.
Introduction by Kate Kelly and Peggy Ramundo
Foreword by John J. Ratey, M.D.
$11.95, Trade paper, ISBN 1-887424-05-9,
240pp, 5 1/2 x 8 1/2

UNDERWOOD BOOKS • P.O. BOX 1609, GRASS VALLEY, CA 95945

QUANTITY DISCOUNTS FOR ADD GROUPS OR PROFESSIONALS: "CUSTOMER SERVICE" (800) 788-3123

ADD Success Stories

A Guide to Fulfillment for Families with Attention Deficit Disorder

Thom Hartmann

Forward by John J. Ratey, M.D.

e first specific guidebook on how to be "successful in the rld" as a teenager or adult with ADD.

D Success Stories is filled with real-life stories of people with ention Deficit Disorder (ADD) who achieved success in school, at ·k, and in relationships. This book shows children and adults n all walks of life how to reach the "next step" – a fulfilling, :cessful life with ADD.

ıd this book and discover:

which occupations are best for people with ADD
how parents of ADD kids successfully juggle work and parenting
how ADD students are thriving - from kindergarten to medical school
how ADDers and their spouses can find happiness in their relationships

$11.95, Trade paper, 272pp, ISBN 1-887424-03-2

Available at bookstores everywhere
Bulk discounts for ADD groups are available at (800) 788-3123

Survival Strategies Fo Parenting Your ADD Child:

Dealing With Obsessions, Compulsions, Depression, Explosiv Behavior and Rage

George T. Lynn, M.A., C.M.H.C.

Children with ADD can have severe and very challenging behaviora problems. Research has shown that some children are *born* difficult to parent. These kids may be unmanageable, have no friends, be full of rage, or take dangerous or destructive risks. They may carry any number of psychiatric labels: "ADD," "ADHD," "Tourette Syndrome," "Obsessive Compulsive," or "Depressed" and their extremely stressful behavior can destroy family unity.

In our society these children are frequently medicated or placed in mental hospitals. But this doesn't have to happen. Author and therapist George Lynn works with "difficult" kids in his practice and he has addressed these problems on *National Public Radio.* Writing from h experience as both a parent and a counselor, he provides parents with methods which can heal the fractures and pain that occur in families with these problems. He believes these "troubled" children are invariab gifted in unusual ways.

Lynn describes six essential strategies parents can use to deal wit their own distress and rage as a result of a child's provocation. He also addresses the problems confronting single parents with ADD children.

$12.95, Trade paper, 284pp, ISBN 1-887424-19-9

Available at bookstores everywhere
Bulk discounts for ADD groups are available at (800) 788-3123

Good News
for
Married Lovers

Good News *for* Married Lovers

A Scriptural Path for Marriage Renewal

CHARLES GALLAGHER, S.J., & MARY ANGELEE SEITZ

Liguori
LIGUORI, MISSOURI

Imprimi Potest:
Richard Thibodeau, C.Ss.R.
Provincial, Denver Province
The Redemptorists

Published by Liguori Publications
Liguori, Missouri
www.liguori.org
www.catholicbooksonline.com

Library of Congress Cataloging-in-Publication Data

Gallagher Chuck, 1927–
Good news for married lovers : a scriptural path to marriage renewal / Chuck Gallagher, Mary Angelee Seitz.—Rev. ed.
p. cm.
ISBN 0-7648-0998-9 (pbk.)
1. Marriage—Religious aspects—Christianity. 2. Love—Religious aspects—Christianity. I. Seitz, Mary Angelee. II. Title.

BV835.G34 2003
248.8'44—dc21 2003044618

Printed in the United States of America
07 06 05 04 03 5 4 3 2 1
Revised edition 2003

Contents

Introduction

Two thousand years ago, Jesus Christ came into the world with a promise. "Give," he said, "and there will be gifts for you: a full measure, pressed down, shaken together and overflowing, will be poured into your lap" (Lk 6:38).

In married couples today, there is a full measure of goodness, pressed down, shaken together and overflowing. There's confusion, too. We've been taught to grab what we can, to satisfy ourselves with things instead of people: with hobbies, careers, clothes, cars.

Thus there are legalistic prenuptial agreements and long-distance two-career families. That's why logic has taken the place of trust, and we seek to fill the emptiness with purchases from the store.

Lord, we're making ourselves so unhappy. And we don't even know why. We need to let go; to trust. To hope and to dream. We need to face the wrongs we've done and forget those done against us. We need to forgive and be forgiven.

There is no easy recipe for happiness, but a promise: of gifts, a full measure, pressed down, shaken together and overflowing. To seek those gifts, we have to reach outside ourselves. We have to have the courage to love, even when it isn't easy. We begin by cherishing those marvelous gifts God has already given us: our husbands and wives.

This book will challenge you to heal each other's hurts, to love each other more deeply than you could ever have imagined, to paint for each other a vivid portrait of God's unbounded love.

Unfortunately, a hurried glance through this book—or any other—won't renew your marriage. But if you read this book carefully, thoughtfully, applying it to your life, the rewards will astonish you. Summer romance, even honeymoon delirium, is nothing compared to the loving, warm, passionate relationship you can share when you invite God—and each other—into your lives.

Ideally, this book isn't for only one of you. It's written for couples. If possible, both of you should read each chapter, pray over it, and discuss it between you. As you read, don't think of yourself as having failed so far. See, instead, how beautiful you are and how much more the Lord is offering you. Growing in love is like learning a language. The more accomplished we become, the more we are able to speak. We are learning to speak the language of the Lord.

That language begins with Scripture. Through the Scriptures, the Lord tells us how we can receive his gifts of happiness and peace. In this book, the Scriptures are applied specifically to married couples to help you think about each other more tenderly, to be more open to each other, to talk with freedom and trust.

In each chapter, you'll find problems and explanations, examples and questions to help you be open: to yourself, to God, and to your spouse. Many of the questions will be for you to ponder in private. Others are to be shared with your love. During your discussions, each of you should express only your own feelings. Describe how each chapter relates to you. Never blame your spouse; always treat his or her sharing with gratitude and respect. Remember, your beloved will be entrusting you with his or her most intimate feelings. No gift is more fragile, or more precious.

At the end of each chapter, you will have the option to write to your love. Please take it. When writing, your words come forth just as you intend them: clear, uninterrupted, unchanged by body language. You will discover hidden feelings of pain and joy, fear and comfort, both in yourself and in your beloved. Chapter by chapter, you'll find yourselves growing closer. In a few months, read this book again. Its meaning will have grown, even as you have.

If you must read alone, by all means do so. Then put this book under your love's pillow, or on top of his or her coffee cup. Speak gently. And pray, really pray, for your love to pick it up.

CHAPTER 1

What Is Love?

"If I Am Without Love, I Am Nothing."

(1 Cor 13:1–13)

If you were asked the question, "What is love?" what would you answer? Many of us would define love in terms of warmth, closeness, or sexual attraction. Others would define love in terms of feelings: maybe the glow we feel when someone is nice to us. Most of us see love as "what's going on inside me."

Philosophical types might define love in terms of action: love is doing the right thing. Married couples often use this definition. It brings to mind phrases like "Love is living up to your responsibilities. Love is fulfilling the commitments you've made."

There's a third definition of love, one that isn't passive and self-centered, contained within ourselves, or dependent on a personal mood. Instead, it is joyful: reaching out, celebrating the good around us, casting off the mundane weight of everyday troubles.

This definition of love was written by Saint Paul in his first letter to the Corinthians. He says love is more important than anything else.

> Though I command languages both human and angelic—if I speak without love, I am no more than a gong booming or a cymbal clashing. And though I have the power of prophecy, to penetrate all mysteries and knowledge, and though I have all the faith necessary to move mountains—if I am without love, I am nothing. Though I should give away to the poor all that I possess, and even

> give up my body to be burned—if I am without love, it will do me no good whatever.
>
> Love is always patient and kind; love is never jealous; love is not boastful or conceited, it is never rude and never seeks its own advantage, it does not take offense or store up grievances. Love does not rejoice at wrongdoing, but finds its joy in the truth. It is always ready to make allowances, to trust, to hope and to endure whatever comes.
>
> Love never comes to an end. But if there are prophecies, they will be done away with; if tongues, they will fall silent; and if knowledge, it will be done away with. For we know only imperfectly, and we prophesy imperfectly; but once perfection comes, all imperfect things will be done away with. When I was a child, I used to talk like a child, and see things as a child does, and think like a child, but now that I have become an adult, I have finished with all childish ways. Now we see only reflections in a mirror, mere riddles, but then we shall be seeing face to face. Now, I can know only imperfectly; but then I shall know just as fully as I am myself known.
>
> As it is, these remain: faith, hope and love, the three of them; and the greatest of them is love.
>
> 1 CORINTHIANS 13:1–13

Most of us don't believe that this Scripture passage is a practical definition of love. That's tragic. This kind of love is, indeed, real. But so many of us pass it by, searching all the while somewhere else.

To understand why Saint Paul wrote this passage, we need to understand the apostle himself. We think of him as a great apostle, a brilliant man who came out with magnificent theology. That's true, but Paul was, first of all, a lover. He was driven to bring Jesus to all those he could reach.

To see how loving he is, read the greetings that close his epistles. They're full of phrases like "Remember me to this person," or "Tell that person I was thinking about her." He closes his first letter to the Romans, for instance, with the hope that, "after longing for many years past to visit you, to see you when I am on the way to Spain" (1 Rom 15:23).

Although Saint Paul was always facing forward, he constantly left his heart behind, among the people to whom he had already announced the glad tidings of Jesus Christ. Saint Paul speaks of love and, in doing so, speaks of his ambition for his beloved people. He wants them to be happy, to live in harmony with Jesus Christ. He offers them a way to truly enjoy life.

Paul knew there were no easy follow-the-directions recipes for perfect love. Paul doesn't say, "If you follow these instructions, you'll be a successful woman, a great man." Instead, he says, "Love is...." He isn't talking about good deeds; he's talking about a quality of life.

Love, according to Paul, is in the very fiber of our being. If we're loving people, anyone who touches our lives will be better off. We simply couldn't resist someone who is living a life of love. In our hearts, we know Saint Paul is right, and even hearing that passage is a moving experience.

Love Is Always Patient

Let's look at the qualities Paul lists in his model for love. Which one does he choose first? Patience. If we were writing that first letter to the Corinthians, would patience have been the first loving virtue that popped into our minds? Probably not. That's why the Lord chose Saint Paul, not us, to write that letter.

Often, we're difficult to live with because we're in such a rush. We want that other person to love us immediately.

We are impatient and now-oriented: "I want you to talk to me *now.* I want supper *now.* I want to go out *now.* I want you off the phone *now.*" How often does this simple lack of patience cause friction in our relationships with one another? Saint Paul was wise when he wrote that love is patient. If we could just get "now" out of our vocabularies, our marriages would be so much happier.

Our urgency isn't confined to small daily concerns. Sometimes we're terribly impatient about serious issues. We withdraw from our loves simply because they aren't changing fast enough. We give up on each other in sex, for instance, or in understanding.

"He'll never change," we say to ourselves, or perhaps, "That's the way she is." Translated, these phrases mean, "I've tried hard enough."

We've given a great deal of attention, energy, effort, persuasion, encouragement, or affection; whatever we thought was needed. We've reached out to the other person and we haven't received a proper response. Nothing seems to be happening, so we decide to leave the other person alone. We don't do that because it's good for that person, but because we're disheartened and weary of trying.

Women are practiced at being much more persistently loving. Take, for example, a day when a woman's husband is angry or moody. She tries to put a hand on his arm, but he shakes it off. She smiles, but he frowns. She backs off, then comes back again with a nice word. Perhaps she tries the hand on his arm again or brings him a drink. Saint Paul was writing about this type of patient love. We have to be willing to stay with each other, not to take no for an answer but to try again in gentleness and tenderness.

Perhaps the husband comes home and sees his wife has had a tough day. She's so down, she doesn't want to talk. He gives her a hug and squeeze. He says, "Honey, what's the matter?"

She says, "Nothing."

He tries again. "Ah, come on, really, what's the matter? I can tell there's something wrong."

"No, I'm fine," she says, with that special overtone to the word "fine."

He rolls his eyes. Maybe he pours himself a drink and tries again. He is a good man. He puts his hands on her shoulders and she shrugs them off.

At this point, he decides, "Well, I did as much as I could." He takes his drink, goes to another room, and reads the paper. "She'll come out of it," he thinks. "When she wants to talk, she'll talk."

But he's really not present to her anymore. He's back in his own world and she'll have to recover alone.

We limit our patience with our husbands, wives, and children to what we think is reasonable. How can something be wrong if it feels so—reasonable?

It is, nonetheless. The devil doesn't tempt good people into doing bad things. The devil always tempts us into doing something less good. Often, we're awfully proud of ourselves because we're avoiding the biggest sins. We haven't robbed any banks or had any orgies.

Reasonableness is one of the most common anti-love concepts in our lives. Why? Because it limits patience. We'll be patient only to a certain point. Once that point is reached, we think we don't have to try anymore.

How many times have we used, "It's against good reason" as an excuse for not being lovers? The lines we draw between reasonable and unreasonable may differ greatly from person to person, but they're always there.

Saint Paul didn't say, "Be patient when it makes sense." He didn't say that love is patient and reasonable either. In fact, reason isn't mentioned once in Paul's entire list. He did say love is patient; it is always ready to make allowances, it endures whatever comes.

We stop being patient because this level of self-sacrifice doesn't meet our needs. Perhaps we get fed up or we don't think we're getting enough consideration. Perhaps anger is starting to churn within us.

"I have really been loving," a wife might say. "What more can I do? He takes me for granted; the least he could do is appreciate my efforts." A man might think, "How much longer is she planning to sulk? I've done all I can."

Love Works Overtime

We're all good, generous people, but even good people tend to ration patience like a precious jewel. We allot a certain amount of time to coax our husbands out of their bad moods or to help our wives solve their problems of the moment. If they don't respond in the proper time frame, we give up. We've done our best, and now we're off the hook.

Remember, it's not whether your effort is reasonable but whether it's successful. If, like Saint Paul, we're lovers, we simply have to keep on until it works.

Patience is other-centered. When I'm a lover, you become my agenda. If, instead, there's something else on my agenda, I can't help but think, "How much more time can I spend with you before I have to leave?" I don't have to leave physically. Maybe my favorite television show is coming on in thirty minutes. Perhaps it's getting late and if we don't wind this up, I won't get my sleep. Maybe I have to make lunches for the kids, fix that faucet.

I simply can't have something else to do when my spouse needs me. If you, my lover, need me to be present to you, I simply have to make you my priority. No matter how long it takes, I'm yours. If later I get around to my other plans, fine, but I'm not counting on that right now because you need me.

That can be very hard to do sometimes. Especially if you're well organized, you might be tempted to think, "But I just can't live that way. There are things that have to be done around here. He understands it as well as I do," or "She knows I can't spend twenty-four hours a day with her."

Our lovers know about all our other obligations; they're very conscious of them, indeed. If they still feel they need us right now, their needs are obviously important. What if the dishes did go unwashed? What if the kids' lunches didn't get made and we had to take them to school later on? What if we did go to work a little sleepy because we stayed up late talking to our spouses? We'd be happier, that's all.

Still, we keep fitting our lovers into our schedules. Think about it. Are our husbands less important than a set of dishes? Are our wives less valuable than the scores of last night's game?

Of course not. Yet our priorities speak louder than our words.

That's why Saint Paul was wise when he chose patience as the first quality of love. If we could just discipline ourselves to give our lovers absolute priority in our lives, our marriages would be so much better.

A "Give" Proposition

We often think of patience as passivity, but Saint Paul's definition has nothing to do with an even temper. "If I don't say anything abrasive," we might think, "I'm patient." Not necessarily. We may be steaming inside, or perhaps we're people who never get angry. It may not be virtue; it may be indifference.

On the other hand, maybe our husbands do shout sometimes, or our wives snap at the children, but they never quit trying to reach out when we need them. Patience is sticking with each other, regardless of response.

That takes trust and sometimes even strength. We can't say, "I love you, but you have to respond to me pretty soon because I have to feel your love, too." That's like saying, "Hurry up and love me before it's too late, because my love won't last."

Paul says that real love loves regardless. Love doesn't say, "I'll give you my love as long as I feel good about it." It doesn't say, "As soon as I start getting frustrated because you're not listening, I'll stop talking to you. I won't say anything nasty, but I'll wait until you're ready." We make love a give-and-take proposition. It's not. It's a give proposition: I give love because I love you.

Love Is Kind

Kindness is a very special gift. Probably the closest we can come to canonizing someone in normal, human terms is to say, "She's really kind," or "He's a kind person." Kindness is something quite different. Saint Paul says love *is* kind. Paul is not talking about performing a number of kind actions. He is talking about living a kind lifestyle, creating that atmosphere in the home. When a husband and wife are living in kindness, there is joy, peace, and delight in that place.

This quality should be the one you most desire for yourselves, because it's the best gift you can give to another. Kindness is a gentle concern for the needs of others, a desire to make them happy and relieve their pain. Affection is a very strong ingredient in kindness.

Kindness can be present in small, everyday actions, but the same actions may not reflect kindness at all. Perhaps you're being kind when you put out the garbage. Maybe not; maybe you're just being obedient or trying to avoid trouble.

The same activity can be good or neutral. Fixing the faucet or dusting a table can be either a chore or an act of kindness. In the second instance, there is an obvious affection in the way you do it. But in the first, you're just doing the work.

This affection, this tenderness, this gentleness, come from a reverence for the other person. That's why kindness is not present merely in our actions, no matter how good they may be. For kindness to be truly present, there must be warmth in our hearts. We can't be thinking only of what we're doing; we have to be conscious of whom we're doing it for, and our feelings of love must be evident.

Do you see yourself as a kind person, not just one who does kind things? We all do kind things, and frequently, too, but that doesn't mean we're living a kind way of life.

Perhaps you are thinking, "I really wish I could look at myself in a mirror and say, 'Yes, you are a kind person.' I can't. I know how wonderful that would be for my spouse. But I just wasn't put together that way."

Maybe you are finding it difficult to even think of yourself as kind. Don't be discouraged and don't give up. Each of us has the potential to be as kind as Mother Teresa of Calcutta.

Kindness is a virtue, not a talent. Talent, I either have or don't have. I'm either six foot ten with a great deal of agility and a good shooting eye or I'm five foot six and I'm just not going to make it as a big-time basketball player. I either have an IQ of 190 and can earn a doctorate in geophysics at a school like Harvard, or I just can't do that.

Virtue, though, is there for the taking. If I go into the bank and take money, I'm a thief, but if I go to an undiscovered island and find diamonds on the beach, they're mine to keep. Like those diamonds, virtue is a free gift.

I can't say I'm not kind because kindness wasn't given to me. I can't think that some people are naturally kind, and I'm not one of them. Some people have better personalities than others, yes. Some people have less abrasive temperaments or are less driven. But nobody, by nature, is kinder than I am.

When someone is kinder than I am, it's because that person has chosen to be kind and I have not. I have to decide: will I be kind? Notice, it's "will I?" This "will" is not the future tense of the verb "to be." It's "will" in the sense of the Latin word *volo:* I will it, I choose; I decide to be a kind person.

I can't value kindness just because it makes me a better man or woman. I shouldn't make a checklist of my virtues, then study it to decide where I score high and where I need work.

I should take on kindness for the sake of my lover, not for my own sake. That's a very important lesson and a very hard one. We humans really are so self-centered, even in our virtues. I'll say, "Yes, this is the kind of person I should be." Then I go out to further my own integrity. Rather, I should be saying, "This is the kind of spouse my partner should have."

We can't excuse a lack of kindness by saying everyone has defects, that we'll make up for our lack in other ways. That's a self-centered response. It's like saying, "Well, I score pretty well when you consider everything."

We can't say, "Well, I'm kind enough to suit my taste. I don't think I'm bad at it." We have to concentrate, instead, on how others perceive us. Do they believe we're approachable? Do they think they have to warm us up—or thaw us out—before mentioning certain subjects? Are they nervous because they don't know how we're going to react? We might discover that we frighten them.

We should all ask ourselves, "Am I a fearsome person?" We're dodging the issue if we ask merely, "Do I sometimes get mad?" Anger is only a symptom of a larger ill. Must our lovers go through all sorts of contortions, building up the courage to risk talking to us about something important?

We can inspire fear in our spouses without shouting. Maybe we're soft-spoken on the outside. Maybe we don't get angry at all, but there is a tenseness about us; our lovers never know when the volcano is going to erupt. It never has because it never has to. Like a nuclear warhead, it's a deterrent.

When we're in the presence of a kind person, we always feel relaxed and at ease. We can be ourselves. We don't have to weigh our words or wonder how to bring up certain topics.

Those around us best experience our kindness when they believe we're pleased with them. When we're kind, they know we're always on their side. That doesn't mean we agree with everything they say, do, and think. It means that no matter what happens, we're always with them. That type of mentality, expressed both verbally and nonverbally, brings our lovers tremendous security and a sense of well-being.

Our natural reaction is to want to do something about acting kind. We say, "Okay, how do I do it?" Ask yourselves these questions: "When I'm sitting on the sofa, reading the paper, or stirring soup at the stove, how tender am I toward my spouse?"

If we find a hardness in ourselves or even just a shoulder shrug, we have to change. We have to stop, breathe deeply, and deliberately build up some kind thoughts about our husbands or wives. We have to reflect on those qualities that originally attracted us to them.

There are many practical ways to be kind. What about the kindness of a truly gentle kiss, or a look across the kitchen table that's misted over a bit with gratitude and affection, or a hug during the evening, for no reason at all? Often, kindness is translated into perfume, flowers, and restaurant meals. That's fine, but it's much kinder to be alert on the days we're not going out or buying gifts.

We have trouble achieving kindness because we aren't spontaneous. We tend to practice it only when it's needed: when something is wrong or when we've hurt someone. More important are the small kindnesses we can do every day, not for any reason but just to be kind. Of course, we do have to respond to our lovers' needs, but it's even better to have kindness flowing from our very being. Then we're going beyond healing hurts. We're creating an environment in which our lovers truly enjoy life.

Love Is Never Jealous

We imagine typical pictures of jealousy, for example, of a woman who tells her husband, "We're going home," because another woman talked to him for thirty seconds; of a man who won't let his wife out of the house unless he's with her. Most of us don't have that type of jealousy. We're jealous in subtler, more significant ways, and we're jealous more often than we think.

What makes us jealous? Usually, it's the small things. If our spouse is heavily praised, we think it's great—providing we get equal time. Sometimes we're jealous when the children bring their needs to our spouse. "Why do they always go to her?" we grumble. "Why don't they come to me?"

Sometimes the jealousy is more serious, an envy of lifestyles: "He has it so good," we think. "He spends money on his clothes and people respect him. I stay home all the time, just like the family dog."

Part of the reason for this jealousy is that we're expected to be that way. Ever since we were little, we've been trained to resent others' good fortune. Sometimes the other person doesn't even deserve our envy. Maybe a neighbor goes on trips and stays in interesting places, but once a person's comfortable with the idea of checking into a hotel, those "interesting" places all begin to look the same, whether in Paris or San Diego, Hawaii or Hartford.

Jealously is anti-love. Jealousy is thinking about me. It's concentrating on what I'm getting out of our marriage. It's not finding delight in the other person's delight. It's a mean, ugly little vice.

Too often we excuse ourselves by saying, "Well, that's the kind of person I am. He knew that when he married me," or "She knew I wouldn't want her spending all her time with the kids."

Jealousy, of course, is not necessarily an overall attitude. It can be restricted to one or a few areas of a couple's life together. Maybe I'm not generally jealous of you, but I am jealous of your relationship with your mother, your success at work, or the way the children obey you. That jealousy strongly interferes with the love and trust that should be between us.

Love Is Not Boastful or Conceited

We have a hard time believing this passage of Scripture was meant for us. Maybe the Corinthians were conceited, but we aren't. To the contrary, Paul knew what he was talking about. We can be conceited no matter what our circumstances.

When does our conceit cause us to obey the loveless rules of this world? When do we turn our backs on the love that could be ours? We could think, for instance, that we're superior in logic. "If he'd only listen to *me*..." we might think, or "If only she'd take *my* advice."

Maybe we're overly proud because of our professional credentials. We might be overly proud of our openness or even our reserve: "I'm in touch with my feelings. Now if he would only get in touch with his, we'd have a great marriage." Or "I don't say anything if I can't improve on silence."

We can even feel smug about our insecurities. We might think, "I'm so sensitive, I'm better at love than he is," or "Where would she be without my support?"

We can also feel superior about our jobs. We might say, "I have to earn a living. I don't have time for...." Fill in any number of things. We can use this as an excuse not to work on our personalities at home, or to dodge out of spiritual growth or church work.

We can put on airs in our faith too. I grew up in an Irish Catholic neighborhood in New York City. My mother went to daily Mass and Communion, had attended Catholic schools, and was very active in church affairs.

My father never set foot inside a Catholic school. He went to Confession on Thursday before First Friday, went to Communion on First Friday and the following Sunday, and that was that until the next month. He worked nights, so he wasn't able to involve himself in church activities. He was a good man, but when it came to "real faith" in the family, we looked to our mother. Only after I had left home, when my dad was dead, did I realize that he was every bit as good a Catholic as my mother was.

Sometimes we can fool ourselves by looking at the externals. We might feel virtuous if we belong to a prayer group, or go to daily Mass and Communion. We're not putting anyone else down, but isn't there a hint of smugness there?

A good personal appearance is a mark of healthy self-respect, but we can also use it as a tool for conceit. We might think, "I'm pretty attractive. It would be a shame for me not to look my best." We can be equally conceited and think just the opposite: "I don't need to look good to feel good about myself. If you think I'm a slob, that shows how shallow you are."

We can also be overly proud of the way we handle money, whether that means spending it or saving it. We may even be proud of the unselfish priority we give our lovers' needs. That's not pure generosity; it can also mean control.

We may seek to prove our lack of materialism by spending little and letting the money pile up in a bank account. Because we don't accumulate visible possessions, we deceive ourselves into thinking we're not acquisitive.

Most of us think we're not attached to money. Paradoxically, most of us also think we don't have enough of it. Money is an addiction; it's even stronger than heroin. People can break away from heroin, but how many of us can break away from money? Most of us probably think the idea's ridiculous. That's an indication of how addicted we really are.

Money can be a real area of conflict even between good husbands and wives, especially if one of them is not particularly good with the budget. Family finances might bore them or they're afraid they don't have any skills for dealing with bills and mortgages. Then their spouses are strongly tempted to feel superior. They may not be especially good at it, either, but they judge they are.

We're also yielding to superiority when we see ourselves as the givers in a love relationship: "Oh, he's a great guy. I'm glad I married him, but I'm the one who holds this marriage together," or "She's a wonderful woman, but she couldn't make it without me."

This feeling of superiority can encompass an entire marriage or only one specific area. In either case, it's not a harmless little idiosyncrasy. If we're going to live lives of love, we must thoroughly explore this attitude of superiority toward each other. Conceit and boastfulness aren't pretty words, and it's hard to be honest with ourselves about them. None of us like to see ourselves as haughty braggarts. Nonetheless, all of us do have feelings of superiority, no matter how good we are.

We're not speaking now of whether I can drive the car better, or sew a better seam, or change a flat tire on the highway. Those are skills; they pale in significance beside our personal qualities: kindness, understanding, listening, thoughtfulness.

Where do I consider myself superior to you? Sometimes we excuse ourselves by saying, "Well, my superiority is my contribution to our marriage. I'm more thoughtful and my spouse is more understanding. We work as a team."

That's not teamwork; it's competition. Superiority, no matter how gracious, is never a plus in a love relationship. Each of us brings special qualities into our love relationships, and that's great, unless they come with a price tag.

Sometimes we don't realize the superiority that hides even behind our compliments. We may say, "Yes, you are much more sensitive than I am. But I'm much better at making money." Or "Why don't you do the entertaining when people come over? After all, you're much better at it than I am." Or "Why don't you discipline the kids? You don't lose your temper like I do."

Conflict grows even more intense when we believe we're superior in the same area. Most often, couples clash over their children, because both of them think they know more about child-raising. But when parents clash over strict or lenient philosophies, a child doesn't see a philosophical debate. He sees the trauma of discord in the home and the lack of guidance.

Love Is Never Rude

Until now, Saint Paul's Scripture passage was serious. What happened here? Love is never rude? That's hardly worth bothering about, is it?

Wait. Let's think for a moment what a gift it would be to have a spouse who was naturally full of small courtesies. When you put all those courtesies together, they're no longer small.

During your dating days, you were delighted by all the little favors you did for each other. You wanted to show your reverence for each other; to let him know he was important to you, that she counted in your life. If we could put our best foot forward when we were dating, why can't we keep it there after we're married?

Why don't you take some time to think of all the tender little courtesies you performed for each other in your dating days and in the early days of your marriage? They really make quite a list, and you did them spontaneously, without thinking too much about them. Write them down, and when you're through, ask yourself a question. How could it be wrong to perform these little courtesies once again?

Maybe by now, you're squirming in your chair or rolling your eyes toward the ceiling. People would wonder what was going on. Even your spouse might be puzzled. But why not do them anyway? People would probably decide you were in love.

Unfortunately, we tend to wonder, "Are these things necessary anymore?" Don't look at them that way; look from the opposite perspective: "How could it hurt my beloved wife, my beloved husband, if I did these nice little things?"

When we think like that, we can't come up with any good reasons. We dropped those courtesies because they cost too much: too much effort, too much trouble.

That's why Saint Paul says love is not rude. When we're courteous toward our spouses, we're never rude. These courtesies may look small, but they create an atmosphere of kindness and concern. How often do we permit ourselves the sharp tone of voice, the imperious manner, the orders given, the demands we make.

Another form of rudeness is name calling. Language doesn't have to earn an "R" rating to be hurtful. Maybe I've cleaned up my vocabulary, but still there's a cynical tone of voice or a biting harshness in the way I say my love's name. It's only a name, I argue. But in truth, I've turned a vital part of my spouse's identity into a curse.

Perhaps I use a term of affection in a bitter tone: "Why don't you do the dishes—*honey,*" or "I hear you—*dear.*" If I do this, I rob the endearment of its power. It will never hold the same loving meaning for my spouse again.

Perhaps we also need to examine our habits of teasing. Teasing can be a gentle gift, but it can also deliver a fist to the face.

Maybe I embarrassed my wife in front of others by a "little joke." At home that night, she told me she didn't like that. Even before she spoke, I knew she was unhappy, but I pointedly told her no one else was bothered by the joke.

If no one had been bothered—my wife included—it would have been all right. But since she was hurt, I should stop that kind of teasing. It's rude to be indifferent to her feelings.

We insist that our children say "thank you" and "please," but when we're angry with our husbands or wives, our "pleases" and "thank yous" become absolutely chilled with ice.

Saint Paul knew what he was saying when he wrote that love isn't rude. We've come to tolerate rudeness on daily basis, and we pay by losing happiness and peace in our homes. We're especially careless of the little courtesies, those small gifts of respect we once gave to each other. Now we're too busy or too "married" to work on them.

Love Never Seeks Its Own Advantage

In other words, love is not selfish. It's easy to be self-centered, to seek our own advantage, no matter how good we may be in so many ways. We certainly want our spouses to be happy, and we'll even help them seek their own happiness. But there's a difference: if they're not happy, we feel sad. If we're not happy, we feel a desperate sense of urgency. Instead of unity, we create a sense of distance, with ourselves irresistibly coming first.

This can happen in sex. We might think, "You want to watch television? Well, *I* want to make love," or "I can't make love to you tonight. I'm angry with you right now, and you wouldn't want me if my heart wasn't in it."

We can be self-seeking in conversation, too. "If your subject turns me on," we imply, "I'll listen. But you can't expect me to listen to a subject that doesn't interest me." In other words, I'm seeking my own entertainment rather than your satisfaction.

An early bird married to a night owl can be (an example of lovers) trapped in the lonely cycle of seeking their own advantage. For example: "For some reason, he likes getting up early," the wife says. "He whistles around the house when it's pitch-dark outside. I can hardly find my coffee before eight A.M., but I have lots of energy at night. I like to watch the late show after he goes to bed."

"I doze off in front of the television after supper," her husband adds. "I can't seem to help it. She threatens to put a construction sign over me that says: 'Man Sleeping.'"

If she worked during the day and he worked the night shift, they would realize how much they were suffering. But they—and many of us—establish such patterns in our own homes. It's a self-seeking way of life. We're really saying, "I'm not going to change my way of life for him," or "She can't seriously expect me to change the habits I've had for years."

God didn't create day people and night people, though. He made all people in his own image; he made them to be lovers.

It's both ironic and sad: many husbands feel despair because married passion "naturally" fades, but they arrange their lives so love has little chance to bloom. Likewise, many women feel lonely for their husbands' company, but create schedules that force their husbands to go to bed alone. No wonder these people are unhappy. But how do they make themselves feel better? By retreating even further into their estranged schedules.

Of course, these schedules often begin as a reaction to hurt or loneliness. A wife may think, "He doesn't pay any attention to me anyway. I might as well read a book," while her husband decides, "I might as well begin that big painting project. She won't want to make love tonight. She'll be reading." These situations call for healing, not retreat.

Who determines the schedule at your house: when meals are served, which activities and social events take place? If you're the one, ask yourself, "Am I being self-serving?" Selfishness often masquerades as efficiency or rightness. Do any of these sound like you:

"Nothing is going to happen around this house until the supper dishes are done."

"I'm not going to have those things hanging over me. I don't want to think about them for the rest of the night."

"Monday night football is my one form of relaxation, so don't plan anything for that night, and keep the kids out of the way."

"I have a right to enjoy myself and I don't care if you're tired. We're going out tonight."

Love Does Not Take Offense

Anger is probably the greatest source of friction in our homes. Its damage isn't confined to the trauma of fighting or even the chill of indifference. Often, anger is held in reserve as a threat, creating an air of constant tension.

How angry are you? That doesn't always mean, "How often do you shout?" You may be a very angry person, even though you never express your anger. Your anger is a method of control.

Perhaps you have to explode only once a year, because when you do, it's earth-shattering. The rest of the time, you have only to threaten to get angry and your lover will surrender.

How many wives are afraid their husbands might lose their tempers? Such a husband may control himself, but the effort is so intense, she'll say, "Settle down. I give in. I don't want you having a heart attack." Either way, he wins, and when there are winners in a marriage, everyone loses.

The threat of anger is especially effective when it promises to undermine the need for peace in the home. When a woman wants peace, she usually means, "There's something between us; let's get it out, even if it means a fight." The man's definition of peace, though, is closer to "I don't want to fight about it. If we have to resolve it in anger, let it lie buried."

A husband and wife could avoid many hurts if they would both think through a problem before talking it through. Often, we calm down when we take time to think. We can see our lover's side and we don't blurt out the first angry words that come to mind. The hurt from those angry words lasts a long time and it causes both of us to be wary in the future.

Many of us have learned to talk through our problems, and that's a marvelous improvement over keeping our problems inside, where they can poison a relationship. It's not good, though, to voice every angry feeling, no matter how much it hurts.

Let's add thinking things through to our repertoire of marital skills. When we know we're losing control, one of us should just say, "Time out." Then both of us should sit quietly holding hands for ten to fifteen minutes, thinking of where we stand on this problem, what we want resolved, and how we can talk calmly and lovingly.

We've talked about coping with our own anger. Now, how about our spouses' anger? Can we do anything about that? Yes, indeed, and not with blame or accusations. Each of us can ask ourselves, "How much do I provoke my lover's anger?"

We look on anger as a small failing, but it's probably the biggest cause of marital unhappiness. Anger is destructive because we use it as an excuse to say things we've been storing inside. We'll let something fester within us until it gets so painful, it spurts out. Then we'll excuse ourselves: "I only said that because I was angry."

The insults we deliver in anger often take months and even years to heal. In the meantime, those grudges poison the happiness of the person who's holding them.

Love Does Not Store Up Grievances

Love is not supposed to be resentful, but all of us do hold resentments at one time or another. How many of us are like the Greek hero Achilles, who sulked in his tent during the Trojan War because the king had taken away his girl?

We may think we're nursing our own hurts. Really, we're punishing our partners. We're creating a miserable environment in our homes, even if we do excuse ourselves with a phrase like "Well, I don't do this very often, but sometimes I just can't help it."

We need to find some other way to air those frustrations. Maybe we should talk them out more frequently, long before they have a chance to build up. If we let resentments silently churn inside, they grow into big issues, which could have been resolved so much more easily.

I remember going home for supper with a man once, a lawyer; when he opened the door and saw his wife's face, he knew a storm was coming. "Honey," he said, "can we have a statute of limitations of five years?" Actually, that statute should be much shorter. Why store up our pain and anguish for years when we can get rid of it right away?

How long should we be able to cling to a slight or an injury? No more than two days. If you haven't resolved a grievance within two days, forget it, and once you've talked it out, don't bring it up again. We can't keep bludgeoning our spouses with the same complaints.

Why don't you make a list of your grievances: grievances against your spouse that are in your heart right now. Be honest with yourself. What grudge do you have against her? What gripes do you have against him?

Think about them, one by one, then decide how you'll get rid of them. You'll be tempted to say, "I'll go ahead and list them, then we'll talk them out. That'll get rid of them." That won't work in this case. You've probably already talked out a lot of them without success. But even if you haven't, if they're more than two days old, consider them dead. Forget them.

You can do it if you truly want to. You remember them because you think about them and bring them up and mull them over. Now stop the brooding and start to ponder the good things instead. Try to remember the positive aspects of your relationship with each other rather than the negative ones. It's hard sometimes, but it works wonders.

If you're feeling some reluctance, don't be surprised. We really don't want to give up all our gripes. We treasure them; they're precious possessions, like wedding pictures or old athletic trophies. We think about them; we take them out and polish them whenever they start to fade.

Often we proclaim our hurts and declare our innocence by airing our marital grievances with our friends. Don't some wives put on halos and say, "That's what men do"? And some men do exactly the same thing, a bit more subtly, when they say, "Aren't women touchy about little things? They're always complaining." But listeners know that the speaker is talking about his wife. Somehow the conversation stirs up trouble. It may make your companions aware of flaws in their own wives—flaws they hadn't noticed before.

How often do wives talk to one another about their husbands? The conversations take different forms, but they usually all mean,

"See what I have to put up with?" Often, we're telling our own version of events, slanted by our own feelings. This is actually detraction and, often, it's slander. We're not free to destroy our spouses' reputations.

Worse, talking about our gripes can establish them more firmly in our minds. When friends respond sympathetically, we begin to feel justified. These friends aren't really friends; if they were, they'd work toward harmony, not division.

We each have a choice: we can continue to brood over our slights or mull over our spouses' virtues. Don't think that you can't stop brooding. That's an attitude of hopelessness. Your negativity is a bad habit, not a personality trait given to you by the Lord. Let today be the day you change. You've probably changed your goals in life, your job, even your values and ideals. Why not change your attitude as well?

We're all afraid to let go of the hurts; we think our spouses will take advantage of us. Even if they did, though, we'd be happier than we are now. Brooding certainly doesn't add joy to our lives. Our rights are very cold bedmates.

We have to be absolutely practical: do we want to live loving and happy lives or not? If we choose, we can be sharp-tongued and on target; our lovers won't get away with a thing. Then what have we accomplished?

Love Does Not Rejoice at Wrongdoing, But Finds Its Joy in the Truth

Sometimes we really do rejoice in wrongdoing: when the kids stand up to Mom or Dad, for instance. Occasionally we rejoice in saying. "I told you so"; "Now maybe he'll listen to me"; "She'll hear me next time and things will get better around here." Sometimes we're glad when we've said something hurtful to our lovers. Rather than feeling their pain, we're smug, at least for a moment. "Well, he hurt me," we say defensively. "She hurt me first. Maybe she ought to know how it feels."

Of course, we don't usually behave this way, but these things do happen, and they happen entirely too often. We'll yield to the temptation to take our lovers down a peg, or we'll be angry with them, angry enough to be pleased when something bad happens. We don't like to admit that about ourselves; it's too petty and mean. That's exactly what it is, and that's what we should remind ourselves when we're doing it. After all, we are people of God; we're truly free to change.

Love Always Makes Allowances

This means no retaliation. That's a real gift in marriage, isn't it? Too often, our spouses will do one small thing and we'll want to send in the army.

Because we're human, there is a streak of vengeance in each of us. We're good people with the strength to conquer it, but first we have to look it in the eye. Most of us don't see ourselves as vengeful, however. We want to believe retaliation is justified. We hold back for a while, but if we don't get satisfaction one way or another, we attack.

Let's ask ourselves, "How do we fight?" Are we all-out fighters? Maybe we pride ourselves on that. We're not peace-at-any-price types; we really fight. Then God help us. There are times when a fight is good to clear the air, but too often we fight so we can hurt our lovers as much as they've hurt us.

How do we react to unfairness? Do we seek fair play? Maybe we shouldn't. Fairness in a relationship is not a good thing. Christ calls us all to be givers, not to establish compromises.

In my study of Scripture, I found that Jesus never used the word *fair,* not even once. Fairness is a pagan standard, rather a nicely dressed "eye for an eye" philosophy. When we love, we're not preoccupied with our fair share.

A little child will pout when his parents say he can't have a toy. "It's not fair," he wails. He really means, "I have to have that toy; I'll be miserable if you don't give it to me."

Unfortunately, our definition of "unfair" is the same. We're saying, "I'm not getting enough"; enough attention, sex, money, time out, or relief from the chores. It really has nothing to do with injustice.

Do we keep score of the hurts in our marriages? Do we keep score in housework and chores?

How about with money? Do we keep mental ledgers on the amounts our partners spend? Usually we don't care how much it is, but if we really want something, we often find we can remember those expenditures.

How often do we keep score on time to ourselves? "She spent the whole afternoon at the mall, so why can't I watch the game for a few minutes?" or "He spent the whole afternoon watching that darned game. I have a right to run out for a few minutes to buy *his* socks."

We keep score in sex: "We made love last night; that ought to be enough to satisfy him"; "Why should she complain?"

We keep score in time spent with the family: "We stayed with his family for Thanksgiving; now it's my family's turn," or "Don't the kids have two sets of grandparents?"

Love Is Trust

Do you trust your spouse to respect and like you, or do you keep parts of yourself secret, afraid they'll provoke scorn or disapproval?

Men, ask yourselves a few questions to determine how you feel about trusting your wives: Do I trust her to make the basic family decisions, or do I decide how much to save and whether to sell the house? Do I discipline the children because I think I'm better equipped or because I don't really trust her with them? Do I trust her with money; with all of it or just the amount I allocate? When we get into the car, do I automatically sit in the driver's seat or do I trust her to drive me?

Wives, ask yourselves: Do I trust him enough to give him his paternity, or do I take his fatherhood away, letting him know the children are my responsibility? Do I trust him to care for myself and our children, or have I limited our family size because I can't handle it all by myself? Do I trust him to care for me better than I care for myself, or do I fend for myself, establishing a home life of my own and expecting him to fit in? Do I trust him to understand me or do I believe only another woman can understand a woman's heart?

Many times, we don't trust because of past hurts or failures. We can't remain locked in our own pain; that's a slow, miserable death. Our Lord is anxious to renew us. We must be willing to open ourselves to his healing.

Love Is Hope

How do you know if you're hopeful? It's not hard. The sign of hope is a willingness to change. I can say I have all the hope in the world, but unless I'm willing to change, I don't have any. If we're hopeless, we decide to continue living in mediocrity and making do with what we have.

Why don't you look at each other and silently ask, "Am I willing to change my relationship with you?" Your answer will show whether you have hope. Be careful with this one. You'll be tempted to look at each other and say, instead, "Yes, we do need changes around here. Are you ready to make them, dear?"

We humans are constantly aware of the good things others are failing to do and the bad things they ought to stop doing. We fail to realize that if we became more understanding, they'd be under less pressure.

Love Endures

We're good people; we really want to love our wives and husbands. So often, though, we think, "He makes it too hard." "She's so difficult to deal with." "I do my best, but how can you expect me to love him when he's behaving this way?" "How can you expect me to love her all my life?"

Saint Paul never asked you to love for fifty years. You can't. It's not human to be able, after being hurt deeply, to love day after day. You don't have to do that. You just have to love for today.

It's not possible to keep talking for thirty, forty, or fifty years to a person who doesn't understand you, but that lack of understanding will only have to be endured for today. We think because we've endured for a long time, we're excused from continuing. Really, that long track record of love is proof we can do it.

Too much of our love is based on our own perceptions. We're saying, "This is the way I want to be loved. Therefore, it must be the way you want to be loved, too." Without knowing it, we impose our style of loving on our spouses.

For example, a man may think sex will make everything all right. His wife may not feel that way, but she needs to know that it will, indeed, make things all right for him. She must heal his hurt the way he needs to be healed. Meanwhile, her husband must understand that sex isn't enough to heal her hurt. He may become frustrated with her renewing desire to talk, but he must realize how important it is to her.

One way isn't better than the other, and we shouldn't trade off: "How do you expect me to desire you when you won't even pay me any attention?" or "Okay, I'll listen awhile—and then we'll make love." Love has the power to endure. We don't want to endure. We'd rather our lovers change instead. Saint Paul calls us to the grace of endurance, to accept our spouses and respond to them in love.

If we're going to be true lovers, we must concentrate on our spouses. We must see love as a means to bring delight to them, not as a gift meant only for ourselves. When we become other-centered, we become happier as well. Small annoyances no longer bother us, and we become more cheerful and full of peace, no longer consumed with worries and regrets.

We can, indeed, live such lives if we ask for God's help. Each of us is supremely capable of patience and kindness and generosity of spirit.

Resources for Reflection

It would be very beautiful to go back and reread that passage from Saint Paul at the beginning of this chapter. As you do, remember that love doesn't exist in the abstract. This beloved woman or man of yours is your love. Then read that passage a second time, saying the name of your spouse wherever you see the word *love*.

You might read, "Jane is always patient and kind. She is never jealous....Mike is not boastful or conceited; he is never rude and never seeks his own advantage.... My beloved husband, you do not take offense or store up grievances....My dear wife, you are always ready to make allowances, to trust and to hope. My darling, you can endure whatever comes...."

Just mull that over. Think of specific ways she lives out her kindness, her hope, her endurance; ways you've experienced his patience, his refusal to be rude, his trust.

Then write these down, specifically listing the ways your spouse lives out these qualities. Don't write generalities, but memories: examples of what you have personally experienced.

Make a full list. The more detailed you are, the more meaningful it will be. Don't remember only the spectacular occasions. The little ones count, too, and they definitely add up.

When you're through, take that list and exchange it with your spouse. This can be a moment of great tenderness between you.

Maybe your love won't write his or her list. That's all right. Write yours anyway, then give it to your spouse. See, we keep falling into that trap of fairness: "If he doesn't write his list, mine will be a waste. Why should I bother?" Your list alone will be a great gift for both of you, giving you an increased awareness of yourself and a greater opportunity to truly understand each other.

My Letter to You, Dear:

This is a love letter; it should be written in your own words, using the name of your beloved. Don't be afraid to use that name as often as you can. The more often you call your love by name, the more he or she will feel truly cherished. Perhaps you would like to write something like this:

My dearest one,

I can't help but remember the many times you have been patient and kind with me. I remember when [examples are added here]... You have a great heart and I see there's room in it for me. Thank you for your compliments and for watching with love when it was my turn to shine....You know I'm proud of you, and perhaps I'm most proud of the times when you stood back and smiled at my accomplishments when you had so many of your own....You are so concerned about me, you treat me with care. You have been unselfish so many times in our years together....

My dear, you are so loving. I haven't been aware enough of your eagerness to forgive me for my mistakes. There are so many times when you could have taken offense or stored up grievances, but you chose love instead....

You are such a treasure to me, beloved. You are always ready to understand....You give me a feeling of self-worth by trusting me, even when I don't deserve it. I have never thanked you for the time when [examples are added here]... You never give up working on our relationship. Your hope for the growth of our love never seems to end; in that hope, I can see my own value. Your love makes you strong; you have endured all the trials of our life together without bitterness. I remember...

I believe your love, dear, will never end. It is more lasting than my finest goals and ambitions, greater than the wisdom of those I admire, even stronger than death itself.

Your love is real to me and, through it, I can see the love that God our Father has for me. Without you, I would be lost and alone. I love you.

Prayer for Wives:

Dear God, I want to thank you for the wonderful treasure you have given me: my beloved husband. Help me to appreciate him and to never take his love for granted.

Please give me the grace to love him as generously as he loves me. Help me love him the way You intend: by making his life worthwhile rather than by selfishly focusing on my own life.

Help us both to grow together in love so we can heal each other and protect each other from the troubles of this world. Amen.

Prayer for Husbands:

Dear God, I want to thank you for the wonderful treasure you have given me: my beloved wife. Help me to appreciate her and to never take her love for granted.

Please give me the grace to love her as generously as she loves me. Help me love her the way You intend, by making her life worthwhile rather than by selfishly focusing on my own life.

Help us both to grow together in love, so we can heal each other and protect each other from the troubles of this world. Amen.

Search and Sharing

The end of each chapter in this book will include questions for self-search to share with your spouse. It will also include a prayer. It's good to respond to the self-search questions with pencil in hand, even though this section of the exercise is private. Most of us think far more seriously when we write down our thoughts. If your spouse does not participate in this, do these questions anyway. Your growth in love will inspire your spouse to a greater love, too.

When working through the sharing questions with your spouse, each of you should write. Write for ten minutes. If you feel you have nothing to say, the enforced timing will often help stimulate your mind. Begin writing immediately and, if you don't know what to say, say so, and try to explain why.

Your written sharing is really a love letter, so begin with "Dear" and end with "Love." Remember to focus on your own feelings and to never, under any circumstances, lay blame on your spouse. If you can insert the word "that" in your feeling, you are expressing a judgment instead.

This expression is all wrong and a love-killer: "I feel that your low-down, selfish way of life makes me miserable and lonely." This one is much better: "I feel miserable and lonely when you tinker with the car after work. I feel a yearning to spend more time together."

After you have both written, exchange your letters. Read them twice, then discuss them with love.

Consider These Questions Privately:

What type of husband, what type of wife, would my spouse like to have? (Make a list.) How can I become that person?

How do I feel about growing in patience, kindness, and generosity of heart? If I am resisting these virtues, why? Am I willing to work and pray for them?

Share This Question With Your Spouse:

How do I feel, knowing that my role as your husband, as your wife, is to make your life delightful and worthwhile?

CHAPTER 2

Do I Love You Enough?

"When the Son of Man Comes...
He Will Place the Sheep on His Right."
(MT 25:31–35)

It was two days until Passover, two days until Jesus would suffer his Passion and Resurrection. He was alone with his disciples on the Mount of Olives, readying them—and us—for that time when he would no longer walk the earth as a flesh-and-blood man.

His disciples still had lessons to learn; none of these would be easy. This last one would be the toughest of all. He said:

> When the Son of man comes in his glory, escorted by all the angels, then he will take his seat on his throne of glory. All nations will be assembled before him and he will separate people one from another as the shepherd separates sheep from goats. He will place the sheep on his right hand and the goats on his left. Then the King will say to those on his right hand, "Come, you whom my Father has blessed, take as your heritage the kingdom prepared for you since the foundation of the world. For I was hungry and you gave me food, I was thirsty and you gave me drink, I was a stranger and you made me welcome, lacking clothes and you clothed me, sick and you visited me, in prison and you came to see me." Then the upright will say to him in reply, "Lord, when did we see you hungry and feed you, or thirsty and give you drink? When did we see you a stranger and make you welcome, lacking clothes and clothe you? When did we find you sick or in prison and go to see you?" And the King will answer, "In truth I tell you,

> in so far as you did this to one of the least of these brothers of mine, you did it to me." Then he will say to those on his left hand, "Go away from me, with your curse upon you, to the eternal fire prepared for the devil and his angels. For I was hungry and you never gave me food, I was thirsty and you never gave me anything to drink, I was a stranger and you never made me welcome, lacking clothes and you never clothed me, sick and in prison and you never visited me." Then it will be their turn to ask, "Lord, when did we see you hungry or thirsty, a stranger or lacking clothes, sick or in prison, and did not come to your help?" Then he will answer, "In truth I tell you, in so far as you neglected to do this to one of the least of these, you neglected to do it to me." And they will go away to eternal punishment, and the upright to eternal life.
>
> MATTHEW 25:31–46

The Hidden Poor

This Scripture passage might cause us to do a bit of squirming. We feel a little guilty; we wish we were more like Mother Teresa. Then we're rather glad we're not. We think of all those we aren't helping: the poor sleeping in the gutters in Calcutta, the junkies in the slums of New York, the abused children on the pornography strips in Fort Lauderdale and Houston. We feel frustrated. We don't even know these people; what does Jesus expect us to do?

The Lord doesn't expect us all to abandon our houses, resign from our jobs, and give our bank accounts to the poor. He works more compassionately than we can imagine. Before we step outside to care for those on the street, he wants us to begin at home.

When we hear this Scripture passage, we never think about our own families. They're well provided for, we believe. Let's think for a moment. We're not cruel people who are deliberately ignoring our husbands and wives, living invisible and dejected right beneath our noses. We've simply slipped into blind thinking. When the Lord speaks of poverty and the desperate needs of others, we look at our lovers' dry, warm homes, their bounteous food and clothing, and say, "Well, they're well provided for—compared to the tough kids on the Minnesota Strip or the homeless in Newark."

It sounds sensible; fair, even, but you can't fill your lover's needs by saying other people are worse off. It would be like telling a heat-struck desert wanderer he doesn't have it so bad; the other guys who came this way are dead.

By taking care of those at home, we aren't sacrificing the needy. We're building spiritual muscle. The more compassion we display toward our spouses, the more our hearts will be moved by all people. If we can live with a husband or a wife and not notice his need, her hurts, how can we be sensitive to people who aren't even close?

When we think of the poor and the downtrodden, we see a vast wave of despairing people on the scale of a Hollywood movie. We feel sorry for them, but they're not real to us. We don't know their names; we don't see their hunger; we don't know when they die. This total anonymity makes them less than human to us.

We can't touch these faceless poor for the same reason we stay aloof from our lovers. We're trapped—as captive as the most wretched prisoner in solitary confinement in a third-world prison. We're imprisoned in a middle-class lifestyle that keeps us enslaved to a false god, money. Money is a jealous god; it demands more and more devotion. We find ourselves working overtime to make money—taking on second jobs just to own newer cars and have dinners out and DVD players. All our purchases would be fair and reasonable, if they weren't paid for with the loneliness of our families.

Another false god is independence. We think happiness is a solo quest, best achieved by becoming more successful, more creative, more fun-loving, but not more loving of others. If we live this way long enough, we find ourselves angry and frustrated, shouting "I am happy! I must be happy, because I finally have all the things I wanted."

What's Wrong?

We don't fully let Jesus into our hearts because we know it means trouble. If we really listen to him, we will have to change completely.

That's why Jesus said no person can serve two masters. We want to live according to the world's standards, but we also want Jesus in our lives. It simply doesn't work that way. We must make a choice.

It's rather like a man who's in love with two women. If he came home and said, "Honey, I can't decide whether I love you or my secretary. Can I have you both?" he'd get quite an answer. Yet we think it's unfair when we have to choose between Jesus and our self-centered ways of life.

We're not doing anything *wrong,* we think. But Jesus didn't say only the wrong things had to change. He came to earth to offer a complete change, a better way. We can take him or leave him, but we can't have him both ways.

When we're dealing with a moral issue, we tend to say, "But what's wrong with... ?" That's the worst question we can ask. It simply misses the whole point. It's an attempt to excuse ourselves; to wriggle by with the minimal amount of work. It's antilove.

"What's wrong with... ?" says our hearts are set on what we want or what we're already doing. To avoid this trap, we must look at what Jesus is offering rather than what we're losing if we follow his way.

The "what's wrong with... ?" trap caught the rich young man in the Bible, too. Remember him? He asked Jesus what he must do to inherit eternal life. Jesus told him to keep the ten commandments. When he replied that he had kept them since he was a child, Jesus said he could do one thing more to become perfect: give up all his money. The young man went away sad; he couldn't do it.

Jesus didn't tell the young man his riches were evil. He didn't say he had to give them up because he was misspending them. He simply offered that young man himself.

It upsets us to read this passage because we know the rich young man wasn't a terrible sinner. He was already a beautiful person, and that's why Jesus offered him more. He's offering us more, too, for Jesus is never outdone in generosity. Our bread cast upon the waters comes back one hundredfold.

Doing Good at Home

That's why when we speak of doing good for others, we must start in our own homes. One of the reasons we don't do better in the inner cities is that we don't do very well where we live.

We certainly can't excuse ourselves from the call to social justice, but it won't be successful unless we personally love the people in our ministries. At best, our work will be a dutiful responding to needs rather than to people.

We may be indefatigable in the way we spend ourselves and our talents, but something will be sadly lacking. We won't be spending our goodness on our families and friends: the people Jesus gave us especially to care for, to make the Gospel come alive in their hearts. If I have a greater concern for the hunger of a stranger than for my lover, something is missing. It doesn't mean I'm a hypocrite; it means I haven't learned to really love.

I Was Hungry; Did You Feed Me Food?

Where are we in our relationship with each other compared to where the Lord wants us to be? Husbands and wives are hungry for the gift of self. Have we given them the food of our company?

Most of us have, over the years, grown separate from our spouses. We relax over the newspaper or the program on television, or we pursue hobbies like golf or reading. We probably spend eight hours a day, at least, earning a paycheck that keeps the family afloat. Our paychecks, though, do not provide the love and companionship our partners so eagerly desire from us.

To be lovers, we must talk with our spouses. We can't tell the Lord we're not naturally loving. He said, "I was hungry. Did you give me food?" We can discuss business topics for hours. Perhaps when we encounter problems in conversation with our spouses, we're simply having trouble with the subject. We can learn to be just as interested in our partners' subjects as we are in our own.

"But it's not natural; I just don't talk that way," we might protest.

It's not natural for a visitor from Spain, Ireland, or Italy to talk about football, but he soon learns, even if he's never seen a football game. Marriage, after all, is a form of immigration; when we take on a new lifestyle, we're living in a new country. There's a naturalization process: we have to learn the language, and that language is sharing with our partners.

Learning to Talk

Marriage, after all, is belonging fully and totally to one person. We simply can't do this without a great deal of verbal communication. Real communication, by the way, is one part talking to two parts listening.

The number one question should be: "How much do I communicate with my spouse?" This question is answered not by looking at other people's habits but by looking at your spouse. Is he or she happy? Does he or she feel thoroughly listened to? That's all that matters.

Don't ask if you're satisfied with your level of listening or whether you're doing your best. Your best can mean "Considering all my responsibilities, I listen fairly well." Your partner may still be lonely.

Marriage partners must also learn to reveal themselves in conversation. We can't speak only when we feel like it; we must always be honest and open. Ask yourselves, "Does my partner feel shut out of my life, shut away and hungry for a fuller part of who I am?" You must look at this hunger, not at the amount you've already given.

Your greatest call as a spouse is to feed this hunger to be understood. So often, we humans want to give on our terms, and only as much as we wish. This turning in toward self is almost as natural as breathing, but it's unhealthy and imprisoning. When we're turned inward, we're not tuned in to our lovers.

How often do we fall into a lonely married holding pattern: we aren't fighting, but we simply stop growing closer? How often do our schedules prevent us from being really present to our partners?

So often, when you come home from work, your partner is less than thrilled with your presence and wrapped up in getting supper, taking care of the kids, or getting tomorrow's events arranged. That's wrong. Where is the eagerness for each other?

But answer this question: if your partner were eager for you, how much would you have to give? Think it over.

Frenzy vs. Freedom

A number of years ago, someone studied the behavior of an infant chimpanzee whose natural mother was replaced with a wire "mother" with a bottle attached. Although the little one's physical needs were met, he was obviously starved for living affection. Covering the wire "mother" with fur helped a bit, but no humane observer could believe it was a good substitute for the real thing. It's frighteningly easy to become a wire imitation of a real parent, to forget how important we are to one another.

This habit of consuming spiritually empty calories is symptomatic of a rush-rush lifestyle that puts priority on the family's itinerary, destinations, and achievements. It sees no value in enjoying one another's company. It says that breaking bread together isn't that important.

If we're in step with society, we don't have time for a sweet, old-fashioned idea like a leisurely meal. It would be great, certainly—but at the cost of piano lessons or soccer or parish council?
Blinded by our options, we find ourselves rushing through our meals so we can chauffeur ourselves or our children to the evening's activities. As Jesus said, we have to choose. Will we choose things or people?

How do we change? First, we must examine our unconscious beliefs. Our friends, relatives, and neighbors will probably think it's selfish, perhaps even abusive, to let a child walk or bike to an activity when he could have had a ride. But they don't realize the virtue of a lifestyle where children burn energy while developing muscle and self-reliance.

We must be in charge of our families. Too often, we allow friends, coaches, instructors, and committees to persuade us their activities are more important than our family love and unity.

Some of us must find the courage to slow down. Sometimes creative scheduling won't work and the only real answer is "No, we won't get involved in that," or even "I resign." This may be the hardest decision of all, especially when it baffles others.

Love's True Food

After Jesus rose from the dead, he visited his disciples near the Sea of Tiberias. They were fishing, and when they came ashore, they found him grilling fish for them. "Come and have breakfast," he said (Jn 21:1-12).

Cooking is a religious ministry. Too often, we neglect a great calling and choose lesser ones instead.

Cooking is a tangible way to tell all four senses that we are nurturers. There's nothing more comforting than the smell, sight, and taste of good food. The Lord knew that; that's why Jesus cooked.

Most likely, one of the partners in your marriage has been chief cook ever since you were married. You, and only you, will have the commitment to get a return to family meals project going and to keep it afloat.

A full dinner can be an intimidating request. It can make us feel we're giving up hard-earned ground. We might think we're being "returned to the kitchen."

I'm not asking you to do KP. I'm asking you to take shelter from the pressures of the world in your own private oasis. You and your spouse need a place of peace, fellowship, and harmony. That place should be the dinner table.

Please don't think of how much time and effort it will cost. That's the world's way, and it's loveless and lonely. Your time together is precious; you don't have much of it. Most of the day is spent at work. How do you prepare for that important time of togetherness? One of the best ways is to plan a beautiful meal. When you spend that time anticipating your partner's company at the table, you'll be much more sensitive to that person. The meal will be the high point of your day.

Please don't compare your family to others' families, and don't fall into the trap of saying, "But no one really cares," or "That kind of meal just doesn't fit our lifestyle." Instead, explore the alternatives.

Just how many chores can the kids truly do? You can teach them to shop or pare vegetables. You might also discover that some of your adult or family activities really sapped energy rather than adding to everyone's quality of life.

My Beloved or My Life?

It's a difficult choice: our activities or each other. Most of us attempt to compromise, although it doesn't make us happy. Both husbands and wives keep their freedom at the expense of their relationships. Too often, they schedule their lives the way they wish. They accommodate their spouses when it seems terribly important or when there's an emergency, but basically they live side by side rather than in unity. They try to avoid clashes. They're not fighters, but are they lovers?

Your life's success is determined not by your happiness but by your beloved's. How much is your spouse getting from your marriage? It isn't enough to ask, "How does our schedule improve the quality of my own life?" or "How does our conversation please me?" We must be lovers. We must ask, instead, "Am I filling my beloved's hunger?"

I Was Thirsty; Did You Give Me Drink?

Paternity and maternity are thirsts. How often do we control our lovers' childbearing and child rearing? Perhaps we're worried about finances, poor health, or the long burden children will lay on both of us.

So often, men and women assume that our only real value in the world is to bring home paychecks. We ask at parties, "What do you *do?*" If the spouse works outside the home, then a sophisticated speech that implies that work is more important than people is supposed to follow. If the spouse doesn't work outside the home, we conclude that person doesn't have anything to add to the conversation. So often, we're so very, very thirsty, and no one even knows how to give us a drink.

Is my wife, my husband, thirsty for love? There's no doubt about it: our spouses' throats are parched. Each of us should ask ourselves, "How do I rate today as a lover?" Just today, not generally. Rate yourself on a scale of one to ten. Don't explain why you chose a number: "I only rate a two today because my spouse was bad-tempered," or "I only rate a one because I had a terrible day."

Now then, how does today compare with my average Monday love? What's my number on Thursdays? How do I rate myself regularly as a lover? How do my spouse and I rate as a couple?

When we say, "How are we doing in our marriage?" it usually means, "Am I satisfied?" Sometimes it means, "Are you doing well enough for me?" When we truly rate ourselves as partners, we don't even face ourselves. We face our lovers instead.

Right now, forget how the other person rates. What's your score? Wives, ask yourselves this: if you were a man, would you like to have a wife like yourself? Husbands, ask yourselves: if your daughter brought home a man just like you, would you say, "Wow, is she going to have a great life!"

We really are good people, and we do make resolutions: "I need to talk to her more." "I ought to spend more time with him." "I need to pay more attention to her." "I ought to get home earlier." "I ought to be more positive." "I shouldn't shout so much." "I shouldn't nag."

Those are good resolutions, and they come from our sincere desire to please our lovers. But do we ever go all the way and resolve to be full-fledged, no-holds-barred, all-out lovers, with no ifs, ands, or buts?

We tend to compromise just a little. We admit we're wrong in a certain area, so we'll clean up there and do a little better. But we don't go for broke.

We should be lovers, not judges who look at the defendants' records and decide what's fair. When we're lovers, we don't ask, "Am I satisfied?" or "Am I doing all right?" Instead, we ask, "Is she totally loved?" "Does he experience every ounce of love I have?" Only this depth of commitment will slake our beloved's thirst.

Resources for Reflection

I hope you recognize that I don't want you to feel like a failure. I want you to see how beautiful you are and how much more the Lord is holding out to you. It's like learning a language. The more accomplished we become in a language, the more we are able to read and the more full of thought we become in that language. As we learn the language of love, the language of the Lord, we become more aware of our possibilities.

I don't want you to close this book, discouraged, or feel that you have such a long way to go. Instead, celebrate how far you have come and how good you truly are. If you weren't already blessed in your love and openness, you wouldn't still be with me here on this page. So thank God, because you are wonderful.

Consider These Questions Privately:

How do I worship materialism and independence? In what ways do I follow the world's standards instead of God's?

What will I do to feed my wife's hunger for my companionship? What will I do to feed my husband's hunger for affection?

How do I rate today as a lover? How do I rate through the week? How do we rate as a couple?

Share These Questions With Your Spouse:

How are my schedule, my priorities, and my conveniences excluding you from my life? How do I feel about my answer?

What will I do, dear, to make our love life a "10"? What are some of my best memories of time we spent together?

Express Your Love:

Husbands, when you come home from work tonight, take a good look at this woman the Lord chose for you. Feel how delighted you are to be with her this evening.... You are so happy with her, you don't want to be anywhere else. You want to spend time with her, to hug her and see her smile.

Wives, prepare tonight's meal as if it's the last one you'll ever make for him. Sprinkle it with love. Use the best tablecloth; use candles. Tonight is your night to celebrate because the Lord has given you this man to love and to love you.

When it's appropriate, you can suggest a commitment to a special family meal. Don't worry about doing this every day. You only have to do it tonight. When tomorrow comes, that will be tonight. You won't have to face a long and weary future. You'll merely get to celebrate tonight—again and again.

Finally, Let Us Invite God Into Our Marriages:

Dear Lord, thank you for this wonderful gift of my wife. Help me realize she is the most important part of my life. Let me delight in her; let me enjoy our time together above all other things. Help me tell her how much I love her, not only with those words, but with every word I speak. Help me give her the gift of myself: my enthusiasm and affection for her, my eagerness to be with her. Amen.

Dear Lord, thank you for this wonderful gift of my husband. Help me realize he is the most important part of my life. Let me delight in him; let me look forward to seeing him when we are apart. Help me enjoy our time together above all other things. Help me show him how much I love him, how worthy he is of my time and my attention. Help me show him that he is indeed the center of my life. Amen.

CHAPTER 3

Welcome Home, Beloved Stranger

"For I Was Hungry and You Gave Me Food."

(Mt 25:35–46)

In Matthew 25:35, Jesus said, "I was a stranger and you made me welcome." Strangers are living in our own households. We know their faces intimately, but we don't understand their hearts.

We men and women come into marriage with a myriad of goals and values. That's normal, but fiercely clinging to those differences is a love-killer. We may think our ways are right, but rightness isn't the issue. Love and happiness are the issues.

So now let's read the list below, putting ourselves into each area and thinking, "Where do we stand? How much have we changed to become one couple? How much are we willing to change?"

Be wary of finger pointing here. It's easy to say, "Yes, if only he'd stay home a little more," or "If only she'd learn to save a little." Think, instead, "Do I really want to give up my own values?"

If you don't, beware. You're forcing your spouse to remain a stranger in your home. You'll each retreat to your own corners, clinging to your beliefs instead of to each other. You'll be separate but equal—but it won't make anyone happy.

So now read these over carefully, opening your hearts to change—and love:

Money. One of us might have a freewheeling "spend it now" philosophy while the other saves for a rainy day. One thinks we have enough; the other believes we need more. One is careless; the other is a precise household accountant.

Housing. To one, a house could be the center of life; to the other, it's only a place to sleep. To one, it's "mine"; to the other, it's "yours." For one, a house needs square footage; for the other, cozy comfort is best.

Faith. For one, it's an experience; for the other, it's a practice. In one of us, it's increasing; in the other, it's stagnating.

Friends. To one, they're pleasant but not that necessary; to the other, they're vital. To one, they're only social acquaintances; to the other, they're like family.

Families. For one spouse, they're people to enjoy on holidays; for the other, they're part of daily life. For one, they're a support network; for the other, a problem.

Children. To one, they're "yours"; to the other, they're "ours." To one, they're a pleasure; to the other, a burden. To one, they mean responsibility; to the other, love.

Lifestyles. For one spouse, livelier is best; the other seeks peace. One wants a busy social life; the other is a homebody. One likes single pursuits; the other wants to go out as a couple.

Charity. For one, it's terribly important; for the other, it's only an option for spending extra time and money.

The neighborhood. To one, it's just a place where we plant ourselves; to the other, it's part of our way of life.

No Surrender

Differences can cause doubt and pain, so we just surrender. "He's going to believe what he wants," we think, "so why bother?" "She's going to get her own way, so I'll get mine, too."

That's hopelessness at work. It's also stubbornness, camouflaged so well we don't recognize it. It's probably good to surrender at this point, because we haven't been trying to meld with our lovers. We've really been trying to change them. We'd really be thinking: "You need to be thinking my way." Of course that doesn't work, so we back off in frustration and disappointment. We had the right idea: becoming one in our goals and values. We simply had the wrong method.

It can be frightening to think of changing to your lover's point of view. You sincerely believe that you are right. So, first, work on the areas you can easily change.

Then when you get to the tough subjects, try to see his point, her view. Talk it through until you understand where your lover's coming from. There could be hidden hurts—or hidden wisdom. Suppose, for instance, that your husband embarrasses you by wearing torn-up jeans to a party. He may be happier than you are; he's looking forward to seeing his friends, and he knows they'll be glad to see him no matter what he's wearing. He'll have a great time, but you'll spend the evening worrying about the run in your hose. You don't have to dress like he does, but you do have to understand his heart. Why not let him teach you to be carefree?

I Lacked Clothes and You Clothed Me

In other words, my husband, my wife, was naked. Did I clothe my spouse?

There's more to clothing than driving off to the mall. So many of our wives say, "He never notices how I'm dressed. I could color my hair chartreuse and he wouldn't comment for weeks."

Men, it's important to notice, for instance, that she's dressed up tonight, or even that she's wearing her favorite pin. You must notice her vocally. You must compliment her until she believes the compliment.

How many spouses are so self-sacrificing, so concerned about watching the family budget that they won't buy anything for themselves? That's wonderful but if self-sacrificing spouses won't buy for themselves, the other partner must buy for them.

You may say, "How could I ever buy women's/men's clothes?" As with everything, you learn with practice. Buying clothing for your spouse is an art form. It can, indeed, be learned. First, when you can do so unnoticed, go through the closet. Find something that fits and look at the size on the label. If that doesn't work, look for a salesperson who's knowledgeable about sizes and styles.

You don't have to buy an entire outfit each time. You could bring home a tie, a piece of jewelry, a scarf. Something that doesn't fit can be exchanged, but if you never buy your spouse anything, there's nothing to exchange. And, don't just give money to sponsor a shopping trip. What is wanted is your praise, and money can't buy that.

In the beginning, there will be times when your gifts are opened and your spouse gasps, "You've got to be kidding." You'll learn not to buy *that* again.

Unfortunately, we learn not to *buy* again. That's wrong. Clothes, after all, are important. They announce us to one another, saying, "I'm this kind of guy"; "This is the type of woman I am." Our clothing tells everyone how we're feeling.

Stripped by Insults

We can use an attitude about money to strip our husbands and wives of clothes, hairdos, accessories, and the like. Perhaps we make pointed comments like "How much did that cost?" Our robbery could be subtle; it could voice itself in gestures or comments: "It's a good thing I don't spend like that"; "I'm glad both of us aren't clotheshorses."

We can also fail to clothe our spouses in ways that don't involve wearing apparel. Is your spouse criticized by friends and neighbors, perhaps because of the size of the family or because the in-laws live with you? Is your wife put down because of her faith, her tenderness toward her children, or her love for you? Most likely these putdowns are subtle barbs, which are much more devastating than frontal attacks.

Do you stand aloof while friends strip your spouse naked? Do you think they're just petty insults and you shouldn't get involved?

Do you believe that? Do you merely nod your approval when told about the hurt over these insults? When we do this, we're fooling no one. Our partners know we aren't serious about their pain.

Sometimes we're right there on center stage when someone attacks our lovers. What do we do then? If we say nothing, we're letting our spouse stand there, naked and hurt and vulnerable.

We can't just comfort our lovers later. We must stand up right away and tell that hurtful person, "This is my wife; you don't talk to her like that." "This is my husband; I love him and there is no way I'm going to let you get away with that." We certainly do not want to protect false friends at our lovers' expense. After a while, digs and insults become less motivated by malice than by habit. They become habits because we don't say, "Stop."

Not all criticism comes from outside, however. Sometimes we ourselves are the hurtful people who criticize our lovers in front of friends, relatives, or the children. Sometimes we merely criticize them in private; that's harmful enough by itself.

We must be strictly on guard against being critical. All too often we make excuses for this failing.

We may say, "Me? I'd never do that kind of thing. I never criticize my husband"; "I never say anything negative about my wife." By "never," we really mean "not at parties" or "not before strangers." We feel perfectly free to criticize in front of the children, with our mothers, buddies, or very close friends.

We're stripping our lovers when we do that. We're exposing them to embarrassment and shame. We're tempted to defend ourselves: Our children, relatives, and friends are close to the situation. After all, they understand.

Quiet criticism before friends and family does far more damage, though, than the angriest screaming match in public. After all, we'll walk away from those strangers and won't see them again. But our children are right there, and they'll remember that Mom isn't so special; that Dad is a grumpy man. Our friends and relatives will remember, too. Every time they see our lovers, they'll recall the defect that upset us so.

I Was Sick and You Visited Me

How do we treat each other when we're sick? Is our lover's sickness an inconvenience? How sensitive are we to each other's needs in sickness?

Have you ever seriously discussed what it's like to be sick and what your spouse could do to please you then? How does your husband want to be treated when he's sick? "Very, very carefully," you may say. "It's like tending a wounded bear." Why? Perhaps that last time he had the flu, he felt humiliated because you were fussing over him. He became annoyed, so you backed off, neither of you understanding each other's feelings.

How does your wife want to be treated when she's sick? "Not how. How much. She wants me there all the time, even when she doesn't need me." Perhaps she wants all those little attentions she tried to give you. She doesn't want you at her bedside holding her hand; she just wants more of you than you're giving. She feels lonely, thinking that her physical pain doesn't matter to you. Why not talk to her about it?

Since we're good people, we try to guess why our lovers act so oddly when they're sick. But often we can't, so we shrug our shoulders and give up. When we surrender like this, we're giving up any real effort to take each other into our lives. That would mean change, and sometimes we don't want to change. We prefer our own attitudes, values, priorities, and goals. We'll let our lovers work on their own goals; we won't interfere with them, but neither will we give up ours.

In doing so, we miss our overriding goal as a couple: to take our husbands and wives into our own lives; to become one. A marriage is not composed of two people who get along well with each other. It's composed of two people who become part of each other.

Sickness is a part of marriage; it will happen increasingly as the years go by. So we must concentrate on being "married" when we're sick as well as when we're healthy.

In marriage, tending the sick includes tolerance for each other's small flaws. How do we respond to baldness, thinness, fat, buck teeth, warts, an extremely heavy beard, a large nose, or excessive height? Do we ignore these little flaws? If so, we're really reinforcing the idea that they're disfiguring.

Maybe we tease our lovers about their flaws. It proves we're open about them. After all, it's just affectionate teasing. It's also a good way to avoid revealing our feelings. That may be all right for acquaintances, but couples are called to do more than evade an issue. Do we comfort each other about our flaws? It's extremely important to handle this well, because these little defects make a significant difference in our spouses' lives.

Our flaws may not be visible, either. Maybe we're afraid of flying, or snakes, or of driving a car. Maybe one of us is an easy crier. Maybe the other one can't cry at all. Either of us could get unnerved in a crisis.

We each seem to have married a person with a flaw. Sometimes, we're not very sympathetic. We think, "He believes he's so calm, but when trouble starts, I'm better off without him," or "She's had these cramps every month for twenty-five years, so why should I get upset?"

We humans have a very high threshold of others' pain. We need to be sensitive to our spouses' needs. First we must realize what those needs are. It's not hard; all we have to do is think awhile. The evidence is everywhere.

It's easy to say, "Yes, she's always that way," or "I know exactly how he's going to behave." How are we using that knowledge? We shouldn't be trying to change our lovers, but we should be responding to their needs. Jesus said, "I was sick and you visited me." I was hurting and you reached inside to heal the hurt.

If we choose, we can use our illnesses to manipulate our spouses. It's an effective way to get the attention we need, to inspire feelings of guilt, or change plans that seemed unchangeable.

This is one of our most typical and most devious ways of controlling each other. We might withhold affection or sex, or begin showing signs of an emotional crisis. We're saying, "Look how awful I feel. How can you do this to me?"

I Was in Prison and You Came to See Me

This one can't possibly apply to matrimony—can it? After all, we didn't marry criminals. No, we didn't marry criminals, but our spouses are still in jail.

Men, how many of our wives are imprisoned by the children? How often do they feel cut out of life? There is a slice of your wife's life from age twenty-one until fifty that just disappears. Those kids are always there. She can't think of anything else.

If she works in the home, she lives and breathes kids from dawn until bedtime. If she works outside the home, she lives in a state of exhaustion, worrying about everything from child care to when she's going to find time to sleep.

The heart of the problem isn't mere physical "imprisonment," but the intellectual prison she's experiencing. Even if she works outside the home, whom does she spend time with at a family picnic? The children, of course.

Part-Time Fathers

No wonder so many young women today are skeptical of motherhood. Today's mothers see themselves as having the whole burden of child-rearing because many men are part-time fathers.

We men don't take full responsibility for our parenthood. We're relief pitchers, waiting in the bull pen. We'll come in if she gets hit, but until then, it's her ball game.

By now, you're tempted to say, "I pitch in when the going gets rough. But I can't do it all the time. I have my responsibilities." You do. They're called Johnny, Mary, Frances. "But I couldn't do more if I wanted to. She likes things the way they are. If I tried what you're suggesting, she'd tell me to go away."

If this is true, you need to find out why. Maybe she doesn't believe you'll do as well as she does. Maybe she's right; maybe not. Maybe she wants you to pretend to care, but she doesn't want real changes.

That's when you both need to talk. She is probably afraid to change because she doesn't believe you'll stick with your new role. She's afraid you'll start with a big fanfare, then let her down. Your change has to be a real commitment.

Maybe you're the one who doesn't want change. You think the present system is fine: "I do my share; now you want me to do my wife's work, too." If you put it that way, yes, I do.

You can't say "I love you" to your wife if you're not a father to her children. It's just not believable. I'm not speaking just of time spent with the children, either. I'm speaking of the whole mentality in the home. Many men are tempted to see the home as a place of rest where we gather the strength to be our best when we go out in the world. We should want to be our best when we're at home with the people who love us.

You might say, "That's not realistic. My boss won't understand that." Your boss is no sacrament. You and your wife are, though. You're supposed to belong to her. Let's hope you don't belong to your boss.

You're not filling your wife's needs when she does most of the work and you merely give her the money to do it. That's when the home becomes a prison. If you're really as much of a parent as she is, the children are not a burden. She realizes how much you're missing when work takes priority over the children. She won't feel that way, though, until *you* realize how much you're missing.

The Chain Gang

Spouses, are you both in prison? If you're both employed, you probably are. Your jobs take away almost all your spare time. You're on treadmills, wearily going nowhere, unless it's to newer or bigger treadmills. Spending day after day at jobs in which you can have no real fulfillment results in no real sense of purpose.

Materially, this generation's families are doing better. We have better homes than our parents did while we were growing up. Our children's educations are far superior to our own. We have more vacations, better meals, and more expensive clothes, but we aren't any better off. We need to see the poverty behind the wealth; we need to see those chains attached to our husbands' well-dressed ankles.

How often does one spouse chain the other to their jobs? They're imprisoned so the children can have what they need in order to have a better life. Ironic, isn't it?

The culprit is our expectations: the homes we think we need, the possessions our children are supposed to need, the expenses we've created. Now, I'm not speaking against basic living expenses or good things for our children. I'm speaking against a middle-class mentality that looks only at purchases and never at the peace and happiness of the buyers. Use this mentality to buy the best house you can "afford" and a couple of new cars, and the prison walls grow even thicker.

Earlier, I told husbands especially to save their best for home. Be careful, wives, that this remains his gift, not something you feel he owes you. You don't want to judge him. Besides, no matter how good his intentions are, maybe he doesn't have anything to give when he comes home. Maybe he has to be filled before he can even say anything to you. He needs human warmth: compliments, gratitude for both his job and work at home, knowledge that you enjoy his company, peace, and cheerfulness.

What about the peace and justice we need at home? You might say, "He does his job and I do mine. I do have sympathy for him, but I work as hard as he does. It's tough being a woman today."

We're not running a contest to see who has it tougher. What's important is this: do wives always see the call to treat their husbands specially? Do we see his needs and lack of freedom?

Often, men don't really know what they need. It's not because they're refusing to be open. It's because needs are a weakness in their eyes. The average man has been trained not to have any needs. At least if he does, he fills them himself.

Wives, not husbands, are supposed to want things. It's a man's job, they think, to respond to his wife's needs. Now, that sounds generous and loving. It isn't necessarily so. It can be a way of saying, "I won't let you in; I don't need you. I will take care of you, but I won't allow you to take care of me."

Husbands, don't be proud that you ask her for nothing. That's a way of putting her out of your life, of not responding to her fully.

When we're working on our marriages, we must be careful when it comes to "fairness." We're always tempted to say, "When do we get to change the other person?"

I'm asking marriage partners to reach out to heal each other without worrying about fairness. If you say, "I'll change if you will," we'll get nowhere.

Should you change or not? If the answer is yes, it doesn't matter whether your spouse changes or not. That's a hard saying, isn't it? But it's God's honest truth.

A Different Kind of Marriage

In Matthew 13:11, the Lord said to his disciples, "To you it is granted to understand the mysteries of the kingdom of Heaven, but to [others] it is not granted..." or, in other words, "I'm telling you some things I don't tell the world." Too often we live the world's way with holy water. We have the sign of the cross hovering over our heads, but the world is imprinted in our hearts.

The Lord is really saying, "I'm offering you a different kind of marriage." He's offering you a greater marriage than others have. His offer isn't a marriage in which you get along better, but a marriage in which the whole value system is different. It's not a marriage with improved communication, but a sacrament of unity which celebrates different decisions about the outside world.

He's offering you a happier marriage. All you have to do is begin. Begin with simple actions like defending your spouse if somebody criticizes him or her. It's your call not to tolerate such insults. Or begin by welcoming your spouse back into your life by learning to understand his or her thinking about family, children, religion, housing....

There are so many graces in this Scripture passage. Ponder it in your hearts, so you can freely let the sacrament of matrimony be present in your lives.

Resources for Reflection

Don't look at this marital soul-search as a weighty obligation. You shouldn't have to gather courage for it. Rather, look on it as an opportunity. Because you have been so good as a husband or wife, you've now discovered even more potential. You have even more ability to respond to the needs of your lover and to the Lord. What you have just read has meant something to you, and that's a gift from God. The fact that you thought, "Gee, I should do something about this" shows how tremendous you are. It's in no way, shape, or form an indication of any failure. It is a definite sign of your success.

It's best if the two of you can talk these ideas over. You can't become a good wife, for instance, by yourself. Why? Because you're not "a wife." You're *his* wife. He needs to be fully involved in your plans. Men, each of you belongs to a special woman. If you decide in private how to be a better husband, you're missing the whole point. Your change must be based on what she's seeking from you, what responses she desires, how she believes you can improve the quality of her life.

If your spouse doesn't want to read this book, don't be judgmental. Try to talk to him about what you've read, ask her how she thinks you should change. Don't hit your lover with a statement like, "I see you're dehumanized by your job, dear." He'll say, "What are you talking about?" or something even less polite.

Say, instead, "I read this book today, and it says... Do you feel like that? Does it hurt your feelings when I...? How would you feel if I changed in this area...?" And of course, never, ever say, "I think you should..."

See if you can get your spouse to write on the sharing questions that follow, or at least talk about them. And pray. Our Lord is a loving God who wants us to be happy in our marriages; he will certainly hear your prayer. Trust, too, in the goodness of your lover. Our spouses are good men and women who perhaps have been hurt in the past and are afraid to be open and trusting. Your sincerity and willingness to change create a greenhouse effect in your home: it becomes a place of light and warmth where souls can bloom.

This book is not a think book; it's a love book. It's written so you will feel more tender toward each other, be more open to each other, speak more freely. It's intended to help you think of subjects that need to be talked over. In order for it all to work, you have to go to each other, so turn to each other and enjoy.

Consider These Questions Privately:

Is my husband, my wife, a stranger in our home? Am I willing to change that?

How is my spouse naked?

How do I treat my lover when he or she is sick? How can I improve?

Do I comfort my lover for those little flaws?

How is my beloved spouse in prison, and what can I do about that?

Share These Questions With Your Spouse:

My love, when do I treat you as a stranger in our home? How does my answer make me feel?

When do I feel most vulnerable? When would I like your support?

How do I plan to make you feel clothed, dear? Am I on target?

How do I want to be treated when I'm sick?... How am I going to change to fill your needs when you're sick?

How am I in prison?...What will I do to free you from your prison, my love?

Finally, Let Us Invite God Into Our Marriages:

Dear Lord,

Thank you for giving me the grace to realize I've been hurting my beloved spouse. Please let me see this truthfully, and let me see with equal truth my goodness and generosity of heart. Help me understand how much you love me, just as I am.

Lord, please make me willing to change. Help me understand that you want me to be happy and that following your way will enrich the lives of both myself and my beloved.

Help me fill my beloved's life with love and warmth and acceptance. Help me treat my dear spouse as I would treat you. Amen.

CHAPTER 4

How Delighted Is Your Life?

"Love Your Enemies,
Do Good to Those Who Hate You."
(Lk 6:27–29)

It would be an exciting day, not only for his disciples but for Jesus as well. He had passed the entire night on a mountain, praying to his Father. Now it was dawn and he would come down to the foot of the mountain and preach to the crowd. He already knew what he wanted to say:

> … I say this to you who are listening: Love your enemies, do good to those who hate you, bless those who curse you, pray for those who treat you badly. To anyone who slaps you on one cheek, present the other cheek as well; to anyone who takes your cloak from you, do not refuse your tunic. Give to everyone who asks you, and do not ask for your property back from someone who takes it. Treat others as you would like people to treat you. If you love those who love you, what credit can you expect? Even sinners love those who love them. And if you do good to those who do good to you, what credit can you expect? For even sinners do that much. And if you lend to those from whom you hope to get money back, what credit can you expect? Even sinners lend to sinners to get back the same amount. Instead, love your enemies and do good to them, and lend without any hope of return. You will have a great reward, and you will be children of the Most High, for he himself is kind to the ungrateful and the wicked.
>
> Be compassionate just as your Father is compassionate. Do

> not judge, and you will not be judged; do not condemn, and you will not be condemned; forgive, and you will be forgiven. Give, and there will be gifts for you: a full measure, pressed down, shaken together, and overflowing, will be poured into your lap; because the standard you use will be the standard used for you.
>
> LUKE 6:27–38

This passage of Scripture is magnificent, isn't it? If everyone could live this one, no unhappiness would be left in the world. It would end the get-ahead mentality that leads to such aggressiveness and aggrandizement. We'd all stop looking over our shoulders to see who was gaining on us.

The Golden Rule is such a wonderful plan for living. Jesus makes a great deal of sense, but everything he says is not so easy to accept. If we're honest, most of us will admit that Jesus' "turn the other cheek" message is most comfortable when we keep a safe distance.

There's No Place Like Home

We can almost imagine Jesus' message being given in a major television address or United Nations forum. We see global implications. But implementation of his message really starts at home, in the context of our own lives. Further, Jesus spoke to each of us individually. It's not as if he finished his sermon, then muttered, "Whew. I'm glad that's over. I hope someone gives it a try." Instead, he's whispering in your ear right now, something to the effect of "I'm serious about this, and I want you to go first." And he's holding this message out as a gift, not delivering it like a jail sentence. He really wants us to live our daily lives this way.

For husbands and wives, Jesus wants us to pay strictest attention to his words when we're in communication with each other. It's unfortunate but true: sometimes your lover is your enemy, at least for an hour or two. That's when she's angry with you; he won't talk to you. When we think of enemies, though, we think of someone with a gun. It's sad, even frightening, to think our enemies share our beds.

Our enemies are people who hurt us emotionally, who take away things we believe are ours, like attention or free time, or who make our lives less rewarding than they ought to be. Who's in the best position to hurt us in these ways? Our spouses, of course.

Often enough, we make the tragic mistake of retaliation. We follow the world's way instead of letting go as the Lord suggests. The Lord said, more or less, "It's easy to be nice to a husband who's romancing you." When he's buried in the computer or glued to the Super Bowl, though, he becomes your enemy. Are you afraid to be nice to him then? How about a spouse who's on your back, who never seems satisfied. Are you hesitant to follow the Lord's message then, afraid you'll encourage even more antagonism? Luckily, it doesn't work that way. There's a difference between encouraging anger and encouraging love.

So often, spouses shout simply to let us know they're there. They wonder if they really come first. We say they do, but we seem to put our jobs first during the day, while the other responsibilities come first at night. Perhaps dinner is taken for granted. We're certainly glad to have it, but we don't often praise our spouses' efforts. Maybe we should but, after all, people don't *really* thank each other for daily chores or for going to work. Do they?

The Lord has told us in no uncertain terms that we must love, even when someone is making us angry and taking our peace away. In other words, when someone is an enemy, even if that enemy is a marriage partner.

Besides, why get into an argument? It merely upsets both parties, and makes everyone feel guilty and uncomfortable. The basic question is simpler: Will we really live the Lord's way, or will we follow society's footpath? Will we continue to take each other for granted?

Now I'm asking you to praise your spouses for coming home at night. Consider this: your spouse's presence is a gift to you, and deserving of praise for faithfulness.

We must begin by seeing our spouses as the Lord sees them: as wonderful, beautiful children created by the Father to be our beloveds.

Then we can't help but find delight in them, from the smallest shrug of their shoulders to their biggest accomplishments. Our partners deserve praise just for being themselves.

We pledged to praise each other when we were married, yet we're very grudging with our compliments. We reserve them for special occasions. When we withhold our praise, though, we signal that we are wary and distrustful, not wanting to commit ourselves. We're not acting in anger or malice; we're simply withholding the beautiful gifts we have to give.

Normal, Everyday Saints

Why don't we live the Gospel more fully? Partly because we think we're not supposed to. At least, not while we're doing the dishes or going through the bills. We're supposed to live the Gospel on Sundays. The rest of our lives are filled with normal, everyday events.

We draw a sharp line between the great bulk of the world and those few items that fit into a spiritual category. We may practice those spiritual pursuits fervently and faithfully, but the world takes up most of our time.

In the worldly category, though, we let Jesus in reluctantly and carefully. We don't want his idealism ruining our relationships with other people.

The rules we use to govern our worldly lives are gathered from our peers. We strive toward good common sense. Common sense is defined as whatever the average, normal person would do under the circumstances.

But Jesus didn't come to proclaim good common sense. He came to tell us salvation was at hand. If we'd let him, he would change our lives, but we often don't give him free reign. Jesus is calling us to himself as whole beings, not just when we're in church or doing volunteer work. The glad tidings apply to every facet of our existence and every relationship under all circumstances. If we accept him wholeheartedly, it will be a conversion experience.

It's the Good News

Today, Jesus' message is just as new—and as difficult to accept—as it was when he first preached it. Our world still doesn't believe the Good News. Husbands and wives are still treating each other with fairness and common sense. When everything's going smoothly, they're smooth; when things are rough, they're rough, too. They're not responding to each other, they're responding to themselves. They're unconsciously deciding, "I feel upset, so I'm going to behave that way."

Jesus is saying, "Let's do it differently. Let's not talk about how you're feeling or how she's treating you. Let's talk about loving her, not because she deserves it, but because I'm asking you to."

He's asking us to question ourselves: "Do I love her when everyone would say I ought to withdraw? Maybe I won't be nasty, but I won't hear a thing. I'll just let her voice roll off me like water off a duck. Then she'll learn."

When we behave this way, we're playing a power game with each other. We're saying, "I won't punish you if you act the way I want." We're forcing our lovers to meet our approval—or else. "My obligation toward you is absolved," we add, "if you don't live up to your obligation toward me." We're trying to "teach" our spouses to treat us better, but we're really teaching them anger, hopelessness, and resentment.

We're behaving like children then. We're not trusting our lovers' goodness. We're saying, "I really don't believe she'll respond; I don't think he cares enough to change. Furthermore, I really don't believe in Jesus' way. I have to use force; it's the only thing I trust."

Perhaps you're thinking Jesus' way is the right way, but it's a big change. It could leave you looking foolish and it might not work: "If I'm nice to her when she's in a rotten mood, she'll die of the shock." What a way to go.

You Are So Nice, Dear, What Do You Want?

I'm not promising instant success. It might take some time for our new behavior to affect our lovers. At first, our lovers might not notice we're acting nicely. They might be suspicious, waiting for the other shoe to drop. So we must be patient, knowing it takes time to undo the previous training.

Sometimes we'd rather look for another way to happiness. Sometimes we even prefer hard work. We keep the house clean and painted, we cook or do repairs, take good care of the children and carefully watch the budget. Yes, we're very good to each other.

That's still a policy of loneliness. We need to add compassion to constant, relentless love. Both men and women crave that type of love. Let's be generous with it. Our lovers need our goodness the most when they're angry or unhappy, and having trouble being lovers themselves.

How could weak human beings ever succeed at such an idealistic program? Basically, because we're the Lord's own people. We have been chosen to reveal him through the way we love one another. Jesus has raised us to the dignity of children of God. That wasn't a reward for good conduct. It was a free gift, made possible by his passion and death on the cross.

We must see beyond our lovers' pouting, shouting, or anger. We must see that immortal being whom God calls his son or daughter. Above all, we must rise above our own feelings.

Feelings are neither right nor wrong, and we shouldn't deny our resentment or hurt. But we must decide whether to love, and that decision can't be based on our own feelings. It must be based on others' needs. We must ask ourselves, "What expression of love does my spouse need right now?" "Right now" should be in the middle of an argument or whenever it is hardest. It's a tough thing to do. If it came naturally, Jesus wouldn't have had to tell us about it.

The real test of a marriage is not when everything is sweetness and light. Then it's easy to do things for each other. The real test of a marriage comes when we're disillusioned with each other. How do we respond when our spouses aren't responding to us? How do we reach out when they're pushing us away? How do we speak to them when their language is harsh and rejecting?

Bless Those Who Curse You

It's tragic but sometimes we curse each other. Some of us are too proper to use so-called bad language. But bad language is not the use of certain nasty words. It's the intention behind the statement. We could cut someone to ribbons with perfectly respectable language.

When we curse people, we're taking away their blessedness. We're depriving them of our approval. Sometimes a curse is best accomplished through silence, or by politeness or pleasant chitchat.

We can also degrade our lovers through sarcasm. We can demean others by superiority or scorn. We can humiliate them by the simple, unspoken assumption that they're not worthy of our attention.

Do we pray for those who curse us, or do we handle them without any help from God? Do we wish God would help us, but doubt that he will? Do we feel that prayer is such a weak little tool when used toward a cold, selfish spouse? When we do pray, what do we pray? "Lord, make him straighten up. Make her see how she's hurting me."

Instead, let's ask the Lord to bless them. How about a prayer to celebrate their goodness, to make us see the log in our own eye rather than the splinter in theirs?

Next time, let's ask the Lord to help us respond rather than react. Let's seek the graces of tenderness and love rather than the knee-jerk defensiveness of coldness and rejection.

We must ask him to help us respond on his terms, not ours. We must listen and wait as he gentles our hearts and pares the calluses off our tenderness. This type of prayer breaks the vicious circle of negativity. Soon we will see our spouses responding to our love with love of their own.

If Anyone Slaps You on One Cheek, Present the Other Cheek As Well

We slap each other, too, don't we? Not physically, but we find other ways to let our lovers know we're upset. For a while, we put up with these hidden negative messages. But sooner or later, we reach the end of our rope. "I've run out of patience," we think. "I've had enough."

We don't always put it into words. Sometimes we say it with angry looks or the way we slam the pots and pans. Our lovers know these signals.

Again, we're measuring out our generosity. It's as if marriage is a recipe, and too much love will ruin the batter. The Good News is this: the more love you add, the better it gets.

So often, though, we find ourselves searching for some minimum standard of behavior: "What is the least I can do and still have reasonable peace at home?"

We must get away from that miserable trap of being satisfied with the minimum. We aren't satisfied with the minimum in anything else. We don't say, "More clothes? No; I don't want 'em. I'll wear what I bought last year." We don't say (at least, without a twinge), "A vacation away? Why would I want one of those?"

Yet we're comfortable with our limited generosity. We believe we're virtuous because we don't lose patience right away. Actually, we're not concentrating on our lovers at all. We're simply being "good."

Jesus is telling us, "Stop concentrating on yourself. Don't see things in terms of how much is 'reasonable'; see your lover's needs instead." He really intends for our unbounded love to be an everyday occurrence.

We want to listen to the Lord, but we have learned this world's lessons all too well. We do the kindly thing: we tune him out. We decide he's not talking about us. If he is, he really can't be serious. He'll understand, we think, when we don't live up to his godlike ideals. Our problem, then, isn't failure. It's that we don't even try.

If Anyone Takes Your Cloak, Do Not Refuse Your Tunic

Do you really give your tunic to the spouse who takes your cloak? There's a good way to find out. What happens when you're both in the car and it's time to pay for gas or a toll? Do you look at each other, waiting for the other one to pay?

Free giving doesn't always involve money. It can involve our lives at home. Maybe I have my chair, and God help you if I catch you in it.

Do we really give the tunic when the cloak is taken, or do we just establish a nice way of life in which both of us can keep our cloaks? Maybe my cloak is smaller than my lover's, but I like smaller cloaks.

The Lord has great ambitions for us, and scorekeeping is not part of his plan. Yet we carefully measure the minimum amount of satisfaction we'll tolerate in a relationship, and we spend tremendous amounts of energy making sure we get it. We all recognize how sad it is when a divorcing couple divides their property, each of them trying to get an edge on the other one.

Too often that can be just as true in a marriage. It doesn't necessarily involve property. We may be perfectly willing to concede a greater amount of time, money, or energy, but we're going to get at least a minimum amount of what we want. Nobody had better take that away from us or we'll let them know about it.

Resources for Reflection

From time to time, we hear stories of the saints who loved their persecutors. We tend to wonder if these people were for real. They were; now go and do likewise.

I am asking you to be saints. The community of faith needs you; you embody our sacrament of matrimony and we need you. It may be difficult for you to realize that you are, indeed, a sacrament. But it's true. The Lord always calls us to greater things than we could imagine on our own.

Once we realize our importance in God's plan, we're called to action. Do we live God's plan with each other? Remember, the man you're angry with is half that sacrament; the woman you wish would go away is the other half.

Do we ever turn the other cheek with each other? Yes, we often do. It's not fair to ourselves, nor is it helpful, to call ourselves failures. There are many times when we are most understanding and compassionate toward each other.

I'm not suggesting that we're reprobates and it's time to shape up. I'm saying, let's expand our goodness. Let's make a real campaign of being our best. We sometimes think if we can't do our best, we might as well give up. That's hopelessness, though, not the Lord's way. Jesus didn't say either we're flawless or we flunk. He expected our goodness to be a journey of growth.

We should ask ourselves whether we're turning the other cheek more frequently than we did last week, last month, or last year. We should ask: "Am I limiting my growth in goodness by thinking I'm already generous enough, or am I willing to push myself a little beyond."

That's all. Don't tell yourselves, "I won't be impatient with him again, ever"; "I'll turn the other cheek with her from now on." The step beyond today's success, however small or large it may have been, is a big stride ahead.

Consider These Questions Privately:

Do I love my spouse when everyone would say it's all right not to?

When am I my spouse's enemy?

What specific steps can I take in order to do better than I did today?

Share These Questions With Your Spouse:

I remember a certain time when you reached out to me, even though my actions or words were pushing you away. Let me tell you about it....How does that memory make me feel?

Which parts of my life did I once think were worldly, and now realize are spiritual? (Make a list and explain why.)

My dear, you are God's immortal son or daughter. I can see this because of your goodness, which shines forth when you... I remember when you....

Finally, Let Us Invite God Into Our Marriages:

Dear Father, I ask you today for the grace of trust. Help me realize your plan is one of happiness and strength, not hopelessness. Help me see my lover's needs, not mine; lift me beyond the trap of my own hurts and resentments. Let me see the pain behind my spouse's anger; fill me with mercy and forgiveness.

Please give me the patience to wait while you gentle my heart, replacing the hardness with tenderness, and the rigidness with happiness and love.

Thank you for my wonderful spouse, who is so good to me. Bless my spouse and fill her (him) with peace. Amen.

CHAPTER 5

We Are Instruments of His Love

"Give, and There Will Be Gifts for You."

(Lk 6:30–38)

This guy didn't look much like a psychologist, she thought. He was too young, his hair was too long, and he was entirely too cheerful. "Don't smile at me," she told him. "We're talking about misery here, you know."

"I understand," he said. "I understand it all."

For a strange moment, she believed he did. Behind the smile, his eyes were full of compassion. But wait a minute. He hadn't heard her story yet. "How can you—"

"You don't have to leave him, you know," he said. "I know how to repair your marriage."

"You do?" For a moment, she felt a surge of excitement. Then practicality took over. No; it was too late now. She wouldn't indulge fool's hopes.

"Don't think that way," he said. "Listen to me."

"You know what I'm thinking? But—you can't read minds."

"You're the one who said it. Now then, dear, I want you to turn the other cheek."

"Turn the other cheek? No one does that."

His gaze was steady; she could see he didn't agree. She began to feel a little guilty. "I mean—well, I know we're supposed to, but we can't really do it. It's not realistic."

The counselor went on as if he hadn't heard. "You need to be good to him, even when he hurts you. You need to say nice things to him; things that make him feel good about himself, especially when he's cold or sarcastic. I also want you to pray for him."

"Pray that God straightens him out?"

"No, pray that our Father blesses him, makes him happy, gives him peace. It wouldn't hurt if you prayed for yourself, too."

She shrugged.

"When he insults you or snubs you, don't fight with him. When he trespasses on your rights, don't hold back. Give him what he seems to need."

"Now you're insulting me," she said. "That's nonsense."

"No it's not. All I'm saying is to treat him the way you wish he'd treat you. It's not enough to love him when things are all moonlight and roses. Any woman could do that."

"Moonlight and roses?" she said. "We haven't had moonlight and roses since the garden show."

He didn't look happy. "I'm not excusing him. But if you're good to him when he's good to you, that isn't love. That's common sense. His wife should love him more than that. Now then, I want you to give him everything he needs without expecting him to return any favors."

"And what do I get out of it?"

"How about holiness?"

"I don't want holiness. I want love."

"Love is the same thing."

She didn't understand that at all. "You're saying it's all my fault."

"No, I'm not. Not at all. I'm complimenting you. You have the goodness and the strength to turn this marriage around—with the Father's help, of course. If I didn't have faith in you, I would have said, take a cruise. Pretend things are going well and be satisfied with mediocrity. But if you do what I'm telling you, you two will have the best marriage on the block. You'll have such a good marriage, everyone will think you're crazy."

"I almost believe you," she said.

"That's almost good. Why don't you pray about it?"

"Pray about it? Who, me?"

"Yes, you." He walked her to the door. "I think you'll do well."

"Am I supposed to make another appointment?" she asked.

"No. I'll see you in church."

She stood outside on the sidewalk. "Church? He doesn't even know if I go to church." She flung open the door to confront him with it. Of course, he wasn't there.

Give to Everyone Who Asks You

Jesus said, "Give to everyone who begs from you, and do not ask for your property back from someone who takes it." We may not like the idea that our husbands and wives have to beg from us, but all too frequently it happens. How often do our lovers have to beg us to pay attention? Are they afraid to initiate lovemaking because they know we might reject them?

There are so many things our spouses like us to do, yet they never seem important enough for us to remember. We're sporadic with our thoughtfulness, which makes our lovers suspicious, sometimes rightly so. When a husband brings home flowers, his wife is tempted to say, "You've quit your job, haven't you? Or have you done something else?"

If a wife does something special for her husband, he runs through a list of occasions to discover if he forgot one. When he realizes it's just an ordinary weekday, he thinks, "I wonder what she's up to."

Sometimes our thoughtfulness is a form of apology: "I'm sorry I fought with you." Why don't we expand our repertory? Let's add, "There's no particular reason for this; I'm just so glad I have you. Let's have a party." The Lord doesn't want his people to wear long faces or think only about "serious" spiritual things. He wants us to be happy.

We force our spouses to beg when they want something we don't approve of, when their needs are a burden on us, or when we think their requests can't really be important to them. Sometimes we make them beg because we're still concentrating on our own satisfaction. We might even withhold something deliberately because our spouses aren't responding to us, and turnabout is fair play. For whatever reason, we humans do a lot of withholding. When we do give, it may be grudging, partial, or seldom. Again, we're not bad people. We're good people who don't see our bad habits. Now that we do, we're free to change.

We're often quite generous with each other. I don't want to imply otherwise. But, often, our generosity is only for special occasions. Many men graciously pitch in with the dishes, the children, or the housework, but pitching in is exactly what we re doing. We're helping our wives do their own jobs; we're not taking responsibility.

Wives can also limit their generosity. Maybe they work outside the home, and when they come home, they feel they ought to be off duty. They may not go anywhere, but they're vividly aware that it's their time to themselves. If our husbands want time for themselves, too, how do we react?

Sometimes our "property" that is not "shared" is an attitude or belief. Clashes in child-raising philosophies are an all-too-frequent example. Often, we think our ideas are the right ones. If our lovers start to "interfere" by using their own methods, how do we respond? Do we feel they're taking the children away from us?

In a sense, we're like dogs clinging to a bone. Our attention is totally centered on what's being taken away from us. Maybe we growl self-righteously about it, and maybe we just clamp our jaws.

Such bones of contention can be sources of conflict and unhappiness. The Lord wants to free us from that. He's telling us to stop being possessive, not just about money or belongings, but about attitudes, preferences, and styles of living.

Let's stop and examine ourselves now: what hidden demands do we have of our spouses? Do we have mental lists of their responsibilities, which can only be postponed under special circumstances? What happens when those special circumstances are over? Do our spouses shoulder the same loads once again? Do they have to carry even more for a while to pay us for our help? "Remember how nice I was to you?" we imply. "Well, now you can let me off the hook."

Jesus reminds us, "If you love those who love you, what credit can you expect? Even sinners love those who love them." If you love your spouses when they're lovable, how different are you from any other couple? How are you a sacrament in anything but name?

Prickly Pair

We have been so carefully trained to be prickly, defensive, and, above all, in charge. When we can't control others' responses, we worry: are we getting our share? Yes, we're less defensive with our spouses than with others, but our training has been so thorough, we unconsciously bring it into our homes.

I'm not suggesting a debate about who's right and who's wrong. What I'm calling for is a surrender of defenses, a throwing down of arms, and a lasting, peaceful embrace. It's indeed not a fool's hope. It's God's plan.

The Lord is saying, "Let go; be free. Don't treat others as they treat you. That's the world's teaching."

"But I'm afraid. My spouse is hurting me. If I don't look out for myself, who will?"

The Lord isn't as heartless as we sometimes think he is. "Why, I will, of course," he answers. "I'm looking out for you right now."

The more we require, the less satisfied we become. We see how much we're not getting, and that certainly doesn't make us happy. The Lord is offering us happiness. He's offering us fullness in life. If we follow his way, there will be much more joy in our marriages. Our husbands and wives will certainly respond to our goodness if we'll only let it shine forth.

If the truth be known, we desperately want our spouses to love us freely. When we force "love" from them, no matter how subtle we are, we're fooling no one.

Besides, if we wait for our lovers to earn our trust, we'll have a long wait indeed. Our lovers simply cannot prove they're trustworthy. They, like all of us, have faults. Our trust must be our gift to them.

We All Have a Stake in Your Marriage

No matter how adeptly we extort good behavior from our spouses, we still can't make them into the people we want them to be. Many a fiancée, for instance, thinks, "Oh, I can make him stop drinking (attend the symphony/enjoy family life/change in other ways)." Of course not. Only he can change himself. Likewise, a husband can't force changes on a wife.

Our sacrament calls us to love our spouses, whether or not they earn it. Your relationship is not just a marriage; it's the sacrament of matrimony. Practically anyone can be married, but your relationship is more significant than a document in city hall. We, the church, have a stake in your marriage. Your good relationship nourishes us, and its rough moments drag us down. You are our community, and we need you to be your loving best.

Perhaps you're satisfied in your marriage. That doesn't necessarily mean you're answering your call to be sacramental. All too often, we compare our marriages with the failures around us:

"Thank God our marriage isn't like Joe and Mary's. They just endure each other. They never go out together, and when they're home, they're in opposite corners of the house. We're not perfect, but we still have some passion in our marriage. At least we still fight."

Maybe we're not judgmental, but just a little smug: "We have a date every Saturday night. We go to dinner, take in a movie. We don't know any other couple who does that." The idea's a great one, but the pride in that sentence can be blinding.

Put the Pedal to the Metal

Let's not ask ourselves, "Am I a good wife?" or "Am I a good husband?" if it means, "Am I living up to certain minimal standards?" or "Am I doing all right?"

Let's do ask, "Is this the best I can do? Am I really going all out, every moment of every day?"

Don't ask, "Does he gripe?" "Is she reasonably pleased?" It isn't enough to wonder, "Am I living up to my responsibilities?" Ask, instead, "How delighted is his life?" "How full is her life?" "How can I add to that enjoyment?"

If you compared many of today's marriages to schoolrooms, you'd find a lot of students content to earn Cs, sometimes a D, or even an F. But we didn't marry to get passing marks. We each have the capability to make our marriages an A+.

The Lord said, "Treat others as you would like people to treat you." We don't want others to do the minimum for us. We need so much more than that. We want to know that our husbands and wives are eager for us to be happy. We want to know that they'll treat us kindly, make sure our lives are filled with wonder because they love us so much.

If You Do Good to Those Who Do Good to You, What Credit Can You Expect?

When do we exercise our good qualities? If it's mainly when our spouses are appreciative or when they're good to us, we've changed loving into banking. We're lending to each other and expecting repayment.

The Lord says, "If you lend to those from whom you hope to get money back, what credit can you expect? Even sinners lend to sinners to get back the same amount."

So many couples practice a system of trade-offs. They may be very good people; it may be all they know. How are we different? Do we live Christian lives during the week and not just on Sunday? Are you living your sacrament right this minute?

If you live as a sacrament, you and your spouse will naturally benefit more than anyone else does. But you're living for more than your spouse's sake, though. The Church is only as credible as you are.

The words of the Bible are great and certainly necessary, but people aren't drawn to God because they're impressed with his book. They are drawn through a love relationship, beginning with his love as it is lived in you: your willingness to seek the happiness of others instead of yourself. That's best demonstrated by the way you love your spouse.

Love Your Enemies and Do Good to Them

In full, this passage says, "Love your enemies and do good to them, and lend without any hope of return. You will have a great reward, and you will be children of the Most High, for he himself is kind to the ungrateful and the wicked."

Our defensive instincts urge us to reject this teaching. We want to say, "Wait a minute. That's a nice thought, but we have to live in this world. My spouse is a good person; better than I am, most likely. But if you let people get away with rude behavior, they'll just get worse."

That's a little crude, but it gets to the point. How do we overcome the tendency to follow such love-killing advice? By telling ourselves, "I am not that kind of person. I am a loving person, and I will be a lover no matter what anyone else says or thinks."

We must teach ourselves that sulking, shouting back, the cold shoulder, forgetfulness of anniversaries—whatever—is unacceptable in the Lord's plan. We'll still make mistakes. We're human. But we must resolve not to lower our standards, even when we can't live up to them.

Prayer opens us to the Father's love. By understanding that love, we better understand how to love others. Prayer can be quiet thought in church. It can be meditation on the Scriptures. It can involve the rosary, spontaneous group prayer, or any number of expressions.

We Catholics, especially if we're older, are familiar with the concept of penance. Penance strengthens our prayer lives and the goodness within us. It is our widow's mite of suffering offered to the Father.

The strength to live his way is also found in trust. We humans are tempted to rely on force, making marriage into a power struggle.

Instead, we must truly trust our partners to want to love us. And the best way to encourage your spouse's desire to love you is to love your partner with everything you've got.

If we allow ourselves even a little laxity, we're being less than we can be. We're called to love each other as much as we can. That exuberant maximum will be different for each person. You might find yourself excelling in gentleness and forgiveness while your spouse grows in spontaneity and joy. Each of us is stronger in some graces, needing more prayer in others.

How to Grow a Lover

Some years ago, researchers placed two sets of plants in separate parts of a greenhouse, making sure the physical conditions were exactly the same. For one set of plants, they made life as miserable as possible. They constantly played harsh music, yelled, and insulted the poor things. To the other plants, they played soft, gentle music and offered constant praise.

The second set of plants blossomed incredibly, way beyond the capacity of the soil, fertilizer, sun, and water. The first set of plants withered and died.

The way to grow a lover is to talk gently and lovingly and in praise. The more criticism you dish out, the more your prophecies will be fulfilled. The harsher you are, the less love will be returned.

The following statements are, in a twisted way, the kind that usually turns into self-fulfilling prophecies:

"You don't care about me. All you care about is yourself."

"How could you *do* such a thing?"

"I don't know why I bother (...with you)."

"I forgot (...because you aren't important enough to make me remember)."

Our spouses are much more likely to become the kinds of people we "speak" them to be than the kinds of people we're trying to make them. Pressure, punishment, and force simply do not work in a husband-wife relationship.

To some degree, we're all guilty, even if we aren't extraordinary scoundrels or suffering in bad relationships. Less than perfect conduct is present even in the best marriages.

If we're clever and we apply enough pressure, we could probably force our spouses to perform as we wish, at least sometimes. But their hearts won't be in it and, after all, aren't hearts what marriage is all about?

It's our responsibility to bolster the good self-images of our spouses. The better their self-images are, the better they'll respond to us. They'll be more capable of loving; freer from defensiveness, narrowness, and rejection.

If our lovers see themselves as inadequate in our eyes, they simply won't have the confidence to love. But if we're frequently telling them how much they mean to us, how much more joyful our lives are because of their presence, the more they'll pour out their love on us. There will be a tremendous increase in their capacity to love because we have expanded them with our praise.

Resources for Reflection

"Words flow out of what fills the heart," Jesus told the Pharisees in Matthew 12:34. Out of those words a home is created. When you provide an environment of unconditional tenderness, your beloved becomes the kind of person who does fit your life. Spouses bloom when they believe they're so wonderful in your eyes that you just can't resist them.

If they receive love only when they perform correctly, they can never believe in that love. When that love is constant, relentless, when it is absolutely, totally poured out, the rewards are great.

There is no man who is loved by a tender woman who does not discover riches in himself that he never believed were there. There is no woman who is loved by a gentle man who does not live way beyond her outward potential. Every bit of love you ever expressed throughout your marriage has been more than returned.

The Lord's way really does work. We're losing so much if we

don't try it. But it won't work if we try a little of it for a little while. We really must make a commitment to love our spouses the way the Lord intends. Husbands, the Lord has specifically chosen each of you to love this particular woman the way he wants her to be loved. Wives, you are each called by Jesus to touch, to heal, to console, and to bring this man to life the way he wants to do it himself.

Do you see the wonder of it? This is an awesome commitment and a great honor. Jesus trusts you the way he trusted his disciples. He wants you to make his Kingdom come alive in the hearts of his people. Matrimony is a magnificent call to love totally and unreservedly.

Consider These Questions Privately:

When do I best increase my spouse's self-esteem? When do I wither my spouse by failing to love? What steps can I take to nourish my lover more?

What is holding me back from being a more perfect lover? Fear of hurt and rejection? Indignation? Fear of losing my "rights"?

Am I willing to incorporate prayer and/or penance into my life for the sake of my beloved? What, specifically, will I do?

Before we cover the next questions, let's review how to share. Remember to focus on your own feelings. These questions are meant to stimulate dialogue between you and to clear up misunderstandings. They are absolutely not a place to lay even the slightest blame. Don't, for instance, say, "I have trouble loving you when you're acting like a jerk, because that's when you make me the angriest." Do say something like "When we quarrel, I feel afraid that you'll stop loving me. I feel ashamed of myself, too. I'm afraid to share those feelings, so I cover them up with anger."

A warning: if you can add a "like" or "that" after "feel," it's a judgment, not a feeling.

Remember: use at least ten minutes to write and at least ten minutes to talk. Enjoy.

Share These Questions With Your Spouse:

My dear, I know that sometimes I love you less than I am able. I want to be closer to you; I want to love you more. These are the feelings that hold me back...

My dear, I want to increase my life of prayer and/or penance so I can love you more perfectly. I am thinking of doing the following... I would like you to support me by.... Will you please...?

What do I like best about you? What are your special goodnesses, the things that fill me with delight?

An Exercise in Happiness:

At least once a month in the next five months, find a way to tell your lover just how wonderful he or she is.

- Bring home flowers or a small gift.
- Plan a surprise dinner out or perhaps brunch on Sunday.
- Spend an evening or a Saturday being completely present to your partner. Do anything your spouse wants, providing you can share it together. A walk on the beach is great; reading books on the beach is not.
- Hide a love note in your spouse's lunch bag/box or briefcase.
- Fix a special food that you know your partner likes.

Finally, Let Us Invite God Into Our Marriages:

Eternal Father, my prayer today is for freedom: freedom from my cage of resentment and anxiety. Please grant me the grace to love as bountifully as you do. Please free me from the fear of rejection and hopelessness; give me the greatness of heart to trust my spouse's goodness.

Thank you, Lord, for choosing me to be the one to love my wonderful husband (wife). Thank you for trusting in me and believing in my goodness. Please help me love my spouse the way you want to do it yourself. Amen.

CHAPTER 6

Beloved, I Belong to You

The Prodigal Son.

(Lk 15:11–20)

One day, while sinners and tax collectors were crowding around Jesus, the scribes and Pharisees began to complain. "This man welcomes sinners and even eats with them"(Lk 15:2). Evidently they thought their virtue made them better company at dinner and probably in heaven as well. Jesus, who didn't agree, told them the story of the prodigal son.

Let's read this parable carefully to see where we fit in, particularly in relation to our spouses.

> There was a man who had two sons. The younger one said to his father, "Father, let me have the share of the estate that will come to me." So the father divided the property between them. A few days later, the younger son got together everything he had and left for a distant country where he squandered his money on a life of debauchery.
>
> When he had spent it all, that country experienced a severe famine, and now he began to feel the pinch; so he hired himself out to one of the local inhabitants who put him on his farm to feed the pigs. And he would willingly have filled himself with the husks the pigs were eating but no one would let him have them. Then he came to his senses and said, "How many of my father's hired men have all the food they want and more, and here am I dying of hunger! I will leave this place and go to my father and say: Father, I have sinned against heaven and against you; I no

longer deserve to be called your son; treat me as one of your hired men." So he left the place and went back to his father.

While he was still a long way off, his father saw him and was moved with pity. He ran to the boy, clasped him in his arms and kissed him. Then his son said, "Father, I have sinned against heaven and against you. I no longer deserve to be called your son. But the father said to his servants, "Quick! Bring out the best robe and put it on him; put a ring on his finger and sandals on his feet. Bring the calf we have been fattening, and kill it; we will celebrate by having a feast, because this son of mine was dead and has come back to life; he was lost and is found." And they began to celebrate.

Now the elder son was out in the fields, and on his way back, as he drew near the house, he could hear music and dancing. Calling one of the servants he asked what it was all about. The servant told him, "Your brother has come, and your father has killed the calf we had been fattening because he has got him back safe and sound." He was angry then and refused to go in, and his father came out and began to urge him to come in; but he retorted to his father, "All these years I have slaved for you and never once disobeyed any orders of yours, yet you never offered me so much as a kid for me to celebrate with my friends. But, for this son of yours, when he comes back after swallowing up your property—he and his loose women—you kill the calf we had been fattening."

The father said, "My son, you are with me always and all that I have is yours. But it was only right we should celebrate and rejoice, because your brother here was dead and has come to life; he was lost and is found."

LUKE 15:11–32

Let's try putting ourselves in the place of each character in the drama: the loving father, the indignant elder son, and the penitent younger one. You don't have to pretend you're an aging farmer or a swinging single. Jesus meant this parable to be generously interpreted. For the purposes of this chapter, then, let's think of ourselves as the loving spouse, the indignant spouse, and the penitent one.

The Wounds of Marriage

Remember the old saying "You only hurt the one you love"? That's because the one you love is the only one who lets you get close enough to cause that hurt.

Rejection isn't ever pleasant, but we can shrug it off more readily if it doesn't come from the ones we love. We all like to impress others, but we aren't seriously hurt when we don't succeed.

Most of the time, we don't expect everyone to have a burning desire for our companionship. But when a husband or wife doesn't desire our company, day after day, night after night, we hurt deeply.

When we love, our defenses are down. We don't want our words to be judged by someone who is supposed to love us. After all, we trust our loves, so we speak spontaneously.

Spontaneous speech is a rare gift, and we don't usually share it. We're always personal with our spouses, though, so when we're faced with indifference, cruelness, or even anger, we're wide open to the pain.

That's why forgiveness is the single most essential blessing a husband or wife can ask from God.

The Gift of Trust

There's a tremendous vulnerability in the love relationship, and often we forget how fragile a gift our spouses are giving us.

Sometimes we don't forget. We may even take advantage of it. A spouse who chooses the newspaper over his partner may say, "I'm not trying to hurt her. I'm just trying to unwind from work." A woman who gives her husband the cold shoulder may argue, "I'm not ignoring him. I'm just busy—doing *his* laundry."

We try to persuade ourselves that we're not deliberately hurting the other person, though we really know better. Once we know our actions will pain our loves, we can't pretend innocence. Even though some of us take advantage of this gift of trust, don't be discouraged. Our goodness is not determined by our flaws, but by our willingness to change those flaws.

Let's Call Ourselves Leaders

Anytime we're tempted to justify our actions by watching our friends' marriages, we're headed for trouble. There are unhappy marriages all around us, but that's because so many around us have already thrown in the towel.

In the parable of the prodigal son, Jesus calls us to be leaders. He calls us to be happy—and to be brave enough to face our mistakes. We're dodging the issue if we say, "There's misunderstanding and pain in every love relationship. We'd be naive to expect anything else."

Why settle for a wounded, hurting relationship when we have a much better choice?

Remember, in 1 Peter 2:9,10, the apostle says, "You are a chosen race, a royal priesthood, a holy nation, a people set apart to sing the praises of God who called you out of the darkness into his wonderful light. Once, you were no people and now you are the People of God...." Jesus Christ came to earth to free us all from the hopeless limitations of humanity. With God's grace, you can, indeed, have a truly loving relationship. It's your choice. Hurry! Your family's happiness is at stake.

The lack of happiness in today's marriages is a life-threatening illness. If a husband was vomiting and feverish, and had a sharp pain on the lower right side of his abdomen, his wife wouldn't shrug her shoulders and say, "Oh, well. Must be appendicitis; that's pretty common. Most people get it sooner or later." Instead, she'd rush her husband to the hospital. When our husbands or wives hurt from wounds we inflict, though, we're much more relaxed.

We humans are much more likely to excuse our own defects, and much less likely to excuse our lovers' flaws. There's a good rule of thumb we can all follow: when we find ourselves making excuses for our behavior, that's when our loves are feeling their greatest pain.

To Love or Be Loved?

We are only happy when we're focused on others, and we're miserably unhappy when we focus on ourselves. We think we would much rather be loved than love. That's not because we're bad people. It's because we've learned to look for happiness the wrong way.

This self focus is a recipe for trouble. Love is supposed to pull us outward until we're taking the other person even more seriously than we do ourselves. As our love grows, we start to find our own well-being in our loves' well-being.

Marriage is not supposed to be a business deal in which each partner receives separate rewards for a joint effort. It's a call for both husband and wife to be totally absorbed in each other. It's a call to spend all our talents, our energy, enthusiasm, and responsiveness for one precious purchase: bringing true joy to our loves.

If we think the purpose of marriage is to be loved, we are clinging to an illusion: that the more we are loved, the happier we are.

If we are experiencing hurt in our marriages, we need to find out why. We must go beyond the specific incident that triggered the pain: "He forgot our anniversary." "She doesn't care how hard I work." We may be choosing to experience the pain. If we have a whole series of hidden expectations for our partners and lists of our own rights, we're headed for heartache.

Sin Is a Four-Letter Word

Ask yourselves, "What causes the most pain in this world?" Terrorism? Cancer? Prejudice? No, sin does.

We don't realize that pain is intimately connected with sin. If we could wipe out sin in a husband/wife relationship, we would eliminate ninety percent of that couple's emotional pain.

"We're sinners." How does this expression make us feel?

Most likely we're probably not too offended, although this statement is worse than any obscene phrase we could imagine.

It's a far more horrible insult to say that we're sinners. Instead, it doesn't faze us in the least. This admission that we're all sinners doesn't make that sinful condition less lethal. When we say, "We're sinners," we're really saying we are people who inflict pain. We are infectious with unhappiness; we make those around us suffer.

We're passive about sin because we don't recognize what it means to be a sinner. An admission of sin is of the greatest and most important seriousness. It's an opening of our hearts to those around us and, for Catholics, a necessary preliminary to receiving the Body and Blood of Christ. Do we realize it's our opportunity for a true conversion experience, or is our admission of sin rather like brushing dust off our coats before we walk into church? For many of us, it's only a lighthearted "I'm a sinner, you're a sinner, all God's children are sinners."

We resist an awareness of our sinfulness because we don't want to go on any guilt trips. We're determined to avoid guilt, even to the point of ignoring our wrongs. It's easier to ignore those wrongs when we don't accept God's view of life. We may admit that, yes, in his eyes we've committed a sin, but we add that we're normal human beings, no worse than anyone else.

That excuse isn't worthy of you. Remember, we're called to be leaders, not sheep following the rest of society on a downhill road. Everyone else's sins don't excuse our own; they merely add to the world's problems.

Ask yourselves, "Do I really stand before God as a sinner and see the pain my sin is inflicting upon his people, especially my spouse? Or do I see it with this world's eyes and pass it off with a shoulder shrug?" Honesty will give you the answer, and your goodness will tell you what to do.

A Way of Life

We must recognize sin as a way of life. It is not merely doing something that is bad in itself, nor is it merely a neutral action that is motivated by a sinful purpose. Sin is a whole orientation toward life: "I am a sinner," not "I did sinful things."

When I say, "I am a sinner," I'm saying I'm committed to a way of life that is self-centered and unloving.

To many of us, that's a threatening truth. We want to deny it; to say, "Most of my actions are good, or at least neutral. They're not bad." Again, we have to stop deluding ourselves. Sin isn't merely action.

We're living a sinful way of life when we're living for our own satisfaction, our own advancement. In sin, others fit best into our lives when they give us these things. That's what it means to say, "I am a sinner." That's why some husbands and wives focus on being loved rather than on loving. We can perform all sorts of good actions sinfully if our attention is fundamentally on us.

In a marriage relationship, the basic choice is between you and me. We sin when we choose me over you. We do this in many subtle ways:

We don't say we're self-centered. We say we're independent. We stand on our own two feet.

We don't say we're indifferent to the needs of our spouses. We say there has to be give and take.

We don't say the other person is less important than we are; we say we have a lot of responsibilities and we can only do so much.

It's no wonder we say such things; it's the way we've been trained. We've all seen tests that measure marital happiness. These tests ask spouses whether they're satisfied in their marriages. A real test should ask, "Is my spouse satisfied? What am I contributing to his or her satisfaction?"

We also need to recognize that sin is never "out there." There is probably no such thing as sin in itself. There are only sinners. Sin is personal. We can't sin when we're asleep or out of our minds. The deed does not make the sin; the person does.

Right now, you're probably admitting that sometimes you don't always do as well as a spouse should. When we think that way, we're still isolating ourselves from our sin. We have to learn a new way of thinking that takes openness and courage. We have to let go of our defenses; we have to stop depersonalizing sin. We have to stop thinking it's outside us, like stained clothes or scaly skin.

The Prodigal Son

We are horrified by the prodigal son's gall. He went to his father and said, "Okay, I'm old enough, I want to be independent. Give me my share." Most of us wouldn't be as generous as his father; we'd put that brat in his place. We'd ask, "What do you mean your share?"

We're indignant that he could have been so greedy and cold-blooded. Our feelings are right. His heartless demand for money was much more sinful than the way he spent it.

We think the sleeping around, the drinking, and the reckless spending were the younger son's sins. They weren't. The sin had already been committed. Those activities were merely expressions of the life-style he had chosen to live; a life-style in which he had divorced himself from his father. Demanding his share of the estate was more than rude. It was a statement: "I no longer belong to you." In effect, he was saying, "I want to live my own way." That's when he decided to be a sinner.

The relationship between father and son is the most important part of this parable. The debauchery is a very small part of the story, like the famine and the degradation of starving while feeding the pigs.

The prodigal son probably could have said, "Look, I don't have anything against the old man. I'm not doing these things because I dislike him. I just want my due. I don't want to live on a farm all my life; I have other plans."

Have you ever really felt yourself to be a sinner with your wife, with your husband? We limit sin in a marriage to adultery, wife beating, and desertion. Most of us find it easy to refrain from those. Often, our virtue is lack of opportunity. Adultery isn't merely sleeping in someone else's bed. Adultery happens when you don't enjoy the bed you're in. Many good husbands and wives would never look at another man or touch another woman, but their sexual response to each other is dutiful or grudging. That's infidelity.

In other words, infidelity is not the actual act of intercourse with another person. It's the severing of relationship with your spouse. It's the putting him or her out of your life. That's because, like the prodigal son's debauchery, an act of adultery isn't the primary sin. It's the expression of a sin that's already been committed.

If you're really involved with your wife or husband, you won't have your mind on adultery; if the opportunity comes up, you won't be interested. Your heart's already taken.

It's much more difficult not to live adulterously, now that we know where adultery really begins. Many of us call ourselves married, but we're really "married singles." That means we don't fully belong to our loves. We just eliminate certain activities like dating others or staying out all night. We're living a single way of life with occasional limitations.

Let's Stamp Out Spouse Abuse

Like adultery, spouse abuse isn't always as obvious as it seems. A husband or wife may not be innocent, even if a spouse has never been touched. Emotional pain is a subtle, terrible thing.

Do you really listen to your spouses—all the time, not just when they talk about something interesting? When you stood at the altar, you didn't pledge to listen to specific topics. You promised to listen to *a person.*

The emotional pain of being ignored is as real as a migraine headache. The pain recurs again and again; it becomes a regular part of life. We can't say, "Well, that's the way I am. My partner will have to get used to it."

Wives can match their husbands blow for blow. More than a million husbands in the United States have been physically beaten by their wives. Many more have been tongue-lashed, and the tongue is a sharper weapon than any fist or pot.

When I say this to an audience, the women will tell me, "If you were married to my husband, you'd do it too!" But I didn't choose to marry those men. They did. Every wife has promised to love her husband without fail until death parts him from her.

Again, remember the prodigal son. Like adultery, tongue-lashing isn't the real sin. The real sin is that we haven't really decided to be married. We're living together with benefit of clergy, but that's not marriage.

Tongue-lashing happens because we store up hurts and grudges. Then we explode. We don't feel any particular obligation to hold ourselves back. It's a shame, but tongue-lashing is what works. What else can we do?

If you're thinking like that, you're asking the wrong question. Don't wonder if your anger is justified. Ask yourself—is your partner afraid of your tongue?

Cast off the right to vent your anger on your love. Don't say, "Well, I know it's not the nicest way to act. I wouldn't do it all the time, but I can only take so much." In those thoughts, the focus is on yourself, not on your love.

Whether you're examining your listening habits, your anger, or any other flaw, don't let yourself be deluded into saying, "Well, I don't do it that often. I'm not like you-know-who." Live for yourself and your own family. Living next door to the neighborhood ogre doesn't make your household any happier. We shouldn't compare ourselves to our spouses, either. Our spouses could be the greatest sinners in the world, but that doesn't reduce our sin in the slightest.

Your Love Is Your Life

Do you really belong to your spouses? We're not talking about whether you love them, whether you're nice or do all the right things. Those are good beginnings, but have you really put yourself in your partner's hands?

The issue is one of trust. Do you really believe your spouse loves you even more than you love yourself? That's what marriage is all about. As anniversaries go by, you should become two in one flesh.

Jesus gives us a great challenge, one in startling disagreement with the lessons of our me-first society. It's a challenge that asks you to give your all. It isn't enough for two independent souls to live side by side. When you're really married, you're no longer running your life. There are two of you inside, and you can no more ignore the needs and desires of your love than you can ignore yourself.

Of course, that perfect oneness is an ideal; most of us probably won't reach it in a lifetime. Instead, begin with a question: Do you really want your spouse to be your way of life?

Have you really decided to get married, or are you taking your portion of the marriage and just not living riotously? Remember, riotous living was not the prodigal son's sin. Refusing the relationship was his sin. Had he been married, he might have run to the store for his wife at midnight, but he would have wanted to live his own life.

How Much Love Is Enough?

No matter how good you are, it's a constant temptation to look toward your spouse instead: to test the waters, to see if he's up to this kind of relationship, if she's responding the way you think she should. Sometimes we all fear that our goodness will bounce off our loves like water off rocks. Then we'll be left alone, with nothing but stark reality.

Of course, behind all those fears is the unspoken judgment that we're better people than our spouses are. That isn't a good way to think. Ask yourselves: "Am I truly willing to be a full-fledged husband?" "Am I truly willing to be a full-fledged wife?" You mustn't decide what that means by watching your friends and neighbors. You must make your decision in accordance with your beloved's needs and your vocation from God himself.

Ask yourself, "Am I willing to accept a life of total love, not of being loved but loving?" If the answer is "yes," then look at yourself clearly. All of us are good people, yet we could all honestly say, "Why, I haven't been married at all. I've been doing married things, the right ones and very well, but I've been expecting rewards. I've been paying entirely too much attention to *me*."

That's when we truly become aware that we are sinners. When the prodigal son chose to be a sinner, to breach his relationship with his father, he was young and single. He used harlots as his sin of choice.

We might choose a job instead of a full love relationship. We might choose our children instead, or the television, a book, or friends. It isn't riotous living, but it's the product of sin just the same.

Now, there's nothing wrong with doing well at your job. There's nothing wrong with being a good parent, being well-read or talented. But don't be an "unwed" mother or father. Don't be married to the boss; be married to this lover you have chosen.

Hitting Rock Bottom

If we're to make the prodigal son's final choice of love over self-interest, we must first become disillusioned with ourselves. The prodigal son hit rock bottom. Then, the parable says, he "came to his senses." It didn't say he recognized debauchery was wrong, that he spent a lot of money on nothing, or that getting drunk wasn't that great, after all. The parable says, simply, that he came to his senses.

Then Scripture tells us what coming to his senses means. Immediately he said, "I will leave this place and go to my father." When he came to his senses, he realized who he was: his father's son.

You see, when we come to our senses, we do more than admit we ought to do better or we've been wrong. This coming to our senses concentrates on the other person, because our spouses are who we are. The prodigal was his father's son. You are your wife's husband; your husband's wife.

We all need to understand that there is no such thing as a full, independent life with relationships on the side. Because we are so intimately defined by our relationships, our coming to our senses makes us look outside ourselves. It makes you, a lover, look to your wife or husband.

We all have selfish impulses. I'm going to outline a few below. And we all need to look at them. Remember; admitting our sins gives us a true feeling of freedom.

Hopeless popular wisdom urges us to think these thoughts:

"I'm not getting enough from this marriage. Why should I stay with you?"

"You're not the person I thought you were. You aren't living up to my expectations. I have plans and dreams, and you're holding me back."

"Darling, I love you so much. But you have to love me, too."

"I'm not going to love you unless you love me. I'll measure out my love."

Or, in a nutshell, "This marriage is about my satisfaction. I married you for my own pleasure, and pleasure is what I expect."

The urge to excuse ourselves is almost irresistible. We want to say, "Oh, no, that's not really the way it is, because I give. I know I have to give, but he has to give too; she has to pull her load."

Again, comparisons only defeat our goal. The prodigal son didn't think about how much he owed his father. He simply faced the truth: he didn't belong to his father any more because he hadn't wanted to.

This parable wasn't a lesson in fairness. It was a lesson in recognition. When the prodigal left home, he stopped being a son, not because his father didn't want him, and not because his father deserved a better son. The breach was his own personal choice.

Resources for Reflection

We have to face that choice. How have we chosen? Are we married, really married, or are we single? Do we live as lovers, as husbands or wives? Or do we live as we wish, earnestly hoping our spouses can accept our decisions?

Consider These Questions Privately:

What thoughts and attitudes of mine keep me from living as a lover: a husband or a wife?

How does my marriage fit my life-style? What changes must I make so my life-style will fit my marriage?

Do I really believe I am a sinner? Why or why not?

Share These With Your Spouse:

What dream has this chapter inspired in me? (Be as idealistic as you choose.) How can you, my love, and I make this dream come true?

"Thank you, dear." Spend ten minutes writing a simple letter to your love, a letter of thanks for that delicate gift of trust. For instance, does she trust you to care about her problems? Does he let down his mask of masculine toughness to be tender during lovemaking? (Remember, focus on your own feelings. Be respectful; never judge your spouse.)

Finally, Let Us Invite God Into Our Marriages:

Dear Lord, let me stop dwelling within myself and live instead in relationship with my beloved spouse.

Let me be grateful for that fragile gift he (she) has given me: his (her) trust. Let me treat it with gentleness and return it in full measure.

Let me forgive my lover's wrongs and ask forgiveness for mine.

Like the prodigal son, let me be open to my sinfulness and yearn for your presence in my life. And like the prodigal, help me realize that we are born to be lovers, not lonely, loveless individuals.

Give me healing and the grace to grow in you. Amen.

CHAPTER 7

I Am Unworthy to Be Called Your Spouse

"This Son of Mine Was Dead and Has Come Back to Life."

(Lk 15:20–32)

Jesus spoke in parables, but he expects us to apply his lessons to our own lives. For us, the parable of the prodigal son might become the parable of the prodigal spouse. But the prodigal spouse may not be the husband who runs off with a young blonde, or the wife who heads down the highway with a salesman from Las Vegas.

Prodigal spouses may spend every night at home. They may be proud of their beautiful home, which both may work overtime to finance, and which they work hard to keep clean. And neither of them seriously thinks of looking for another mate.

But are they married? They may have stopped living as spouses to each other, just as the prodigal son decided not to be a son to his father.

Now, suppose a prodigal couple wanted to reconcile. How would they do it? They might make a catalog of sins: "I worked on the car when you wanted to talk"; "I let you work overtime so I could have a nice house." It would be a noble effort, but it wouldn't even touch their real problem. Their sin was more than a grocery list of mistakes. Their sin was choosing self-centered ways of life.

Instead, they should look to the parable of the prodigal son to find an ideal example of reconciliation. When the prodigal wanted to reconcile, he said, "Father, I have sinned against heaven and against you; I no longer deserve to be called your son." He didn't say, "Let me tell you all the rotten things I've done." He said only, "I no longer deserve to be called your son." He knew that his breach of relationship was more serious than his sleeping around, his drunkenness, or his carelessness with money.

Fairness Doesn't Work

In sin, we deny who we are by denying the loves in our lives. It's the normal, everyday sinfulness that says, "You are a man who's supposed to make me happy," or "You're not flesh of my flesh. You're here because I like what you do for me."

This focus on reciprocal fairness is a pagan standard that has nothing to do with God. We try to structure our marriages in terms of fairness. We say marriage is a 50–50 proposition. That sounds like an ideal compromise, but it's not God-centered and it simply doesn't work. What happens if that perfect balance slips a little? If it's 51–49, our favor, that probably feels all right to us. But what if it's 60–40? Do we think it's about time we got our share, or do we begin to feel a little guilty? What if the scale tips to 70–30, and we're giving the seventy? Do we say, "It's all right; we're just having a rough time right now"?

If we want to become real husbands and wives, we must reconcile with each other. We can't merely say, "I'm sorry I nag you," or "I'm sorry I close up." These are the expressions of sin, not the sin itself.

They're also easy to confess. Instead, we must be honest and trusting, both with ourselves and our lovers. We must say, "I have been unworthy to be called your husband"; "I have been unworthy to be called your wife."

Those are strong statements, but we need strong statements when we're speaking of sin. Sin is serious, and we have to challenge it face-to-face. As long as we resist saying, "I am unworthy to be called your spouse," we're refusing to come to our senses as sinners.

Sin Is Comparing

Sometimes we judge the success of a marriage by the level of unhappiness. We lie to ourselves, saying we're not doing too badly. We have carefully rationed interludes of romance: birthdays, anniversaries, and the like. Forget all that; it's organized misery.

The only way we should be single is in recognition of our sins. Even then, we must be thinking of how our sins harm our lovers. We must come to our senses and say, "I am a sinner." We can't pretend our sins don't exist. The only way to erase sin is to seek forgiveness.

The prodigal son didn't say, "It's normal for young men to sow their wild oats." Instead, he came to his senses and said, "I no longer deserve to be called your son."

We shouldn't say, "I don't deserve to be called your wife because of what I've done." Instead, we should realize, "I don't deserve to be called your wife because I have not *been* your wife, and because I have not allowed you to be my husband."

Sin is the keeping of ourselves to ourselves, whether it's expressed in reprehensible actions or even in praiseworthy ones.

"I am unworthy to be called your husband" may be hard to say. We might disagree: "I always support her, I don't drink up the paycheck." But have we been part of her heart?

We must say, "I am unworthy to be called your husband because I haven't been living for you. I've been living with myself, and you're nearby. I have taken my share of the marriage and squandered it."

Sin Is Reasonable

On your wedding day, you said your body wasn't yours anymore; it belonged to your beloved. Later on, you can't change your mind.

Saint Paul states very clearly in his first letter to the Corinthians that a husband's body belongs to his wife and a wife's body belongs to her husband. In 1 Corinthians 7:3–4, he says: "The husband must give to his wife what she has a right to expect, and so too the wife to her husband. The wife does not have authority over her own body, but the husband does; and in the same way, the husband does not have authority over his own body, but the wife does."

Yet we tend to think it's normal to deny sex to our lovers. We don't realize it's a form of theft. We must stop thinking that marriage is like living with a roommate. Marriage is a real integration. It is truly becoming one in mind, heart, and body.

With today's emphasis on careers and materialism, both husbands and wives are finding themselves too exhausted and even too busy to physically love each other. Doesn't that sound bizarre?

Go make love. It'll keep you out of trouble. The goodness of a passionate relationship spills over onto your friends, your neighbors, and especially your family. A passionate love relationship, for instance, fosters patience. When you're passionate toward each other and your son misbehaves, you'll say, "Ah, isn't that cute? He's just like his father." When you're not passionate toward each other, you'll shout, "You little brat! You're just like your *father.*"

Marriage is more than a piece of paper you signed one, ten, or fifty years ago. It's a sacrament, and your love, including physical love, is sacramental.

Am I Sorry? Or Am I Married?

"I'm sorry" means "I know my action was inappropriate and unworthy of a good person like me." It's a very self-centered awareness. "I'm sorry" can mean other things as well. It might mean, "You're very angry about what I did. I can't understand why; I don't think it was that bad. But you're not going to get over it until I say I'm sorry, so I'll say I'm sorry and get it over with." In this case, I really do want to reconcile, but I'm not admitting I'm wrong.

Or maybe "I'm sorry" means, "Gee, you're hurt and I don't like to see you hurt. I'm not hung up about saying I'm sorry, so if it makes you feel better, I'll say it." It's a remedy, like bringing you chicken broth when you're sick.

"I'm sorry" is a request. We're really asking our loves to say, "Ah, that's all right; forget it. I do things like that too."

That's why when we say, "I'm sorry," we're selling ourselves short, we're not facing the truth that we denied our relationship. We're only facing the symptom: what we did. If the prodigal son had behaved this way, he would have said, "It's not worthy of me to be sleeping around, so I won't do it anymore." That doesn't touch his sin, does it? His sin is against his relationship with his father. The prodigal could have stopped sleeping around and drinking; he could have worked very hard, earned back all the money he squandered, and sent it home to his father, and still he would not have come to his senses.

When we say, "I'm sorry," we're avoiding both the Gospel story and our own identities: those of husband or wife, not just man or woman. When our loves tell us, "I'm sorry," and we answer, "Well, that's all right," we're really saying, "Okay, let's be friends—until this happens again."

We have memory rights when we excuse that way; we're allowed to revive the old hurts whenever appropriate. This way, we can protect ourselves. We don't have to trust as much because, after all, our loves let us down before.

Most husbands and wives excuse instead of forgiving. It's the normal thing to do. It's also impersonal; it isn't open.

Excusing is too shallow an option for two good lovers. Instead, we must forgive and seek forgiveness. The prodigal son said, "I will go to my father and say: Father, I have sinned against heaven and against you; I no longer deserve to be called your son; treat me as one of your hired men." He didn't invite his father to excuse him. He knew better. He knew that "I'm sorry" so often means "I'm hurting too much for any more of this fighting, so let's make up."

We appear to be the heroes when we say "I'm sorry," but we're really looking for something: for peace in the home or for our lovers to be nice to us again. The prodigal son saw through all of it. He simply said, "I'm not worthy to be called your son. Treat me like a hired hand."

That's what it's like to come to our senses. Ordinarily we wouldn't see the need for it unless we'd dealt with a great trauma like physical adultery or beating. That's where we're wrong. The trauma of sin surrounds us every day.

Sin: Not What It's Cracked Up to Be

Most evil isn't glamorous. It's trite and everyday. Adolf Eichmann, for instance, lived quietly in Argentina for more than a decade. His neighbors probably never dreamed that this almost kindly looking man would eventually be hung as a mass murderer, condemned for the deaths of millions of Jews.

Take that idea one step further: imagine yourself living next door to such a criminal, thinking, "I'm not sure I agree, but my neighbor seems happy enough. Well, it must be all right, because there's nothing wrong with him."

As a society, we're obsessed with the desire to be like those around us. Why? Because watching others absolves us of having to try harder than they do. If all our friends are getting divorced, we reason that it must somehow be all right. If they dive into the computer every night or throw dishes at each other, we can decide that's normal, too.

"But everyone does it." The answer comes automatically. Other people work overtime. Other people don't date after marriage; they stay home like old married couples are supposed to. Other people don't hold hands and they don't feel too rotten when they insult each other in a fight.

Now, why did Jesus come to earth? He came to change everyone. There's no Gospel passage that says, "Thou shalt do as everyone else does." Nor did he say that when we appear before him in heaven, he'd reward us because "I was hungry, and you behaved like everyone else."

We're called to a better goal. Everyone else doesn't recognize that we're called to be higher than a blind average. Everyone else doesn't recognize sin. They think sin is the normal human condition; sin is to be expected.

No, it isn't. Sin is why Jesus came to die on the cross. God thinks sin was serious enough to merit the suffering and death of his only Son. He didn't just shrug his shoulders and say, "So this person didn't listen to his spouse, so what's new?"

Rightness is another reason Jesus came to earth. Being right kills a love relationship. Rightness doesn't justify inflicting hurt. The prodigal son didn't say, "After all, Father, I only took what was coming to me. It's my business how I spent it." He said, "I will go to my father and say: Father, I have sinned against heaven and against you; I no longer deserve to be called your son."

Hurry to Forgive

The parable of the prodigal son continues, "So he left the place and went back to his father." His father was standing a long way off, looking, hoping, yearning. The father didn't say, "I hope my kid comes to his senses and knows what he's done to me."

A husband and wife must have that same yearning to embrace. We must also be looking from a long way off, watching and hoping for that first sign that our spouses are seeking forgiveness. When our loves try to reconcile, we too often make them go through their paces: "I want her to realize this is serious"; "I want to make sure he knows how much he hurt me."

The prodigal's father cast all that aside. The parable says, "While he was still a long way off, his father saw him and was moved with pity. He ran to the boy, clasped him in his arms and kissed him." At the first sign of his son, the father was overwhelmed with eagerness to reach his son. He didn't test the waters; the slightest sign that his son was responsive again was enough for him.

Do we do likewise, or do we cling to our hurts and our righteousness? We test our loves' sincerity, thinking, "He has to earn his way back. She has to prove she's reformed." That's not forgiveness.

The father didn't exact any fee from his son. The father was simply drawing him in with love, hoping against hope they could reconcile. Even though the boy saw his father's openness, he didn't feel extremely sure because he was so aware of his sinfulness. He insisted on saying what he'd come to say: "Father, I have sinned against heaven and against you. I no longer deserve to be called your son."

But his father ignored the past. He hugged that boy and leaped up and down for joy. He shouted, "Come on, everyone, get him a robe, get him a ring, put sandals on his feet, kill the best beef on the farm. Let's have a party!"

He wasn't rejoicing because his son was going to change or because he was penitent. The father rejoiced simply because he could touch him. When our loves seek our forgiveness, our response must be the same. It can in no way, shape, or form be judgmental or superior.

The Long Memory

When our loves seek forgiveness, we must pledge to wipe out the memory of their wrongs. As long as we remember those wrongs, we have not yet forgiven. We may be virtuous enough never to bring them up, but their memory can poison our love. When our loves ask for forgiveness, our response in joy is to reaffirm our relationship by saying, "My beloved wife..." or "My beloved husband...." What we remember from now on is his humility, her goodness.

This is a key point. Too often, we give ourselves great credit for being long-suffering. We're long-suffering, though, because we have such long memories.

If you want to know just how forgiving you are, ask yourselves, "What do I remember?" Do we remember our own goodness in forgiving so graciously, or do we recall with wonder our loves' humility? Do we recall the sin? If we recall the sin, our spouses can never be touched by the forgiveness. We could say, "Well, I'm not holding it against him"; "I'm not using it against her." If we're keeping it alive in memory, though, it's more important than our relationship.

We're called to give total forgiveness, not lukewarm excuses and apologies. We are called to remember the sinner's seeking of reconciliation, not the sin. The prodigal's father illustrates this beautifully. He didn't ask, "Are you going to be a good boy now? Are you going to settle down? Did you learn a lesson?"

The father did say, "This son of mine was dead and has come back to life." With that statement, he wiped out the boy's denial and reestablished their relationship. A truly forgiving wife or husband says the same: "Yes, dear, you are my spouse. I could never let you go. I'm so glad to have you back."

That celebration marks not your love's sin, but your renewed belonging. It rejoices: "How good you are in wanting to belong to me. I thought I had lost you. But you are my husband (wife). You're so wonderful, I'm so lucky to have you. Come, let us be merry, let everyone know: not that I who have been offended have finally been justified, but that you are so good, and my belonging to you is precious to me." When we forgive like this, we follow Jesus' teaching and become true lovers.

Sin Unseen

This parable of the prodigal son prompts us to think of a few prodigals we know and hope our spouses get the point. We don't really apply it to ourselves. We don't realize the Lord is seeking to teach us through this story.

Perhaps we mentally cast ourselves in the role of the son who stayed. The older boy wasn't all that gracious, but we might have real empathy for his position.

We shouldn't feel sorry for the second son. He had no more relationship with his father than his brother did. Both boys were sinners. Both boys were living their own ways of life, centered around themselves. One of them expressed it in a spectacular way by going to a far-off country and doing all sorts of extravagant things. The other boy looked good on the outside, but where was he in relationship with his father? Obviously, not very close, since he never shared his father's pain over the other boy's absence.

If the older son had been in relationship with his father, he would have known what the younger boy meant to his father and he would have rejoiced for his father's sake. But he was thinking only of himself for all those years when his brother was gone.

The second son had equal need to go to his father for forgiveness. He might have said, "I am no longer worthy to be called your son, not because I live riotously but because I don't understand you. Otherwise I could not be so cold and indifferent, so wrapped up in myself."

There are plenty of second sons in our marriages. Maybe our spouses do more "bad" things, but we are equally guilty of failing to love. If we've realized this, we can go to our spouses and say, "My beloved, I am unworthy to be called your spouse, not because I've done anything, but because I haven't belonged to you. I belong to myself. I haven't been responding to you, my dear. I've really been responding to my own sense of self."

Remember, in the parable of the prodigal son, the father never gave any grudging replies like "Oh, it's all right," or "I'm glad that's over." When his younger son came to him, he merely reaffirmed the relationship. That's true forgiveness.

Accepting Forgiveness

We should be eager to seek such forgiveness ourselves. First, of course, we must search inside for our sins. One area we all overlook is the memories of our spouses' failings. These memories become our own failing; that of cold-heartedness. If we are guilty of this, we must say, "My beloved, I have been remembering your failings. I am unworthy to be called your wife (husband)."

It isn't easy to accept our spouses' forgiveness. It's easier to keep concentrating on ourselves. Even after we've been forgiven, it's normal to wish we could make up for the hurt. Don't do that.

After your love forgives you, you must simply rejoice at being accepted back. You should concentrate on your love's acceptance, rather than on the sins you've committed. Focusing on your sins may be virtuously self-punishing, but it's also self-centered. Besides, you can never really make up for the pain you caused.

You can avoid this self-defeating trap by welcoming the goodness of your lover. The more you can concentrate on how good she is, how forgiving he is, the more you'll be able to accept that forgiveness. If you look to yourself and try to make up for the past, you'll prevent your own healing. Furthermore, scorekeeping is a subtle method of avoiding relationship. It's a way of canceling sin, not admitting it as a way of life and accepting your lover's goodness.

Often, we don't live in relationship with our loves because we think "husband" and "wife" are job descriptions, like "homemaker" or "diplomat." That's not true. Being a spouse is not an occupation, it's a relationship with another human being.

It doesn't matter how many children you have by each other or how long you've lived in the same house. Only your choice of each other on a daily basis makes you husband and wife. So does a constant seeking of forgiveness, because we are all sinners. We will continue to be sinners, even after we are reconciled. Marriage is a constant offering of forgiveness as well.

Forgive Me? What Did I Do?

You can't offer forgiveness to someone who doesn't ask for it. The father couldn't search out the youngest son and say, "You're forgiven." He didn't know he'd sinned. Likewise, you can't go to your spouses and say, "You are forgiven." They'll ask, "What for?" But when forgiveness is sought, it has to be given generously, as the Lord teaches us.

Jesus said, "Do not judge, and you will not be judged; do not condemn, and you will not be condemned; forgive, and you will be forgiven. Give, and there will be gifts for you: a full measure, pressed down, shaken together, and overflowing, will be poured into your lap; because the standard you use will be the standard used for you" (Lk 6:37, 38).

Ask yourselves: "Can I stand before my heavenly Father and say, "Father, I ask nothing more than the forgiveness I have given my spouse"? Don't worry about whether you forgive others. Concentrate on your spouse; that's where it all begins.

Jesus has placed himself in our hands. We really are the body of Jesus; that's not just a nice theological notion. We have been called to express him, his view of life, and his way of living. We do this by the way we live. Specifically, we do this by the way we live with our husbands and wives.

The Lord says forgiveness is part of the kingdom of heaven. When my beloved experiences that goodness within me, the kingdom of heaven becomes real to him or her. The believability of God and God's way of life is in your hands. Please, search within yourselves to discover how you are a sinner and then spend some real time with each other and seek forgiveness, regardless of whether your spouse seeks forgiveness, too.

Beloved, I Have Sinned

You may be thinking, "How can anyone just presume we're in sin and need to be forgiven?" That very question indicates that we're in the position of the older son. We think because we've been doing the right things, we don't have any sin. We're fooling ourselves. We know that someday we must stand before our Father and say, "I am a sinner."

It's not presumptuous or unreasonable to say that each of us as husband or wife really needs to seek forgiveness, not just in the sense of "Well, I have these little defects," but in the sense of "I am a sinner before God. I am unworthy to be called your spouse because of my whole attitude; because of my whole lack of belonging; because I have lived my own way instead of putting myself in your hands."

Maybe you're willing but you're tempted to tell your spouse, "Okay, I'll go first, you go second." Don't; you're not ready.

If you're really conscious that you're a sinner, you're completely unconscious of your spouse as a sinner. It works in reverse as well: the more conscious you are of your spouse's sin, the less conscious you are of your own. If you're still focusing on your spouse's sin, you are in no state to seek forgiveness, and maybe you should say that. You could say, "Help me, beloved. Let us go to the Lord together to soften the hardness of my heart. How could I be so indifferent to my own sins and so conscious of yours?"

Resources for Reflection

This is a wonderful opportunity to discover each other, to come to your senses. As soon as you finish this chapter, go to your beloved and say, "My beloved, I have sinned against heaven and against you." Then specify the ways. General confessions aren't much help.

You should describe the specific ways you've established your independent lifestyle; how you've shown your indifference; how you've chosen self over your beloved; how you really haven't been married.

If I'm a sinner, I need forgiveness. The more I recognize I am a sinner, the more unworthy I become in my own eyes and the less conscious I become of my spouse's growth—or lack of growth—toward God. I need forgiveness. I need to belong again. I need to come to my senses; I need that awakening to be truly recognized, not only by myself, but by that person I have pledged myself to.

All too often, we'll ask for forgiveness, then add, "Now it's your turn. What? You're not going to say anything? Well, I take mine back." We must seek a healing, not a trade-off. This is not an event where we come together to confess to each other. Here, each of us must come to his senses alone.

Go ask forgiveness of each other, not next week or next fight; do it right now. This reconciliation can be a real moment of grace. It can be a profound occasion for love. Read the questions below and search inside yourself to discover how you have sinned against God and against your spouse. Pray together for the grace to seek forgiveness and to freely forgive.

How Have I Sinned Against God and Against My Beloved Husband or Wife?

- Have I believed the purpose of my marriage is to make my lover happy? Or have I thought this marriage is for my happiness instead?
- Have I been living my own life-style, expecting my spouse to fit into my demands?
- Am I sensitive to my spouse's hurts and needs? Or do I react only to myself?
- Have I kept my lover out of my heart, not allowing my husband, my wife, to truly be part of me?
- Have I withheld my attention and approval?
- Have I withheld my body?
- Have I yielded to the temptation to hurt with words?
- Have I insisted I was right instead of working toward a solution in love?
- Have I insisted on fairness in our marriage instead of unbounded love?
- Am I more conscious of my love's sins than I am my own? Have I refused to forget my love's failings? Do I keep them alive in my heart to use as weapons?
- Have I been imitating the life-styles of "everyone else" instead of imitating Christ?
- Have I made our family meals a real time of sharing? Do I show my love for our children?

A Prayer for Grace:

Lord, let me truly come to an understanding of my own sinfulness. Help me see myself as I really am, not hidden behind a mask of pride, fear, and self-interest.

I want to ask my spouse to forgive me for denying our relationship, for not living as a lover. Give me courage; help me to be sincere.

Help me to not expect my spouse to ask for forgiveness in return. Give me the grace to understand that each person grows at different rates. Let me wait lovingly and patiently until my spouse is ready.

Should my spouse ask forgiveness of me, help me to give it wholeheartedly. Let my love's failings be wiped forever from my mind so we can live together in joy.

Thank you for the wonderful goodness of my spouse. Let us both rejoice in your gift of healing; let us always see each other through your generous and all-forgiving eyes.

Be with us as we celebrate Your love for us and our love for each other. Amen.

The Reconciliation:

Your own words might be similar to this:

"My beloved, I have sinned against God and against you. I can see how wrong, how selfish, I've been. I've been living with myself, not with you, dear.... (Add specifics.)

"My sin has isolated me from your love, and I can see how lonely I've made both of us. I want to truly live as your husband (wife). I love you so much. Please forgive me."

When your spouse seeks forgiveness, your response might be similar to this:

"I forgive you, my beloved. You are such a good, loving person. I thank God for giving you to me and for bringing us closer to each other right now.

"I want to belong to you, too. I love you so much; you are the most important treasure I have. I'm so glad I have you, because my life would be empty if you weren't here. I want to celebrate, to tell everyone how wonderful you are and how much you mean to me. I will always remember your goodness and love in coming to me today. I will never forget it."

CHAPTER 8

My Talent Is Loving You

"A Man...Summoned His Servants and Entrusted His Property to Them."

(Mt 25:14–30)

The scribes and Pharisees provoked Jesus to some marvelous retorts. These were more than snappy comebacks, though, they were lessons. After one fierce debate with the Pharisees, Jesus sat on the Mount of Olives and told his disciples about the Kingdom of Heaven:

> It is like a man about to go abroad who summoned his servants and entrusted his property to them. To one he gave five talents, to another two, to a third one, each in proportion to his ability. Then he set out on his journey. The man who had received the five talents promptly went and traded with them and made five more. The man who had received two made two more in the same way. But the man who had received one went off and dug a hole in the ground and hid his master's money. Now a long time afterwards, the master of those servants came back and went through his accounts with them. The man who had received the five talents came forward bringing five more. "Sir," he said, "you entrusted me with five talents; here are five more that I have made." His master said to him, "Well done, good and trustworthy servant; you have shown you are trustworthy in small things; I will trust you with greater; come and join in your master's happiness." Next the man with the two talents came forward. "Sir," he said, "you entrusted me with two talents; here are two more that I have made." His

> master said to him, "Well done, good and trustworthy servant; you have shown you are trustworthy in small things; I will trust you with greater; come and join in your master's happiness." Last came forward the man who had the single talent. "Sir," said he, "I had heard you were a hard man, reaping where you had not sown and gathering where you had not scattered; so I was afraid, and I went off and hid your talent in the ground. Here it is; it was yours, you have it back." But his master answered him, "You wicked and lazy servant! So you knew that I reap where I have not sown and gather where I have not scattered? Well, then, you should have deposited my money with the bankers, and on my return I would have got my money back with interest. So now, take the talent from him and give it to the man who has the ten talents. For to everyone who has will be given more, and he will have more than enough; but anyone who has not, will be deprived even of what he has. As for this good-for-nothing servant, throw him into the darkness outside, where there will be weeping and grinding of teeth."
>
> MATTHEW 25:14–30

What Are My Talents?

God himself has given us our talents. He generously asks us to use these investments for his people's sake; most specifically, for those people we have chosen to marry.

First, of course, we must realize what capabilities, skills, and graces almighty God has given each of us, specifically as husbands and wives.

Some of us may say, "My talent is in accounting, or finance, or…." But many of us don't believe we have a special talent to love, to be generous or tender or forgiving. Oh, we can summon up that behavior if we try hard enough, but it's work.

However, if we want to live as whole, healed people, we must recognize that God has given each of us a marvelous capability to love our spouses. In 1 Corinthians, Saint Paul tells us that we can do it. Paul wrote, "None of the trials which have come upon you is more than a human being can stand. You can trust that God will not let you be put to the test beyond your strength, but with any trial will also provide a way out by enabling you to put up with it" (1 Cor 10:13).

Now, let's look at our resources from our spouses' point of view. Sometimes we're not good judges when it comes to ourselves. Ask, "Why did my spouse choose me? What was it my partner saw in me that caused a lifetime commitment?"

Some of you will say, "Oh, I suppose I could name a few things." Now, stop insulting yourself. Your lover wasn't that naive. Your spouse saw good qualities in you and was so taken by that goodness that he or she promised to live with you until death. You don't make promises like that lightly.

What is inside you, as a person, that caused your spouse to say, "Will you be mine?" Start thinking of the words that have been said over the years, especially the compliments you don't believe.

One reason we disbelieve compliments is that we've never been taught to think kindly of ourselves. In this culture, criticism is often the only acceptable opinion of self.

Compliments are also challenges. If a compliment has been accepted, for example, for gentleness, then the partner will have to live up to it. Even though it destroys us inside, we find it easier to say, "No, I'm really not gentle (considerate/funny/ beautiful/sexy). I just was this time."

Always Inferior

We humans always find people who are better in one area or another.

"She's so patient. Compared to her, I'm a shrew." "He's such a wonderful person. He must be closer to God than I am." How destructive to think that way.

It simply doesn't matter how we rate compared to others. We're missing the Lord's lesson if we say, "Well, I'm not as good as my mother was with my father," or "I'm not as good as the guy down the block." The Lord has indeed invested in us. Earthshaking talents often look normal, even humdrum.

How about the gift of time? We have time; maybe not as much as we'd like, but we do have it. We each have a certain number of hours per day to spend as we will. There is lunchtime and coffee break time. There is unwind-from-the-day time and recreation time. We also have double time; that is, when we're doing things we don't have to think about. Housekeeping chores like taking out the trash keep our hands busy, but our minds are free to think, to rest, or to share with our mates.

We also have the time that we waste. How many of those moments you call "your own" are your lover's, and how many belong to you?

Too often, we'll measure our marriages against an ideal relationship. The result is wishful thinking, feelings of inferiority, and despair. The Lord didn't ask for such comparisons. In the parable of the talents, he didn't differentiate between the servant with five talents and the servant with two. All that mattered was the servant's stewardship.

So, examine an ordinary day. How much did you think about your lover today? With affection and eagerness, that is? "If I don't call, I'll have hell to pay" doesn't count. That's not thinking about your spouse. That's self-preservation.

Perhaps we call our mates to ask what's in the mail, what our friends had to say, and so on. Our mouths are moving, but we aren't really talking to each other. We're being safe and amiable. But let's be lovers. Let's use our time during the day to plan how we'll be more effective with each other that night.

Time Costs More Than Money

Do we value time together as our most precious commodity? How many hours do we spend worrying about our lack of time together? In contrast, how many hours do we spend worrying about the disposal of our income? We probably spend considerably less time saying, "Dear, when are we going to sit down and talk tonight?" and much more time saying, "What are we going to do about the orthodontist?" or "Dear, how much is in your wallet?"

We all know people who just can't handle money. Some of us are that way ourselves. These people get in terrible binds because the money just seeps away from them. Most of us are like that when it comes to time, not because we lack natural talent but because we lack attention, self-discipline, and even knowledge. Many of us don't realize how many wonderful things our time can buy.

It's much more important to budget your time than your dollars. Get out paper and pencil; write it all down. How much time do you have on an average day? How much of that time is used productively? How much of it is spent sitting on the sofa, dreading to do the chores? How much time is spent pursuing hobbies and outside commitments you "ought" to love, but in reality make you feel weary and burdened?

What are your weekends like? That's when we're together the most, but we don't do well with each other on weekends because we cram them full of activities that aren't family activities at all. They're merely entertainments the family attends, such as the amusement park, the beach, or a swimming party. No wonder our weekends aren't warm and peaceful and happy. We spend our precious hours rushing from one activity to the next and wondering if we're having fun yet.

We may rub shoulders all weekend, but we don't specifically plan how to be with each other as persons. Don't let that weekend slip by. It's a wonderful opportunity to really be present to each other.

My Time Is Your Time

How many of our evening chores could have been done earlier in the day? Do we spend our valuable time together reading the mail, paying the bills, or writing the grocery list?

We have to stop squandering the time the Lord gives us to spend with each other. There isn't that much of it. We're probably awake about sixteen hours a day, but we only have between four and six hours with our spouses.

How much of that time is poured into dry ground because we haven't thought ahead and put each other first? Time is critical if we're going to use our God-given talents for our lovers' well-being.

All too often, though, we think, "How am I going to spend *my* time?" Sometimes, even time with our lovers is really spent for our own sake.

Our gestures may be self-motivated. Many spouses will say, "Look, honey. I know you're upset. Let's go out tomorrow evening; we'll spend some time together..." The unspoken finishing line to that phrase is "...because you've been looking so unhappy and I want to see you smile," or is it more like "...because when you get a break, I get a break too"?

In the latter example, the spouse is only placating. It isn't time spent together on the agenda, but a peaceful relationship that's uppermost.

The Fifteen-Minute Lover

We need to reevaluate our time in minutes, not in hours. How many hours' worth of minutes do we throw away every day?

We treat our minutes with the same indifference as we do pennies. How about that extra free fifteen minutes just before supper? Do we use it to phone friends or take a nap? Or is it the husband's time to sneak off and read the paper?

But when you add fifteen minutes here, fifteen minutes there, and fifteen minutes somewhere else, you've counted almost an hour of the evening. We just fritter away the time we could spend together. The whole evening ends up lost, as far as loving each other is concerned.

We must decide to prioritize our time for each other. That doesn't mean adopting a rigid schedule: "Seven o'clock's our time together, son, so run along. We'll set that broken arm at seven-thirty."

We should value our time, though, the way we do our money.

Businesses succeed or fail because they follow the principle "Time is money." Time is also love. If a business used "Time is money" as earnestly as we use "Time is love," would that business be among the Fortune 500, or would it be bankrupt?

My Talent Is Tenderness

How do you spend your tenderness? Some men may have raised your eyebrows. "Tenderness? That's my wife's department."

Maybe you only have one share of tenderness and she has five. That's all right. We're not asking how you spend five; we're asking how you spend one.

Wives, be careful not to use the same argument: "I'm much more tender than he is, so I relax. I don't need to improve." Are you sure? You may be spending five shares of tenderness, but you have fifty. Don't ask whether you're giving more tenderness than he is. Ask whether you're giving the level of tenderness the Lord has invested in you.

How tender is your relationship with each other? Now, don't compare it with any other couple; compare it with your own capabilities. How tender are you right now? Maybe this isn't a time that calls for tenderness, but that's all right. The Lord didn't say, "Invest the money when the opportunity arises." He said, "Invest the money." Furthermore, when you do invest, you get the interest, and the Lord's return is a hundredfold.

When we don't think much about each other, we react to one another instead of responding. Suppose you went home after work or greeted your spouse at the door with a different attitude: a determination to give every bit of tenderness you have tonight. You may not have all that much. That's all right; just give what you have.

Do we ever really resolve to be tender, not just for some special occasion but because I have this tenderness to spend? How thoroughly do we examine what we've given, and how frequently do we focus on what we're getting? Especially when pain's involved, it's easy to measure out the first by weighing the second.

A woman, for instance, might think, "He isn't very tender, so I don't have to be tender with him. Even if I was, he wouldn't understand it." But maybe he isn't tender because he hasn't experienced much tenderness.

If It Doesn't Earn Money, It Can't Be Talent

Do you ever smother your God-given talents with a cash-flow mentality? You could have natural talent for woodworking, ceramics, flower decoration, or any number of skills you don't pursue.

Every one of us has talents that go unused. "I'd love to do that," we tell ourselves. "Too bad I couldn't make a living at it." Evidently the Lord didn't think we needed regular income before he gave us a loan. Why can't we use it?

He also didn't say we should wait for others' approval. He said we should use the gifts he gave us.

Let's examine the talents we do have. What would we do well, if only we had the time? What do other people seem to like about us? What do we think is fun?

Maybe your talent is writing poetry.

"Yes, but I could never get it published."

Don't worry about that; write for your spouse, your beloved.

Ask yourself: why are our talents worth less if we spend them on our spouses and children? Let's' forget how much we're "not worth" and start spending ourselves.

In order to do so, we must take another look at our expenditures of time. By the way, don't be comforted because everyone else is wasting time, too. Let's just ask ourselves: how much of our time is spent doing things that are not only unnecessary but also harmful?

Children can give a sterling example of how our best efforts can be misguided. We spend a lot of time chauffeuring them from activity to activity. That's bad for them. Dance class, scouts, sports, and music lessons all round out our children's education—and encourage them to be independent, unloving people. By keeping our kids in constantly moving cars, going from "experience" to "experience," we're teaching them a strong lesson about values. We're telling them these experiences are more important than the people in their lives. We're making them value things over people.

When we fill our children's evenings with activities, we're institutionalizing them. We're turning the home into a taxi stand and building up a peer group mentality. Has anyone noticed? Today, kids are socializing with one another at age nine the way we did when we were fifteen. They don't have even an older child's knowledge of how to stay out of trouble.

This chauffeured culture isn't any healthier for Mom and Dad. We shouldn't have time to chauffeur our kids. We should be too busy creating a home and family to spend that much time in the car.

Sex Is a Talent, Too

Some of us don't realize our sexuality is a God-given talent. Others wish our spouses would wake up to that fact. I honestly believe most couples fail to invest their sexual talents far more than they fail to be tender, forgiving, or generous.

When most of us ask, "How well do I use my sexual talents?" we think of frequency. We reduce sex to intercourse, and that's a problem.

If we believe that a husband and wife must communicate intimately with each other on a daily basis—and I strongly support that statement—it must include physical intimacy as well as verbal. They must set aside time when they are free to experience each other physically. And I don't mean at eleven-thirty or twelve at night. Whether that is expressed ultimately in intercourse is not the point.

If a couple does take time to physically experience each other, intercourse will probably happen more frequently. One reason it doesn't happen is that it's unavailable. We're too busy.

God did, indeed, give us sex as a resource. Are we spending it or are we hiding it in the ground? Are we using our full capacity for sexual experience of each other?

Again, I'm not speaking of frequency but of passion. Physical communication is like verbal: it can be intimate or superficial. A couple may talk to each other every night, but perhaps they're just chattering. Are you making love, or are you engaging in sexual chatter?

Some of you will say, "What we have is quality rather than quantity." Quality is good, but this can be a means of avoiding each other. If you applied this phrase to conversation, it could create a pretty chilly relationship: "Find a significant topic, dear, and I'll talk to you."

When you were married, you gave your bodies to each other so you could be healed of your hurts and aloneness. If a husband has to say to himself, "I wonder if she's in the mood tonight," her body is not his. If a wife has to figure out ways to seduce him, his body is not hers.

Again, I want to emphasize that we're not just talking about the completed act. Why don't you set aside fifteen minutes to half an hour each day for physical intimacy? Perhaps just to go into your room and experience each other, skin to skin. Now, maybe "nothing will happen." Isn't that a terrible statement? All sorts of things can happen: in awareness, in sensitivity, and tenderness. Yet we seem to think if we merely grow in love, our lovemaking has failed.

Compliments Are Free

To fully invest in our marital relationship, we should use all the resources at our disposal, and compliments are a powerful resource.

Even if we think we don't notice details, we're probably better at it than we suppose. Do we turn our observations into compliments, or do we keep them hidden from our loves?

Do we note only the negative things? Some of us have been taught that it's "discerning" to see flaws, but it's a weakness to pay too much attention to goodnesses. That attitude smothers our hearts.

Do you give your partners a full measure of compliments? Mind you, I didn't say, "compliments that are deserved." It's arrogant to judge whether someone deserves a compliment. The question is, rather, "Right now, do I have a compliment in me?"

We may be afraid to offer compliments. But if we hold back our compliments, our spouses will think we don't care. We might also hold back our compliments for fear that praise will make our partner impossible to live with. A person can actually be overflowing with false pride because deep and sincere praise—backed by understanding and real affection—are lacking.

Because we've been trained to criticize, it's tremendously difficult for many of us to give compliments. It's even tougher to accept a compliment. Most of us will squirm every which way to dodge praise. "Well, thank you, but...," we begin, "...but I'm not really pretty." "But this is just an old shirt." "But I'm not a forgiving person."

We must understand what's happening behind the scenes when our lovers cast off our heartfelt praise. They may laugh or say, "You don't mean that," or even, "What do you want?" Have patience. Again, the Lord doesn't say, "Spend your resources when they'll be accepted." He says, "Spend your resources."

There is nothing like praise. Our highest call, in relationship with our Father in heaven, is to praise him. How can we praise God unless we praise our spouses? Further, God is really more pleased when we praise the daughter or son he gave us than when we praise him directly.

Now, let's ask ourselves specifically, "Do I give my spouse the praise I have inside? Do I give it all?" We humans tend to hold back; to give praise only when it's appropriate, when we're feeling warm and affectionate, when we've been complimented, or when someone has earned it.

That's wonderful. Now, is it all you have? Is there any more in you? If there is, spit it out. Don't keep it to yourself; it's just rusting in there. Keeping a compliment inside doesn't help anyone, unless you're praising yourself.

Our Talents Are for Eternity

One of our greatest talents is our desire to love each other. We do, indeed, wish to put each other first. The difficulties we face in doing so are just that: difficulties. They're not failures. We can overcome our difficulties with prayer, with soul-searching, and by keeping our eyes wide open to the love-killing lessons society has taught us.

The toughest part is facing the fact that, often, we have to give up something in order to have love instead. What makes it tough is that we don't realize how marvelous and fulfilling that love will be. Our present life seems pretty attractive, even if it is somewhat hollow.

Decide what kind of relationship you'd like to have, then go for it. Don't worry about looking back; there are better roads ahead.

That brings us back to the subject of time management. In order to love each other, we simply have to spend time with each other, and that may mean cutting something out of our schedules and changing our agendas.

Who, really, is more important? Your spouse, or your friends, coworkers, fellow volunteers, or children's sports coaches? You didn't marry those people. The Lord is not going to ask how passionate you were about them. Nor will he ask you if you did the laundry, the ironing, the lawn, or the house repairs after you came home from work. He might ask, though, why you didn't put your feet up for an hour after dinner so you'd be enthusiastic about your lover.

We all have beautiful excuses about time, but they aren't cast in stone. Our problem is that we don't want to find the time: not unless it fits into our current schedules.

That's when we have to cut loose from that love-smothering focus on self; to trust our spouses to make us happy, just as we did when we were first married. We must also trust God, who truly wants us to be happy. He's offering us a way; let's take it.

Resources for Reflection

Let's list the talents God gave us. Let's add all the skills, big and little, that we now realize are ours. Take every talent, one by one, and ask, "Am I using every bit of it for my beloved?" not "Am I doing well?" "Is she satisfied?" "Is he content?" and not "Would he understand if I suddenly did all those things?" "Would she be shocked if I became that full-fledged?"

"How much am I keeping to myself? Am I using my talent for the sake of my beloved, or am I just letting it rust, maybe to disappear in bitterness because I haven't been able to live up to my potential?"

Let's ask ourselves if we're ready to stand before the Lord and say, "You gave me this talent of listening. You gave me five shares of it and I have spent five shares. You gave me two shares of sexuality and I spent it all. You gave me five units of understanding and I poured it all out. Now I have ten because you returned it in abundance."

I have faith in you; you are truly good people. Even now, as you spend your talent of hope, remember the Master's promise: "Well done, my son; well done, my daughter. You have shown you are trustworthy in small things; I will trust you with greater; come and join in your master's happiness. To everyone who has will be given more, and he will have more than enough."

Consider These Questions Privately:

What qualities prompted my spouse to spend his/her life with me? What compliments has my spouse given me that I just pass off?

Make a time budget. How much time do I have with my spouse? What can I make more efficient, shuffle around, or omit entirely to give me more time with my lover?

What talents have I been given for my beloved's sake? There are at least three kinds:

Spiritual (like kindness or patience)...

Enriching (like creativity, intelligence, or humor)...

Uplifting (like lightheartedness, optimism, or sexuality)...

Do I use each of these talents for the benefit of my beloved? What can I do to use each one to the utmost?

Share These Questions With Your Spouse:

What compliments do I give you, dear, that you don't seem to believe?

I want to spend more time with you, dear. I'm willing to do these things... so we can spend more time together.

My beloved, I yearn to spend more time being intimate with you physically. Why don't we do the following...?

Finally, Let Us Invite God Into Our Marriages:

Loving Father, it is hard for me to truly believe that You have given me so much goodness. Please help me appreciate all the talents you have given me, especially the ones I don't yet see. Let me use these every day, to the utmost, for the sake of my beloved spouse. Let me fill his/her life with warmth and joy and trust. When I believe my talents are lacking, gently remind me that, when I have spent all the talents I have, you will fill me with so many more. Thank you for loving me so much. Amen.

CHAPTER 9

We Are One

"Who Among You Delights in Life,
Longs for Time to Enjoy Prosperity?"
(1 PET 3:8–12)

Peter's first letter really was written for you. You'll find it just as relevant today as it was to the early Christians, who were also bearing "all sorts of trials" (1 Pet 1:6).

> *Finally: you should all agree among yourselves and be sympathetic; love the brothers, have compassion and be self-effacing. Never repay one wrong with another, or one abusive word with another; instead, repay with a blessing. That is what you are called to do, so that you inherit a blessing. For who among you delights in life,*
> *longs for time to enjoy prosperity?*
> *Guard your tongue from evil,*
> *your lips from any breath of deceit.*
> *Turn away from evil and do good, seek peace and pursue it.*
> *For the eyes of the Lord are on the upright,*
> *his ear turned to their cry.*
> *But the Lord's face is set against those who do evil.*
>
> 1 PETER 3:8–12

Here, Peter is referring to the whole church. That's a lot to deal with, so let's take it down to the little church: the family. More specifically, we'll see how Peter's words apply to the husband-wife relationship.

Delights in Life, Longs for Time to Enjoy Prosperity?

We certainly don't hesitate to wish for happy lives. As for prosperity, we'd probably translate that somewhat differently from the way Peter would. The key to this prosperity of peace, happiness, and goodwill is found in the next two lines:

Guard your tongue from evil,
your lips from any breath of deceit.

These verses make sense. None of us would defend the virtues of malicious conversation and deceitful talk. Maliciousness and deceit are so repugnant to us, in fact, that we don't apply them to ourselves. It's far more comfortable to see malice "out there" in our coworkers and neighbors.

Maliciousness can crop up when we're hurt, especially if we've evolved a lifelong attitude of defensiveness. It's a way of protecting ourselves first—before someone else runs us down. It can arise when we're called to change but are afraid to let go of the safe and comfortable. It happens frequently when envy gets the best of us.

Personally, I find it difficult to admit I have malice. I don't fall into the trap of claiming I'm perfect, but I do tend to write off the bad things I say: "Well, sometimes I sound malicious, but most of the time it's provoked" or "Maybe I was malicious, but I wasn't nearly as bad as he was."

But Peter didn't tell me, "Guard your tongue from evil unless you're provoked." Nor did he say, "Make sure your deceit isn't as bad as the other guy's."

Silence Can Be Golden

In most marriages, there is usually a silent partner and a speaking partner. The roles can switch any time; one spouse might be the silent partner on politics, while the other is silent on religion. That silent partner may fail to talk, but keeping silent curbs the tendency toward a malicious tongue.

Yet we humans excuse ourselves for thoughtlessly blurting out our problems. After all, we say, we're not "holding it inside." Perhaps you've had a tough day at work, and you just can't wait to get home and vent your feelings. Wait a minute. Maybe it would be better to wait until tomorrow night, when you have a little more perspective.

Maybe you're the type of person who stores up the frustrations of the day until your spouse comes home. You're not on a personal attack. You're just venting what's wrong with your life.

We've all behaved that way at some time, haven't we? It's not that we're mean, it's that we can hardly resist. We know we'll be in pain if we don't vent it on someone, and secretly we decide, "Better them than me."

That takes us back to Saint Peter's use of the word "prosperity." Most of us tend to define prosperity in terms of cash, but also in terms of comfort. Now, some of that comfort is material, but some of it is emotional, too.

It's ironic, isn't it? Our very longing for prosperity is what keeps us from having it.

Talk It Up

We truly must examine our consciences when it comes to our conversations with each other. This especially applies to the talkers.

Free speech—and I mean speech free from fear or shyness—is a real grace in a marriage. But we do want to look at the content of that speech. Sometimes, because we so highly praise communication, we underemphasize the virtue of thinking a problem through first.

Our society tends to make a talker feel superior. Those of us who can lay it on the line feel skilled, and may even consider our quiet spouses handicapped.

Not necessarily. Study a normal day in your lives. How much does your lover enjoy your company? Not your conversation; communication is beyond conversation. Even when it concerns a tough subject, it's beyond merely venting your anger. To twist the old saying, where there's fire, there's probably so much smoke that nobody can see clearly anyway.

Let's take an imaginary scene again. Supposing, wives, that your husband forgot your birthday. He didn't say anything in the morning and he didn't ask you out to lunch. That evening you waited for your surprise, but surprise! It didn't come. The next day you went off to work angry and, as the day progressed, you rehearsed the blistering comments you'd make when you both got home that night.

You weren't able to make them, though; you had to work late. You also had time to think—and to cool off; to remember how busy he'd been at work, with the kids, fixing the plumbing. Now you had an honest chance at communication.

If you'd said what you'd originally planned, there would have been no communication whatever. An angry "Did you intend to forget my birthday, or was that just the best you could do?" would provoke nothing but defensiveness and shame.

A comment based on compassion might have had a different effect:

"Yesterday was my birthday, Joe."

"Oh, no. Not the twenty-first?"

"That's right. Shall we do something anyway?"

Joe is a good man, even if he did forget, and this gives him a chance to exercise his goodness: to take you out, bring you belated flowers. It also gives him a chance to apologize, and for you to express your hurt feelings in a nonthreatening way.

Blurting it out isn't always wrong, but it isn't always right, either. Blurting it out has nothing to do with openness, honesty, or communication. It's a knee-jerk response to pain, an action that is supposed to make us feel better. It doesn't, really. It takes away the feeling that we're going to explode, but it causes anguish in the family, and that can't possibly make us feel good.

Sometimes blurting it out does help rid us of negative feelings. It's like writing a hate letter. By the time we've finished the letter, we've changed our minds and maybe feel a little silly.

So write, if you have to. It's much better to wield that poison pen than a malicious tongue. You can always trash the letter, but you can never erase your lover's memory of your harsh words. If you have to, shout at the mirror. Say those angry things into a tape recorder. Then play it back. Believe me, once you've heard yourself at your worst, you won't be tempted to speak that way again. Then sit down and think your problem through.

Sometimes malice is disguised as self-awareness. We each have years of experience in knowing which subjects, phrases, or tones of voice will pain our lovers. Still, we yield to the impulse to use them again and again.

How about changing that to this statement: "That's the kind of person I am, all right. And I want to do better."

Marriage Means Change

Change is marriage's whole purpose. In matrimony, you become one couple, not two good people being themselves.

The matrimonial union creates a whole new life, just as the sacrament of baptism does. We may not realize it until years after the ceremony, but baptism is a commitment not to be ourselves anymore. It's a commitment to become bodied with the Lord in his people, to become so much more than we could ever be ourselves. That commitment doesn't take away our identities or make us less than we are.

Marriage, in a very real way, is the same. We're called to become bodied with our beloveds; to become bone of his bone, flesh of her flesh.

Those are inspiring words. Many of us will read them with pride and gratitude, perhaps even saying, "Good. People are finally starting to recognize our dignity as a married couple." We have to watch, though, that we don't close this book and return to our old selves: two good people living side by side, except on special occasions.

It's difficult not to do that, especially when we try to force virtue on ourselves. We should do it the easy way: by praying for the grace to become one with our beloveds.

Are We Alike?

We must ask ourselves, "How similar have I become to my spouse in the last twelve months?" Again, we shouldn't ask, "Am I satisfied with our marriage?" or "Do I think I'm a good wife (husband)?" That last question is a fine one, but it's only a beginning. Let's ask, "How much of her has become part of me?" "Do I speak as he does?"

I'm not speaking of tone of voice or even vocabulary. I'm speaking of desiring to converse the way he converses; talking about her topics in her way. Ideally, it should happen spontaneously. The more we become like our spouses, the more sincerely we enjoy their conversation, the less malicious we'll become. This is not easy. That's why you're a sacrament.

If we're like the pagans—good pagans—we get along well with each other, provided there are some understandings: "He's used to my spouting off." "She has to take my ranting and raving in stride."

Instead, ask, "Am I used to talking to her in the tone of voice and in the way that touches her heart? Am I used to listening to myself with his ears rather than just shouting it out?"

We excuse ourselves for our flaws in conversation. We say, "I'm only human," or "Let's be reasonable." First, you're not "only human." The Lord came to make you greater than mere flesh. Second, you're not just a man, not just a woman. You're a husband; you're a wife.

Your marriage license isn't just a contract to support a family, put out the garbage, and cook the meals. Your marriage is a call to put him on like a beautiful garment, to make her an integral, intimate part of you. Too many of us really haven't changed much since we were single. Sure, we'd find it difficult to sleep alone, and we might not want to sit down to an empty table. Those changes are good; they're a beginning. But ask yourselves, "How different am I inside, compared with my single days or with any single person?"

"Well, I'm thinking about him all the time." "She's my whole life;

she's the reason why I do so many of the things I do." That's great. That's also an exaggeration, isn't it? But it's good; it shows ambition.

It's not enough, though, to be thinking about your lover all the time. You're called to bring her inside yourself, to draw him close. In a very real way she has to be doing some of the thinking for you. He has to be so much a part of you that it's difficult to imagine where you end and he begins. That does lead to prosperity and a happy life.

The Marriage Bomb

It certainly isn't easy to keep the tongue under control. If the tongue were a beast, it would be more of a Komodo dragon than a house pet. Saint James puts it bluntly: "Wild animals and birds, reptiles and fish of every kind can all be tamed, and have been tamed, by humans; but nobody can tame the tongue—it is a pest that will not keep still...." (Jas 3:7, 8).

That makes us stop and think, doesn't it? We'd probably agree that a thunderstorm is very powerful. But its aftereffects don't compare with the path of destruction wreaked by a truly nasty tongue. That becomes most clear when we look at the damage in our own lives.

That's certainly true in marriage. How many of us really work on our tongues? Most of us probably don't, except when it comes to extremes.

Now, remember, I'm not addressing the shrews and spouse beaters who make the headlines in the local paper, and I'm not talking about verbally abusive relationships. I'm talking to you: good people who are nevertheless capable of malice, especially when you're wounded by insult, envy, or what have you.

We all have shameful memories of a quickly slung insult that really made him crumble, a cheap word we know she never forgot. Those memories make us feel awful, and we know to work on that kind of behavior. Let's work, too, on the peace and prosperity of our everyday speech.

Let's examine the power speech has over men and women.

For many women, sex lasts longer than it does with their men. These wives are still basking in the afterglow while their husbands are saying, "Let's do it again."

Likewise, conversation usually lasts longer with a man that it does with a woman. When a wife talks out her problem, the talking itself is her cure. Her husband, though, tends to think out his problem. It may take days.

This trait has both positive and negative implications. If she insults him, he may feel the sting for a long time. If she compliments him, he will savor that goodness for a long time, too.

A really sincere compliment lasts longer with a man than with a woman. That's why our women think their husbands are so sparing with their praise. That accusation baffles their men, who protest, "I *said* I loved you. Didn't you believe me?"

Bite Your Tongue

If you're the talker in your marriage, why don't you ask your lover how to stop and think before you talk? After all, marriage is a relationship where we share and learn from each other.

At first, it may sound like asking the leopard to change his spots, but that's not the case. A long history of spouting off isn't virtuous. It's a powerful reason for change.

Choose a time when the two of you aren't in conflict, then ask: "When you want to blow up at me, how do you stop yourself? I'm sure you have feelings as strong as mine, and I know you'd like to blurt it out sometimes. Yet you don't. How do you succeed?"

Next, ask, "How do you stand it?"

Then listen to the answer. Much of it will probably be along these lines:

First, your spouse trusts you. He (or she) knows you make mistakes, but believes you are a good person who honestly loves him.

Second, calmness and confidence are involved. There will be a solution to your dispute.

Third, follow this two-part rule: One, "Don't sweat the small stuff." Two, "Everything is the small stuff." When you think about it, it really is.

Fourth, focus on learning to forgive. Sometimes it can be rough on our pride, but it always pays off. In a real crisis, forgiveness may be a pure act of will. The forgiving person may say silently, "Lord, even though I am furious with this person, I forgive her (him). At least, that's what I want to do, even though I don't feel it now. So help me to really forgive; to really have compassion."

Forgiveness also frees us from a myriad of unconscious reactions; it is a way of choosing life-giving thoughts and rejecting the negative thoughts induced by someone else's behavior. If your next-door neighbor drives you absolutely up a tree, forgive him or her; think of pleasant things instead and silently insist that you won't let him bother you.

If you don't do this, you'll remain a puppet on angry strings. If you relieve that tension by dumping it on your spouse, both of you will be trapped.

Discussion or Slander?

Evil or malicious speech isn't always kept within the four walls of our homes. Sometimes we defuse our anger at our spouses by dumping it off with friends. It's all right, we think, because we've purged ourselves of it and now we won't fight with our lovers.

Like nuclear waste, the poison of complaints doesn't just disappear. It can seep and spread and remain constantly virulent. Even the nicest, the noblest, of friends won't refrain from looking at your spouse and thinking, "Why does he leave her at home when he goes out on Saturdays? Just selfish, I guess," or "Boy, I'm glad I don't have that old spendthrift pulling the purse strings."

Do your girlfriends wish they had married your husband, or do they think he's a lot like their own men: partly good and partly bad? Is every man at work anxious to see the paragon you go home to, or is she just another woman?

It's ironic; we say things about our spouses that no one else would even dare hint. If a friend said, "Your wife couldn't balance the checkbook if she tried. What an airhead!" we'd bristle instantly. If a neighbor said, "Poor dear. Your husband must not love you very much. He's always going off to play poker," we'd let her have it. But we'll deliver similar insults ourselves. What in the world are we doing?

What kind of reputations are we crafting for our lovers? It doesn't matter if our complaints are true. That just makes us guilty of detraction instead of calumny.

Like nuclear waste, it's difficult to erase the poison once it's spilled. Once we gripe to our mothers, neighbors, bosses, or the people in our car pools, we find it difficult to retract that gripe. We rarely say, "You know, my back was really aching and that's why I was so mad at my wife," or "He said one wrong word and I made a whole paragraph of it."

At best, we just don't repeat it again. If our friends bring up the gripe at some later time, we'll probably support it again. Especially after ten or twenty years of marriage, we don't want people to think we're too much in love. Too much in love? What a terrible cage we've locked ourselves into.

Of course, when we criticize our spouses to others, we wind up feeling guilty. Whenever we think of our lovers or see those friends we complained to, we remember our hasty words. The result of it all is definitely not prosperity.

Turn Away From Evil and Do Good, Seek Peace and Pursue It

Do we seek peace in our homes or do we seek personal satisfaction? When someone asks you how your marriage is do you say, "Yes, I have a happy marriage," or "Well, it could be better, but in general, I'm happy"?

A man or woman of peace should answer, "I honestly believe my wife is happy"; "I truly think my husband has a happy marriage."

Now, if you believe your husband or wife truly isn't happy, don't feel like a failure. You are here, loving that person, ready to change. Praise the Lord for your goodness.

This focus on self begins in our dating years. When I went on a date, my mother, father, and aunt always waited up for me. "Did you have a good time?" they asked. They were sincerely interested, and that was beautiful.

Never once, though, did they ask if my date had a good time. Maybe it's good that I didn't get married. My whole preparation for marriage was to enjoy myself. That's an exaggeration, of course. But we are indeed trained to judge our romantic relationships by how well we're satisfied.

That's also true for our priests. If you asked me, "Are you satisfied with your priesthood?" I would not automatically look at you, my people, and ask in return if you're pleased with me. Instead, I'd say, "Well, gee, I couldn't imagine myself doing anything else. I feel very fulfilled."

My answer is a denial of our relationship. It becomes "my" priesthood, not "ours." Then it's reduced to a ministry instead of a network of love relationships.

Likewise, a marriage becomes "my" marriage instead of "our" marriage. It becomes a list of duties, balanced by the benefits of the spouse living up to their responsibilities, too. That's good business. True peace in the home comes, instead, when we find satisfaction and joy by experiencing our spouses' happiness.

We have to bow reverently to our husbands when it comes to love-making. Most good husbands simply don't enjoy sex unless their wives do. Without her delight, he has only the minimal physical satisfaction.

Conversation should be the same way. But, too often, we evaluate a conversation by asking, "Did she listen to me?" "Did he understand what I was saying?" Instead, we should be thinking, "I truly believe I understood her tonight"; "I really think I listened to him." That's when conversation brings joy.

Our homes aren't truly at peace when we're merely getting along or when we've succeeded in hashing out an issue. Peace doesn't come when we're doing all the right things by each other. Peace comes when we're more interested in our lovers' well-being than in our own.

It sounds great, but we find ourselves saying, "Yes, that's nice, but it's unreal. I'd like to be that way, but I'm human and I fail."

We keep concentrating on our humanity. Remember, Peter said, "You are a chosen race, a royal priesthood, a holy nation, a people set apart to sing the praises of God who called you out of the darkness into his wonderful light. Once you were no people and now you are the People of God..." (1 Pet 2:9, 10).

He didn't say we're people. He didn't even say we're good people. He said we're a holy people, a people set apart. Frankly, we don't accept that. We don't deny the theology of it, but it sounds too good to be true. Why not take Peter's word for it? We're so used to limiting ourselves. In material possessions or career goals, our society is insatiable, but when it comes to something like love, we throw up our hands and say, "Infatuation doesn't last forever, you know. Real love is—uh, comfortable."

Agree With Each Other

Peter's First Letter was directed to the whole Church, but it also applies to our fellow Christian (our spouse) with whom we sleep.

How much do we agree among ourselves? How much do we disagree? We may even say, "Ah, but opposites attract." That explains why we get married. It doesn't explain why we're still married and reading this book.

After one, ten, or thirty years together, are we still opposites? In marriage, we're not called to be rugged individualists. We're called to be one in the Lord, models of how Jesus loves his church.

Do we live in harmony, or do we ascribe to the "separate but equal" philosophy: "She takes care of this part of our life together and I take care of the other part." Do we agree among ourselves or do we just avoid fights? Giving in isn't enough. That's a good start, but we have to become part of the other person.

An obvious area to consider is the struggle between a silent partner and a talker. If a talker is overwhelming a thinker, they must both examine that situation and decide how to fix it. The thinker can't just say, "Well, he (she) always takes the stage. I'll just have to live that way." That's not agreement. That's toleration.

Another area of disagreement may be love-making. One partner may have more physical desire than the other. That's fine; that's the starting point. After ten years, the gap should have narrowed a great deal. Has it?

Sex with teeth gritted and a false smile would be a form of prostitution. You don't have to pretend, though; it can happen naturally. You can pray for passion. You can ask your spouse how to yearn more for him or her. If exhaustion or worry is sapping your energy, you can address those issues as well. You can also work at it. In this case, practice has a great deal to do with desire. But, too often, the person who doesn't have the desire says, "Well, when I get the desire, I'll practice."

There are a myriad of other possible disagreements. For example, how do you both feel about working overtime, hobbies, furniture buying, faith, friends? In Chapter 4, you found a list of possible disagreements. Go back and read them over with a new eye.

Now, ask yourselves where you need to agree more. Don't ask what conflicts you need to resolve. Many of your disagreements will be hidden within your lifestyles. They don't always surface as conflicts. After all, you are good couples, and whether or not you realize it, you've already begun your search for peace.

Over the years, there may have been a great deal of polarization of views between partners. Many, weary of it all, have taken refuge in indifference. Have you settled into indifference about in-laws, money, the number of your children, the raising of those children? That's not agreement.

Remember, I don't recommend artificial smiles pasted over angry faces. Start with "I want to agree with you." That may sound trivial, but it isn't. Once we say, "I don't agree with you," we've closed a door. We don't even want to agree.

So, first, build up the desire to agree, not because our lovers are right but because they're our lovers. Loving each other will help us agree.

Don't think, "I'll lose my integrity if I knuckle under all the time." As a married couple, your integrity is formed not by maintaining opinions but by becoming one with each other. Think instead, "I just can't understand why she feels this way, but I want us to work it out." "I love him so much, I don't want there to be anything between us."

Of course, we're not talking about violations of conscience. If your spouse wants to rob a bank, agreement is not an issue. Instead, we're talking about the kind of opinions that are a dime a dozen. What isn't a dime a dozen is your spouse. He or she is infinitely precious.

Sympathy for Spouses

Saint Peter is telling us not to take each other's sacrifices for granted. Perhaps your husband's most magnificent trait is his consistency. That's what attracted you to him. You knew he would never let you down. Do you still delight in that, or do you sometimes feel there's no excitement in your life?

Perhaps you married your wife because she was so practical and level-headed. You knew she'd take good care of a family. Do you still bless her for that, or do you feel weary because she keeps suggesting financial and home improvement projects?

Too often, we can take for granted the goodness that we deliberately brought into our lives. Instead, we focus on the miserable.

How sympathetic are we toward our lovers' trials and responsibilities? Sometimes we're too envious to be sympathetic. So often, we believe our lovers' ways of life are much easier than our own.

Our lovers' responsibilities are more than drudgery. They're gifts. Unfortunately, though, we rarely see them that way. Instead, we're always focusing on what we don't have. Deep down, we think we're supposed to be that way. If we're too grateful, someone might say, "Pollyanna, get your head out of the clouds."

We deliberately torture ourselves with hurtful fantasies; ones that aren't even true. How about the old classic "I wish I'd married...." So on we go, having our "fun," making ourselves feel terrible. That isn't what Christ called us to do.

Are you sympathetic toward your lover? I'm speaking of more now than doing the housework or watching the family budget. Let your lover know you appreciate his or her work. Find meaningful ways to say: "I'm so grateful that you do all these things for me, and for the children, too. You do them so well, and I know they're not easy." This must be more than an occasional pat on the back or a nice word that almost sounds dutiful.

Sympathy needs a little imagination. To convey it, speak your thoughts a little differently from the way you otherwise might; use, maybe, a change of intonation or facial expression. Your lover is used to hearing you say, "Yeah, thanks." You want to convey an added message: "How wonderful you are to do that."

Have Compassion

Compassion is deeper than sympathy. Husbands, do you really know your wives' pain? Wives, do you experience your husbands' suffering?

How compassionate are you because her father never hugged her; because she just doesn't feel comfortable with her body? How much tenderness is in your heart because his mother nagged him to pieces? It doesn't have to be that extreme. Maybe a husband just doesn't see himself as all that lovable, or a wife doesn't see herself as all that capable.

Maybe our lovers' wounds are long buried, but still alive and painful. Our lovers probably don't complain of them; they don't realize how much they hurt. Maybe he lost his father at twelve, or she always wanted a sister and was raised with six brothers. We can't rectify these lifelong hurts, but we can help the healing process by giving our lovers our compassionate hearts today.

Maybe our lovers' hurts are physical. We're usually more compassionate about physical pain, but how often do we stretch ourselves to be as compassionate as we can be?

It's especially hard when physical pain becomes a way of life. Maybe a wife has constant migraine headaches. After a while her husband gets used to them. He encourages her to lie down; he takes over around the house, then entertains himself with the paper until she's up and around again. He isn't fully suffering with her.

What happens when a husband has a touch of bursitis? Perhaps his wife thinks, "What can I do about it?" She notices the flash of pain across his face and says, "Pretty bad tonight, isn't it?" She's sympathetic, but she isn't fully suffering with him, either.

In both cases, these actions are good. They're probably better than someone else's actions, but they're not filled to the brim with compassion. We have much more compassion than we use, amd we are asked to use that compassion to the full.

Be Self-Effacing

This command of Saint Peter's is probably the hardest one in this Scripture passage. Can we honestly say we're self-effacing?

Now, I'm not speaking of a milquetoast. I'm speaking of a person like John the Baptist. If you'll recall, his thundering denunciations and unswerving proclamation of the Lord's message were anything but spineless. He was also self-effacing. In John 3:30, he said of Jesus, "He must grow greater, I must grow less."

I'm not speaking of becoming a slave to others. I'm speaking of selflessness, of seeing that our lovers get the attention, affection, and healing they need, while we cease being preoccupied with our own.

For instance, who gets the attention at home? Maybe we make sure it's us. On the other hand, maybe we're a bit shy, so our spouses really do get the lion's share. That may not mean we're self-effacing. We may merely lack assertiveness. Perhaps we don't need much attention, but when we do, everything screeches to a stop while the family gives us our due.

On the other hand, people who are not self-effacing—let's call them proud—may not demonstrate that pride by ranting and raving. The proud person can be a quiet type who controls the atmosphere in the home by his or her very quietness. The proud person can be dedicated to fairness or even generosity. "In fact," he or she seems to say, "I'll give you even more than you give me, but I have to have mine."

We also need to look at that notion of "You deserve it." We "deserve" all kinds of things that cost money; everything from hair color to exercise equipment. In order to get the things we "deserve," we work harder and harder at jobs we like less and less. We set our sights on objects like restaurant meals and cars and clothes; there's no time or energy left for the God-given people in our lives. We feel more and more out of control, so we wander the shopping malls in search of inner peace. "After all," we say, "I deserve that much." When we're exhausted and broke, have we gotten what we deserved?

"Deserve" crops up sometimes as an excuse. "After all, I pull a double shift. I deserve a break now and then." But when it comes to God's generosity, none of us is more deserving than the rest. If we struggle for what we "deserve" in a relationship, that struggle can deprive us of God's peace.

Let's not ask ourselves what we deserve. Let's ask, instead, "Is my life about him, is my life about her? Or is it about myself?" We have a natural tendency to think that happiness starts with ourselves. "If I'm happy," we think, "I'll make her happy. If I'm pleased, I can be so much more responsive to him." Unfortunately, it doesn't work that way.

Now, I'm in no way suggesting that you allow yourself to live in anger, unforgiveness, or self-loathing while trying to please others. Not only is that hurtful, it isn't necessary. If your focus is on the loves in your life, you will naturally be happy. You'll be like a physically healthy person who feels great without thinking about it. If you're constantly focused on your need to be happier, you'll be like a hypochondriac who's miserably absorbed in minor aches and pains.

Never Repay One Wrong With Another

Now Saint Peter's really hitting below the belt, isn't he? We don't like to think we do this. The truth is, we will graciously put up with a certain amount of trouble. Then our dignity becomes at stake. This happens especially when we're under attack. Suddenly our husband or wife is angry. He's furious; she's shouting—and not kind words, either. What do we do? Shout back. Tell them off. After all, they have no right to do this to us.

We're responding to a challenge to fight. What we're not doing is thinking. On a calmer day, we'd realize he or she is naturally a good, loving person who doesn't really hate us. So what's wrong? It must be something.

Saint Peter says in this passage, "Never repay one wrong with another, or one abusive word with another; instead, repay with a blessing."

What does he mean? That we should be mealy-mouthed? Not at all. Saint Peter is not recommending this type of exchange:

"You silly ninny. Can't you do anything right?"

"God bless you, dear."

That's not good-hearted; it's unnatural. Instead, Saint Peter wants us to respond with a kind word, a gentle word, a soft word. That will, indeed, turn away wrath. We're called to see behind the anger, to learn what our lovers are really trying to say.

If you do this, Peter says, you inherit a blessing, because the eyes of the Lord are on the upright, his ear turned to their cry. That means he won't abandon you to an eternally angry spouse.

Resources for Reflection

Are we really taking our values from the Lord, or are we taking our values from the world around us, saying: "Well, I'm not doing badly"?

You are a holy people. You are not called to be a "not bad" people. You are saints. I'm not just writing nice words, and I'm not just repeating them because they were good enough for Peter. They really come from the depths of my heart because I couldn't have written these words to any but a holy people.

Consider These Questions Privately:

When have my words at home caused unhappiness or hurt? What would have happened if, instead of blurting it out, I had taken time to think? Exactly how would I have done that?

When have I complained of my spouse to others? How could I have stopped myself?

What are my spouse's hurts and responsibilities? How can I show sympathy and compassion for my spouse?

What steps can I take to be more in unity and agreement with my spouse?

Share These Questions With Your Spouse:

Each of us takes turns being the speaking partner and the silent one. With that in mind, ask: Dear, how do you keep from blurting out harsh words?

Saint Peter said we are a holy people, meant to sing the praises of God who called us into his wonderful light. How would I think, speak, and act if I really believed that?

Finally, Let Us Invite God Into Our Marriages:

Glorious Father, we ask you to be present in our marriage this day and always. Thank you for your gift of grace, which allows us to see our flaws and gives us the courage to become more loving and selfless. Help keep us from hurting others with our anger. Let us see each other's goodness so we can speak gently and with love. Give us your peace and prosperity, and help us to truly become one. Amen.

CHAPTER 10

Scriptural Marriage

"I Am Here, Beloved, to Give You Life."

(EPH 5:21–33)

In this chapter, we're tackling that most misunderstood passage in the New Testament, the one where Saint Paul is supposed to tell husbands they have dominion over their wives, and that wives should be their submissive servants. Do I have your attention?

Honestly, Saint Paul doesn't say that at all. Saint Paul was inspired by God to make not a document of slavery, but a case for equality of the sexes. He's recommending peace, love, and great respect. Trust him as you read this passage of Saint Paul's letter to the Ephesians:

> Be subject to one another out of reverence for Christ. Wives should be subject to their husbands as to the Lord, since, as Christ is head of the Church and saves the whole body, so is a husband the head of his wife; and as the Church is subject to Christ, so should wives be to their husbands, in everything. Husbands should love their wives, just as Christ loved the Church and sacrificed himself for her to make her holy by washing her in cleansing water with a form of words, so that when he took the Church to himself she would be glorious, with no speck or wrinkle or anything like that, but holy and faultless. In the same way, husbands must love their wives as they love their own bodies; for a man to love his wife is for him to love himself. A man never hates his own body, but he feeds it and looks after it; and that is the way Christ treats the Church, because we are parts of his Body. This is why a man

> leaves his father and mother and becomes attached to his wife, and the two become one flesh. This mystery has great significance, but I am applying it to Christ and the Church. To sum up: you also, each one of you, must love his wife as he loves himself; and let every wife respect her husband.
>
> EPHESIANS 5:21–33

Saint Paul's message is this: husbands, be one with your wives; love them as fully and completely as Christ loves his Church. To wives he says, let them love you as Christ loves his Church.

Neither of these commands is easy. They both require dying to self. But as you well know, dying to self means opening your heart to others and especially to our good God. It's like Jesus' parable of the mustard seed. That smallest of seeds—our sin-bound, hurting self—when healed and allowed to bloom, becomes the biggest of trees.

Pass the Dynamite

Before we do some honest soul-searching, let's blast, once and for all, some centuries-old misconceptions about this passage of Ephesians. First, it doesn't mean that the husband is Lord. It doesn't say the husband's decisions, ideas, or attitudes represent the will of God.

Second, this passage is concerned only with relationships, not with gender issues. It certainly does not say, "Women, be subject to men." That would be completely out of character with the freedom and dignity Jesus offers all men and women. The idea of prostrating oneself before another in order to be dominated is alien to the message of the Gospel.

None of Scripture relegates women to the role of passive rag dolls. Women played an active role in Jesus' life and he always responded with reverence and respect. Submission, as expressed in Scripture, cannot mean a lessening of women as persons.

Paul's words, then, speak to a couple who have already chosen to love each other. He and she have already established a relationship of understanding, communication, and responsiveness. They're totally committed to each other. Only then could he consider treating her as he treats his own body; only then could she be called to be respond to his love as she is to that of Jesus.

Because of the uniqueness of sacramental marriage, a wife's role is shaped by her interaction with her husband. She can't be subject to him unless he draws forth that response. The two of them must be bonded together in making this happen.

This bonding happens in love. The husband loves his wife as his own body; he gives himself up for her. The wife becomes responsive to that love because its invitation at this depth is irresistible. Her joyous response inspires an even deeper love from him.

We should keep this in mind at all times. Paul's Letter to the Ephesians isn't a burden; it's a game plan for joy. We have to work to get rid of our own game plan and the world's game plan. We have to integrate the Lord's plan into our way of living.

Marriage Is a Prayer

Now let us reexamine our call to the sacrament of matrimony. Do we believe our marriages are spiritual? Are we sure? It's easy to say a quick yes.

Marriage is spiritual twenty-four hours a day. It's not spiritual just at Christmas, at Mass or church services, or after a wonderful sexual experience. Marriage is spiritual on Tuesday, even if it's spaghetti night and the food is all over the floor. It's spiritual on Friday when we come home shell-shocked from the week.

Too often, we see God's plan as a list of "shouldn'ts." We shouldn't fight, we shouldn't be angry with one another or hurt one another.

God's definition of love, though, isn't like calf roping. We're not supposed to subdue our anger and annoyance like a wild beast. We're supposed to transcend our humanity by, again, dying to self and believing in the wonderful goodness of our lovers. That is our spirituality.

We Catholics are invited to attend Mass and receive the Eucharist every day. We consider the Eucharist a sacrament. Matrimony is a sacrament, too. Do we see marriage as a grace that we receive daily?

Sometimes we think loving others is more in tune with the Gospel message than is loving our own spouses. If someone works in the inner city, Appalachia, or the local Sunday School program, we think they're being especially spiritual. If we, on the other hand, spend time with our families, we're only doing what comes naturally.

Do we realize our marriages are spiritualizing us, or do we merely see our spirituality helping our marriages? There's a difference.

Do we realize that our marriages are our fundamental prayer, or do we merely believe prayer helps our marriages? Of course, we should certainly use prayer to help our marriages, but our first prayer is our relationship with one another. The best way husbands and wives can acknowledge God is by loving one another in his name.

Our relationship is more than a series of actions that please God; it's more than doing the right thing, as he commanded us. It's an act of liturgy. All the normal little everyday acts of love in the living room, bedroom, dining room, and kitchen are religious acts because we are faithful couples.

Husbands loving their wives as they love their own bodies—or of wives trusting husbands to do that—seems so extreme that we tune this Gospel message out. It's like one of those oldtime prayers we Catholics used to say after Holy Communion. They sounded beautiful and they were appropriately spiritual for the occasion, but we had no serious intention of living the type of life they spoke of.

People who hear Saint Paul's message that "Husbands should love their wives, just as Christ loved the Church; wives should be subject to their husbands as to the Lord," shouldn't think it sounds bizarre. They should be able to say, "Oh, you mean Christ loves us in the Church as much as we love each other? You know, that's really something."

Vocation to Love

Sacred Scripture really does give couples a vocation to love each other with the same passionate faithfulness that exists between Christ and his Church. Imagine Saint Paul looking you right in the eye and saying, "Will you love her as you love yourself? Will you treat him as you'd treat Jesus?" Not just "Are you doing a good job?"

We, the people of the Church, are calling you to a totally different relationship. It's not a lofty ideal that an occasional saint or two might embrace. It's just as attainable as reconciliation with God, Holy Communion, or the sacrament of baptism.

When you're baptized, you seek admission into the community of God, the very body of Jesus. We, the Church, respond to you with trust and confidence. We baptize you into the death and resurrection of Jesus: we immerse you in the saving waters of baptism.

That's not fantasy; that's a fact. When we call you a matrimonial sacrament, that's a fact, too. When we say that we, God's chosen people, believe you are to love each other as Jesus loves his Church, that's not an exaggeration. We're serious.

We are called to be prophets. A prophet, despite the popular misconception, is not someone who predicts the future. A prophet is someone who announces God's presence in our midst by living an exemplary life. As married couples, we are specifically called to live out those words of Saint Paul. We are called to a scriptural marriage, not just a human marriage.

That means a total lifestyle change; it's more than being a little kinder to each other today. Instead, we're called to be moved toward God.

The Heart of Matrimony

Imagine yourself being interviewed by a newspaper reporter who says, "My editor thought your life would be worth a story. Why don't you tell me about it?"

What would you tell the reporter? Would your story center around your job, your avocation, or outside interests? Better, you might mention a cause you've lived for or some people you've served with responsibility and love.

Even better, you might describe your personal qualities: "I'm a very prayerful person," or "I'm really good with children." Now, that's an improvement but, still, is that all? Would you tell this reporter, "The most important thing I've ever done is become a husband or a wife"?

Too often, we think marriage is something each of us accomplishes separately: the wife does wifely things and her husband does husbandly things. The two halves somehow equal one whole.

It doesn't work that way. Marriage is purely a relationship, and that relationship is determined by how much we become each other.

The heart of matrimony is the community of life we establish in each other. The key to that community of life is not merely to live in the same house, sleep in the same bed, eat at the same table, or go together to the same party. The key is to have the same goals and values. It's not merely avoiding conflicts or disagreements; it's two hearts beating as one. It has to be a constant effort, not just something that's nice when it happens.

We may have very good and lofty dreams; probably the dreams we had even before we were married. We should take on our lovers' dreams, not because the dreams are so good, but because our lovers are.

This kind of unity is possible, but we must be open to God's grace. Saint Paul admits that this is not something we would think of ourselves. He says this is a mystery of great significance. He also explains why we are called to it. When we accomplish this or even strive to accomplish it, we are revealing Jesus' love relationship with his Church.

Husbands Should Love Their Wives Just As Christ Loved the Church

We must take Saint Paul's teaching to heart. He says, "Husbands should love their wives, just as Christ loved the Church...." How did Christ love the Church? He "sacrificed himself for her." In other words, he submitted himself to her.

From the very beginning, Jesus submitted himself to his people. He came down to earth and became one of us. As a child, and even as an adult, he was subject to Mary and Joseph. He was also obedient to his Father's will. In John 8:28–29, he said, "...I do nothing of my own accord. What I say is what the Father has taught me; he who sent me is with me, and has not left me to myself, for I always do what pleases him."

He died in submission to us, too. He didn't have to be mocked, beaten, and crucified, but he let us do that to him. You'll recall that when Jesus was betrayed by Judas in the garden of Gethsemane, one of his followers cut off the high priest's servant's ear. In Matthew 26:53,54, Jesus asked that disciple, "...do you think that I cannot appeal to my Father, who would promptly send more than twelve legions of angels to my defense? But then, how would the scriptures be fulfilled that say this is the way it must be?"

If a husband is to answer the Lord's call to sacramental marriage, he must take the leadership in submitting himself to his wife, exactly as Jesus submitted himself to the Church. He must surrender himself profoundly, relentlessly, and totally to this woman who is flesh of his flesh.

A sacramental wife is called to subject herself to her husband *in response to his subjection to her.* If she seems to have difficulty doing this, it's because she has no model. The Lord says that model is you—her husband. He's calling you to take the lead.

Sacrament of Marriage

A sacramental marriage calls a man to become incarnate with his wife just as Jesus enfleshes himself with us. A sacramental husband makes no distinction between his wife and himself. Saint Paul says, "...husbands must love their wives as they love their own bodies; for a man to love his wife is for him to love himself." Ask yourselves, "Do I see her as my body, or as an important but very separate person?"

Husbands may acknowledge their responsibilities toward their wives and admit to opportunities to make their lives more pleasant. Beyond that, though, husbands may live their own lives because they don't want to take on the responsibility for the kind of overwhelming intimacy Jesus is calling us to.

Husbands are tempted to say this total intimacy isn't real; it's something no one really does. Before we actually voice those words, let's take a good look at our wives. Do we see their needs, their search for oneness?

A man has to ask himself, "How married am I?" Sure, we do a lot of married things and we've stopped a lot of single ones, but are we living a married way of life? Or are we merely two nice people who have affection for each other, some concern, a history together, and are living side by side in peace and harmony?

Married to the Job

Many husbands form their identities watching other men rather than by becoming one body with their wives. These men tend to judge success by their nonmarital accomplishments.

If a man lets others determine his identity, his wife is an outside interest. She has rights, and he respects these. She has needs and desires, and he knows his responsibility to respond. He does his best, but his wife is definitely a distinct entity. This undercuts Paul's whole message. If different and distinct, she's not part of a man's own body. She's a separate body, albeit an attractive one.

Many men are married to their jobs. We can't just say, "Well, that's the way things are." Saint Paul is saying very clearly that sacramental husbands are *not* supposed to be that way.

We can allow the job to keep us from relationship in other ways. For instance, we can bring the job home with us. Sometimes we do it literally: "I just have a few plans to make, honey," or "I have to go over these reports."

Even worse, we bring home the job's atmosphere. This happens more frequently, drowning the whole family in work-related anger or depression. Maybe the boss has been on our back, or maybe we're the boss and we've been on everyone else's back. When we come home, everybody has to deal with our job traumas.

Show a Little Tenderness

Physical, mental, and spiritual tenderness is such a beautiful gift from a man to his spouse. Sometimes we husbands are tender physically but not mentally. Tenderness means so much to a woman. Ask any woman what qualities she wants in her lover, and tenderness is always there. Some women will say they want certain qualities, but all look for tenderness in their partner.

Men are inclined to be tender only when we feel like it. If we're in a tender mood tonight, we show our tenderness. But that's a response to ourselves, not to our lovers.

Tenderness, whether mentally, physically, or psychologically, can be a decision. Its reward isn't the mere pleasure of feeling tender, but the fulfillment that tenderness gives and the unity it helps achieve.

We have to start thinking about how we can improve our tenderness quotient. We have to force ourselves to do this just as we force ourselves to jog, study for an exam, or drag into the office when we're sick. We can ask for the grace to create an environment of tenderness within our homes. It won't happen overnight, but each day we'll improve a little. In time, we will truly see the results.

First, we must remember when we've been tender, what helped create that feeling and helped express it meaningfully. We should recall what destroys a tender mood or an attitude that would lead to tenderness. Then we must take steps to eliminate those destructive influences, thoughts, or behaviors.

Men are called to take the lead in creating that tender environment in the home. To do so, they have to be as willing to work on tenderness in their marriages as they are to work on success in their jobs. We can't leave our marriages at the mercy of accidents, and we shouldn't leave the initiative to our wives.

Tenderness of heart and soul, mind and conversation, is an inestimable gift to our beloved wives. To give it, we should place three thoughts where we'll never forget them: a memory of how much she desires our tenderness, how significantly that tenderness impacts her, and how much more it would mean if she could look forward to tenderness as a normal, everyday occurrence.

Heavenly Treatment

Since we've been called to treat our wives as Jesus treats the Church, let's examine Jesus' life. Let's take some cases in point.

In John 15:15, he said, "...I have made known to you everything I have learned from my Father."

Do we men let our wives know what is inside us? Many husbands keep private places within themselves. Can we truthfully say to our beloved wives, "I have told you everything that's inside me. There isn't any of me today that you don't know"?

"But that isn't so easy to do," you might want to say. "I'm naturally not too reflective a guy. I don't look inside myself that much, much less talk about it."

That's all right. That's where you are right now. But you should start being different for your wife's sake. She needs to be part of you, and she can't be part of you unless you tell her what's in there.

In John 10:10, Jesus said, "I have come so that they may have life and have it to the full."

Why have you come into marriage? Many husbands don't understand that their life's purpose is to give their beloved wives abundant happiness. They believe they can add to her well-being. But her fulfillment is her own responsibility, they think.

Jesus doesn't think that way. He doesn't teach us a little more than we knew before; he doesn't improve things. He came to give us a totally new way of being, and he did this because we are his flesh.

Likewise, your wife's whole life should be totally different, fresh and new in hope and joy because she is one with you. You have let her into your life so she wouldn't be alone any longer. Now she is full of you and your love for her.

Jesus said, "Come to me, all you who labor and are overburdened, and I will give you rest" (Mt 11:28).

Many husbands offer their wives every refreshment but themselves. They suggest a night out with the girls, a trip to the mall, freedom from the children for a Saturday.

When our wives are frazzled, lonely, disturbed, or not feeling up to par, do we say, "Come to me," or do we offer all sorts of suggestions to take them outside themselves? We do this largely because we don't believe in our power to heal. Saint Paul doesn't agree. Neither does the Lord. They not only believe we can do it, they are calling us to.

Without question, our wives' heaviest burdens are the children. That's partly because of the children's natural demands, but also because they don't have full-time fathers. Many husbands are well-intentioned, but they're not really there.

A wife is not fundamentally refreshed if her husband pitches in only when she's desperate, or if he gives her little rewards like praise and an occasional dinner out. The only true refreshment a loving husband can give is to become an actively involved father.

A woman can't believe her husband truly loves her unless he loves those children. No matter what else he may do, she's going to feel deserted and alone.

Women can receive a lot of negativity about having children, especially if there are more than two. These insults come from family, friends, neighbors, even strangers. It hurts our loves when others think they are foolish or lacking independence and creativity because they have families. If a woman's husband is as involved with the children as she is, those attacks don't bother her. If they do sting, it's because they are echoed at home.

In John 10:14, Jesus said, "I am the good shepherd; I know my own and my own know me."

Often, husbands don't really know their wives. Do you *really* know your wife, not just know about her?

"Sure, I know her; we've been married for twenty years. She likes to sleep with the window open and she likes anchovy pizzas. She gets mad when I'm five minutes late and even madder when she hears about cruelty to animals."

That's fine; it has to start there. But really knowing the other person is a much deeper matter. Often, a husband doesn't take enough time for that.

Jesus was referring to the Lord's knowledge: the knowledge of belonging. He said, "I know my own," not merely "I know this person because we've lived side by side for two decades." Do we know with intimacy, and do ours—our wives—know we belong to them, or are we very much our own men? We may do all the right things by them; we may live up to our responsibilities in marriage. That's good for a start, but Jesus went much further when forming a love relationship with his Church.

In John 15:11, Jesus said, "I have told you this so that my own joy may be in you and your joy be complete."

How often do we talk to our wives to bring them joy? In comparison, how often do we talk to provide information or a suitable response?

Do we even want our speech to make our beloved wives joyous? Then that's where we must concentrate. It isn't as difficult as it seems, nor does it call us to do all sorts of exotic tasks. We must simply tell her who we are. We must believe our wives have a need to know us. Nothing brings a wife more joy than for her husband to let her inside.

Resources for Reflection I

Near the end of Saint Paul's passage on married love, he wrote, "This is why a man leaves his father and mother and becomes attached to his wife, and the two become one flesh."

If I were to ask whether you were living in accordance with this passage, you'd sincerely say yes. You'd be puzzled, wondering why I even asked. After all, you left your father and mother's house years ago.

Why not put a new slant on the question? Ask yourself this: "Have I left myself and my habits, attitudes, and demands? Have I left my single way of life and become one with her?"

"This mystery has great significance," Paul added. A mystery is never understood completely; it's only gradually revealed. That's why the Lord gives you fifty years to love your wife.

Consider These Questions Privately:

Below is a list of Scripture passages. Each describes Christ's intimate love for his Church.

Read and interpret each of these. How do they apply to your relationship with your wife? What are you doing well? What can you do better?

Matthew 11:28: "Come to me, all you who labor and are overburdened, and I will give you rest."

Matthew 19:13, Mark 10:13–16, Luke 18:15–17: Jesus and the children.

Matthew 26:6–11, Mark 14:3–6, John 12:1–7: The woman and the oil.

Luke 10:38–42: Martha and Mary.

John 8:2–11: The adulterous woman.

John 13:3–16: The washing of the feet.

John 13:34, 35: "Love one another as I have loved you."

Share With Your Spouse:

After you and your wife finish reading Chapter 10, write to each other on these themes:

Beloved, you are such a delightful spouse; I have such wonderful memories of your goodness. I can see you following God's plan for our relationship when you...." (Write on more than one if you wish.)

My dear, I realize I haven't always followed God's plan for our relationship. I am going to make the following change(s). This makes me feel....

Finally, Let Us Invite the Lord Into Our Marriages:

Almighty Father, I truly want to follow your plan for our marriage. I know that, without your help, I don't have the grace to do what you ask of me. Please send me your Spirit so I can fully live out your plan with my beloved wife.

I thank you for her beauty and goodness, and for the graces you have already given me: the grace of openness to your word, the grace of trust, the grace of generosity, the grace of hope. Thank you; praise you for your gifts to my beloved and myself. Amen.

I Am Here, Beloved, to Give You Life

Wives, Saint Paul's passage from Ephesians 5 calls us not to servitude, but to healing. Our Lord wants us to be free to live in the warmth of his love, and he shows us that love through our beloved husbands. He wants us to be free; free to share ourselves with others, free to believe we are wonderful and good, free to accept and give love, free to use our talents.

Let's review that Scripture passage again (on pp. 143–144). Some of it describes what the Lord is asking us to do. The rest describes his promise.

For years, many women have listened to Ephesians 5 in anger and despair. They thought it was just another demand that they continue to be passive.

It's not that at all. Allowing yourself to be healed and loved is anything but passive. It's tremendously hard work. It will take everything you've got, spiritually, intellectually, and emotionally. It's rather like a crisis, except that exhilarating things are happening instead of traumatic ones.

The sad truth is, many people will never be healed. Terrified of trust, they develop alternate ways of dealing with—and sometimes manipulating—others. Each victory through masquerade or manipulation is another nail in their spiritual coffins. Ultimately they can turn away from God and humanity, living half-lives of empty loneliness.

Allowing yourself to be healed and loved, though, takes more than courage. It takes self-confidence, love, and trust. All these are graces from God, and we should pray for them. God loves it when we ask for his graces. He'll give them to us every time. Pray for them every day; it may take hours, weeks, or even a few months, but you'll begin to notice changes. Grace, by the way, snowballs. It may start small and slow, but if you're willing, it picks up depth and speed until it's a magnificent avalanche.

Some of you must be wondering why the Lord places such emphasis on self-stroking. If our purpose on earth is to love others, why are we wasting time in these selfish pursuits?

Now, that's a put-down par excellence. Who are we to say we don't deserve healing and wholeness? The Lord made us, he wants to heal us, and that should be enough.

There's another reason why we should allow ourselves to be whole: we must be healed and loved before we can give love. Maybe it doesn't seem logical, but it's like this: Trying to love others while neglecting your inner self is like trying to draw water from an empty well. You can put mud in the bucket instead, but people who drink it will be able to tell the difference.

Healing Us

Now that we've talked about individual healing, let's apply that to you as a couple. The Lord is calling you as a couple to be healed, to be one whole body, just as Jesus is one with his Church. He wants you to give each other his life to the full. When that happens, you can show his love to all other people.

Before we tackle the world at large, though, we should be healing our husbands. Many of our husbands have hidden wounds, too, and are suffering from lack of love. As you both begin to grow, him loving you, you accepting that love and loving in return, your bond of oneness will grow stronger.

By the way, your husband needs love the way he defines it. That's not because his idea is right and yours is wrong. It's because love happens not with the giver, but with the receiver. For instance, imagine you and your spouse have been conversing, and he was doing most of the talking. Now, have you listened to him? Only he can say for sure. You can tell him, "I have tried to listen to you," but only he can say, "I feel listened to." Likewise, you can say, "But I did love you. Didn't you feel it?" He's the one who decides, "Yes, I feel loved by you," or "No, it's not getting through to me."

Know You Are Loved

Saint Paul's message calls us to accept our husbands' love, to let them consider us part of their own bodies and to make absolutely no distinction between us and themselves.

After all, we're celebrating the sacrament of matrimony. It's much more than marriage, which is a secular contract. In marriage, two people who love each other merely come together to their mutual advantage, Instead, we've taken on a whole new way of being; we're living in, with, and through the other person.

Matrimony is not two people doing nice things for each other. It is two people *being* each other. This is Saint Paul's meaning when he says the two become one flesh.

The Gospel calls your husband to live for you. It asks you to let him make you his world and his happiness. You are the woman for whom he pours out his life, just as Christ poured out his life for his Church. As his center, you are the place where he discovers his true identity. Your scriptural call is to accept his gift and support him in giving it.

Saint Paul calls each of you to complete, absolute, and relentless responsiveness to your chosen husband. You must draw from him a willingness to share totally in your life. Ask yourselves, "How can I belong more deeply to my husband?"

As you read this, you may be thinking, "I just can't respond that way forever. It's too much."

But you can respond today. We live only in the present; right now, today's love is all that matters. C. S. Lewis, in his book *The Screwtape Letters,* says, "... the Present is the point at which time touches eternity... in it alone, freedom and actuality are offered...." Tomorrow doesn't exist yet, and the past is over. Besides, God gives us graces on a daily basis. He even told us that the burden of our whole future is too much for us to bear.

What If the Leader Gets Lost?

By the way, what if your husband isn't impressed with God's plan and isn't interested in following it?

Then you are called to pray for him, and for yourself. Not a prayer like "Dear God, make him do what he's supposed to do," but a prayer to bless him, to surround him with God's infinite love, and to help him feel that love. He needs compassion, as much as you can give. He isn't making the first move for a number of reasons.

First, he may not know what he's supposed to do. If he does, he may believe it's too challenging or too wonderful to be real. He may be alienated from God by suffering or negative experiences with organized religion.

Perhaps you have been sending out signals that say, "Love me, but don't get too close." Maybe you unknowingly have sent him the message that his best—that is, what he considers his best—isn't enough for you. Perhaps he feels inadequate.

Perhaps he needs healing. This will come with time, prayer, and effort.

Perhaps he's afraid of the depth of involvement that would happen if he followed Saint Paul's message. Not only would it drain his resources, he wouldn't know how to handle it.

Each husband may have a different combination of reasons for reluctance. In all cases, your prayer is a good first step. Especially, pray for compassion. As Jesus said in Matthew 6:8, "...your Father knows what you need before you ask him." And as he said in Luke 11:9,10, "Ask, and it will be given to you; search, and you will find; knock, and the door will be opened to you. For everyone who asks receives; everyone who searches finds; everyone who knocks will have the door opened."

The Many Faces of Anger

Now let's examine the ways in which we fail to follow God's plan for our marriages.

First, we tend to finger-point. Be careful not to think that way because it will throw a whole lot of heat and not very much light. If you tried to keep score, you would have to list which of his actions caused the flaws he's accusing you of: "Sure, I yell sometimes. It's because he doesn't care; but he doesn't care because...." You'd need a full notebook to keep track of all the blame and misery, and when you finished, you'd have two wounded hearts and no resolution.

The second way we lose track of God's plan is in our expression of anger. When we speak of anger, we're usually speaking of fights.

Let's examine how each partner reacts to a fight, and how these natural, harmful reactions damage love relationships and clear no air anyway. In most fights, good men and women will behave in ways that only worsen the conflict.

Men dread their wives' anger; it makes them feel hopeless and leaves heavy lumps of anguish in the pits of their stomachs. Worse, it makes them feel unloved.

Anger is a feeling, and feelings are neither right nor wrong. But the by-products of anger are definitely worth giving up:

First is the desire for retaliation. Perhaps a man hurts his wife by being indifferent to her needs; by ignoring her, working overtime, whatever. She feels betrayed; she believes he doesn't care. There's no way she can *make* him care or repent his actions. He just walks all over her any time he feels like it. So, partly in despair, partly in indignation, she delivers verbal punishment for his crime.

Second is the urge to provoke guilt. If a wife yields to this impulse, her husband will feel like an absolute blockhead by the time the fight is finished. This is certainly easy for a woman to achieve, and a natural human impulse, but it doesn't come from God. She would never do it in cold blood; if a friend tried to make him feel equally worthless, she'd go in swinging to defend him. After the fight is over, the man may insist he still feels good about what he's done, but he nevertheless feels like garbage. This lowers his self-respect and his ability to love. It starts a downward spiral.

Third, this anger can be ongoing. We don't think, "Yes, he failed me, but that's okay. It's over. I'll forget it." Instead, we have a panic reaction: "Dear God, he really worked me over. Is this a trend? I have to deal with it or my life will fall apart." The hurtful emotions that accompany this don't rise to the conscious surface, but they do come out in the fight.

In a fight, a woman's emotions are in full swing. She's upset; she's hurt; she's afraid and downright furious. She gives vent to most of her impulses.

The man feels attacked. The person he loves most in the world suddenly hates him from the inside out. He knows that isn't really true, but if she doesn't hate, loathe, or blame him, she's certainly giving a good imitation of it. He decides to stay calm; his getting angry won't solve anything. He tries to apologize, calm her down, tell her the situation isn't that bad. In other words, he placates her which increases her anger.

The fight escalates from there until the man really is angry. As his adrenaline flows, he wants to fight or flee. He can't do either. If he leaves, the trouble will be waiting when he comes back. And he certainly can't hit her. All he can do is survive the situation and swallow that heavy pit in the center of his stomach.

Eventually, harsh words fly back and forth. Everyone is hurt; both parties wish it had never happened.

So often, though, it happens again. What can be done about it? There's no quick answer. Understanding and compassion for each other work; so does prayer. So does a calm, nonfrantic life-style. The biggest healer, though, is trust.

Fear of Trust

Trust is like quadruple bypass heart surgery. If you don't get it, you'll live a restricted life and you may even die. But the thought of climbing onto that operating table is equally terrifying.

Many women don't trust. They have a deeply ingrained fear that they don't have equilibrium in the relationship. The details may be different. Perhaps there's a fear of being mastered, of losing one's identity, of being taken for granted or becoming a servant. Certainly there's the fear of not being loved and cherished. Often, at the bottom of it is a feeling of worthlessness—that we're not important and deserve no more than second-rate love. We're constantly on the watch for skirmishes in the disputed territory of self-worth and lovableness. If we can defend ourselves vigorously enough, maybe that empty feeling inside us will go away.

It all boils down to lack of faith in our spouses. Because we cannot trust, we deny ourselves the life-giving, self-affirming knowledge that our husbands will always love us and will be there for us, no matter what.

"But he does let me down. I'm not imagining that." That's true. But you let him down, too. You're both good, imperfect people who love each other. Flaws don't stop healthy, whole people from trusting. None of us can earn trust; it's a free gift. In fact, it's an essential gift if we want to follow God's plan.

This trust is, in a nutshell, the subjection Saint Paul speaks of. Paul asks us to say to our beloved husbands, "I am yours; I belong to you. I find my true self in your love. I place myself in your hands and I give myself over to you. You will determine the quality of my life."

The reward for trusting him isn't betrayal; it's peace of mind. It's happiness. It's trading that heavy burden we all drag around for the lighthearted freedom of God's plan.

Lack of Enthusiasm

How often do our husbands go out with their own friends? For all the talk about nights out with the boys, it's probably pretty seldom. Often, when a man gets married, his whole social life becomes restricted to his wife and her choices of what to do.

Take one example: wilderness trips. They're a typical male recreation, but many men don't get to experience them because of their responsibilities at home. If he goes off with the boys to fish or hunt, he feels guilty because his wife is left at home with the children. But often, he can't take her with him because she doesn't enjoy the rugged outdoors. Now, she rarely says, "Don't you dare do that to me." She may not even mind if he goes, but after years of her unenthusiasm, he is so dispirited, he decides he doesn't want to do it anyway. It remains a wistful dream or a memory of his youth.

A lack of enthusiasm, by the way, is devastating. It's every bit as effective as disapproval; it just takes a little longer. If you hear yourself laughing about "men's stuff," take note of it. Stop, because once he's convinced that the things that turn him on are worthless, he'll be partly dead inside. You'll then have less of a husband. He'll love himself less, and he'll be less capable of loving you the way God wants.

A lack of enthusiasm is particularly devastating in sex. When a wife tells her man "No," or even "Oh, I suppose so," he feels alone, even abandoned. Especially if he's afraid to speak of his love and desire for unity, so he expresses it physically. When you imply "I'm not really interested in you right now," you've done more than deprive him of his evening's entertainment; you've told him you don't love him. He takes it personally, and he's right to do so.

The Hebrew word for *memory* means "make me present to you." In sex, you make yourselves totally present to each other through your bodies, which are no longer your own but are given up for the other. When you make love to your husband, you are saying, "I have given up my body for you. It is yours. Make me present to you, and become present to me, as we speak to each other physically."

It sounds like a paradox, but we humans are happiest when we forgo control and become truly one with our lovers. If the oneness is a coming together in sex, it suffuses our being for a long time afterward. We are not lonely because we are no longer alone.

"Time to Think"

"I just want some peace," says the husband. "So do I," responds the wife. "That's why I want to get this problem solved."

That, in a nutshell, is the difference between men's and women's views of peace. What's defined as "quiet" to a man is, to a woman, the final solution. To her, remaining quiet when there's an unresolved problem is as silly as sweeping dirt under the rug. Her husband, though, just wants time to think. How can he solve anything when he doesn't even have the silence he needs to ponder the problem?

Wives, let's have compassion. Let's understand they're not stonewalling us. They just work differently. They need that silence in order to love us as Christ loved his Church. Even if it feels sometimes as if we're living with the emotionless man from outer space, let's give them thinking space.

Both husbands and wives need an atmosphere of peace and harmony in order to let Christ's love flourish in our homes. Only when there's peace—peace for both parties, peace because we show compassionate understanding—can he work on loving you.

Peace is particularly difficult to find in our tense, driven society. We don't allow ourselves any time to think, and we make sure our lives are crammed full: so full, our tempers fray. "I shouldn't feel this upset," we tell ourselves. "Mary (Melissa/Joanne/whoever) works much harder than I do. *Plus* she has an exercise program and that wonderful hobby. She seems so happy and cheerful. Why can't I do it, too?"

Search for Happiness

Of course, that other woman isn't as happy and cheerful as we imagine. She's working like a field ox; how can she possibly be happy? She—and we—are like Richard Cory. Do you know the poem by E. A. Robinson? Richard Cory was the rich man who had everything: women, money, honor in the church, the respect of his fellow men. But, as the song says, Richard Cory went home one night and put a bullet through his head. He ought to have been happy, with all his achievements and luxuries, but in fact, he was in despair.

We simply can't be superheroes, yet we don't allow ourselves the dignity of our own limitations. We deny our feelings of frustration and, instead, dance to the piping of "You'd better do it or you'll be inadequate."

Let's ask ourselves a question: "What do I need to do in order to feel really good about myself?" Most likely, the answers will be in the form of exacting demands: lose twenty pounds, dress better, have thicker hair, wash out that gray, make more money, be able to do more work in a day, take up an exotic hobby like jewelry making, increase my IQ....The grind goes on and on. When we do get a color, lose twenty pounds, and buy some clothes, we'll find another reason to feel inadequate.

Of course, the problem goes much deeper. At the root of it are two facts: we don't value ourselves as ourselves, and we are lonely in our personal relationships. If we asked ourselves, "Would I rather lose twenty pounds and keep my relationship with my husband just as it is? Or would I rather my husband was wildly romantic and after me all the time just as I am?" what would we answer? We'd have to think about it, wouldn't we?

What are we doing to ourselves? We're saying, "No, I won't subject myself to freely given love. It can't be worth anything unless I earn it."

We don't seem to place a very high value on plain and simple happiness. Furthermore, we don't even know what it is. We think happiness comes when we have what we ought to have. The idea that we ought to take time to watch the sun go down sounds romantic and rather frivolous. We don't do it very often because it wouldn't get us anywhere.

Part of our pain exists because we think we're not worthwhile people unless we do worthwhile things. We have to have our own hobbies, do our own housekeeping and child-raising, make our own money. It's like a computerized formula for self-worth.

Imagine feeding this into the computer: "My greatest accomplishment is loving my husband with everything I've got." Where does that fit in? In our society, if we said it out loud, people would answer, "What are you talking about?" or "Oh, you can do that anytime." It's time to reprogram ourselves.

We're happiest when we're in love. Remember your courtship and your honeymoon? People are desperate to recapture that feeling. They'll rip their lives apart trying to do so. That's why there are so many divorces, so many affairs, so many lonely women lost in beautiful novels. We all wish like crazy to be in love, but we work like crazy at things that drive us apart. We love love, but it isn't "worthwhile" according to society's standards. We don't agree out loud, but our actions speak louder than words. Love is a waste of time, a waste of ambition.

Now, I'm not saying we should abandon our talents. God gave them to us to be used. I am saying that your transcendent calling in life is to love that man; your calling as a couple is to echo Christ's passionate love affair with his Church.

Are you ready? The world—and your lovers—are waiting.

Resources for Reflection II

Dear wives, dear husbands, it has been such a pleasure writing these words to you. So much of God's presence in this world is shown through loving couples like you who are willing and courageous enough to embrace his way. The world needs you so much; your spouses need you; your children need you. Our society desperately needs you as an example and a guiding light. We hope these words will take root and grow in you, so that Christ's joy may be in you and your own joy may be complete.

Love, Chuck and Mary Angelee.

Consider These Questions Privately:

Below is a list of Scripture passages. Each describes a response to Christ's love for His church.

Read and interpret each of these. How do they apply to your relationship with your husband? What are you doing well? What can you do better?

Trusting the goodness of our spouse:

Matthew 11:28: "Come to me, all you who labor and are overburdened, and I will give you rest."

Accepting unconditional love:

John 13:3–16: The washing of the feet.

Relentless love:

John 13:34, 35: "Love one another as I have loved you."

Oneness:

Acts 4:32–35. The early Church.

God's will for our love:
Romans 8:28–39.

God's great love for us and our response:
1 John 4:7–19.

Share These Thoughts:

After you and your husband read this chapter, write to each other on these topics:

Beloved, you are such a delightful spouse; I have such wonderful memories of your goodness. I can see you following God's plan for our relationship when you...." (Write on more than one if you wish.)

My dear, I realize I haven't always followed God's plan for our relationship. I am going to make the following change(s). This makes me feel....

Finally, Let Us Invite the Lord Into Our Marriages:

Dear Father, I truly want to follow your plan for our marriage. Please help me to trust my husband's goodness; give me your peace, your patience, and enthusiasm for your will. Please send me your Spirit so I can fully live out your plan with my beloved husband.

Thank you for his wonderful goodness and for the graces you have already given me: the grace of openness to your word, the grace of compassion, the grace of generosity, the grace of hope. Thank you; praise you for your gifts to my beloved and myself. Amen.